Conser.
Design

Socially inclusive process

Christopher Day

with

Rosie Parnell

Architectural Press

OXFORD AMSTERDAM BOSTON LONDON NEW YORK PARIS
SAN DIEGO SAN FRANCISCO SINGAPORE SYDNEY TOKYO

Architectural Press
An imprint of Elsevier Science
Linacre House, Jordan Hill, Oxford OX2 8DP
200 Wheeler Road, Burlington MA 01803

First published 2003

British Library Cataloguing in Publication Data
A catalogue record for this book is available from the British Library

Library of Congress Cataloguing in Publication Data
A catalogue record for this book is available from the Library of Congress

ISBN 0 7506 5605 0

For information on all Architectural Press publications
visit our website at www.architecturalpress.com

Produced by Gray Publishing, Tunbridge Wells, Kent
Printed and bound in Great Britain by MPG Books, Bodmin, Cornwall

Contents

ST. JAMES'S PALACE

For the last fifty years it has been very difficult to talk about the human and spiritual elements of building. These have been passed over in favour of the purely physical aspects of the environment where buildings are designed as 'machines for living in'.

With new breakthroughs in the area of science, showing that matter moves through both space and time, it is no longer so difficult to talk about these less tangible aspects of the relationship between mankind and place-making.

In this wonderful and unique book Christopher Day sets out to explain the process of Consensus Design, which is used to explore the resonance of a place and show how this can be reflected in built form. As Michelangelo set out to discover what lay beneath the surface of a piece of marble, so Christopher Day helps the inhabitants of a place to discover what 'wants' to be built by 'listening' to the place in which they live.

This gentle response to building, through the distillation of ideas, may lead us closer to the secrets of how past generations managed to build places that touch our hearts and strike a chord in our souls.

Preface: Consensus Design in context

Christopher Day's soul-affirming architecture deserves all the attention it has received in recent years. His books on the subject have helped many to appreciate the potential value of an architecture whose primary concern is the well-being of individuals, 'place' and the wider environment. In these books, Day has alluded to the type of creative social process which he believes is integral to the incarnation of such an architecture. The following pages are devoted to this unique process.

Day's design process has evolved through his commitment to collaborating with others. It was other people who first began referring to his method as Consensus Design: the name has stuck. A preliminary explanation is straightforward enough: Consensus Design involves a group of people who strive for consensus through design. But achieving consensus is by no means straightforward in normal circumstances. There may be several ways to reach this goal, but this book focuses on Day's particular technique. On the surface the use of a technique is puzzling, since Day himself is wary of the term, sensing that the idea of an imposed structure 'makes it sound awfully doctrinarian and limiting …'. Indeed he is wary of techniques generally. And yet, this technique, this structure, is key to the Consensus Design process: it is the discipline of the structure that holds back premature thought. This principle permeates the four-layer structure which lies at the heart of the process.

Consensus Design potentially involves design and construction professionals, clients, users of architecture, and anyone else who might be affected by specific environmental and architectural developments. In this sense it builds on the tradition of co-design. Design participation, community participation, community architecture, advocacy, neighbourhood planning, community planning, community-based development … for each term there is a body of associated work – writings and action. Each has its own qualities, whether defined by scale, method, motive or degree of involvement – some terms subsuming others. Each term can itself have different meanings for different people. What they all share is the principle that non-professionals are involved, to some degree, in decision-making about issues which will affect them. Of key concern here are those issues relating to the development of the built environment.

A recent history of co-design

The roots of co-design are often traced back to the 1960s when a number of different forces converged to produce a climate conducive to community participation.

Radical architects and planners rallied against the dominant technical-rational approach of the day and called not only for a new professional practice – one with moral and political content – but also for social justice and citizen empowerment. Public protest to imposed urban renewal, on both sides of the Atlantic, resulted from what was essentially a political crisis. US grass-roots activity led to the development of community design centres, from which community advocates[1] worked with local people to fight against federal developments threatening to destroy existing communities.[2] Radical activity in the States was mirrored in Britain through the work of activists such as Colin Ward. In his book, *Tenants Take Over*,[3] he argued for the transfer of municipal housing from local authorities to their tenants. He acknowledged the political nature of his proposition, which ultimately demands a transition from a paternalistic to a participatory society.

The 'radical' position[4] lies at the heart of what Comerio has called 'the idealistic phase' in community design.[5] In their struggle against authorities, disillusioned design and planning professionals of the day were essentially driven by leftist utopian ideals. It is this political ideology which defines the phase – the search for universal solutions to society's problems. But critics have pointed to the failing of this approach. While aiming to transform both society and the profession, its proponents found they lacked the necessary political power.[6]

In Britain, the 1969 Housing Act, took a tentative step toward participation, demanding that 'people be consulted before rather than after final plans'. In the States, participation in planning and design gained inclusion in federal law in the 1970s. But some argue that the institutionalization of participation did more harm than good, only galvanizing the view held by the general public and many designers of participation as the *end*; not as the *means* to environmental justice, but justice itself. And so, with the ultimate goal of justice attained, the focus of participation shifted away from the big political picture toward the improvement of living conditions through specific projects. Eighty community design centres opened across the States during the 1970s, providing technical assistance for communities involved in such projects. By then, participation, formerly confined to the realm of the 'underclasses', had also been adopted by mainstream middle-income Americans, demanding a say in decisions about their environments. Meanwhile, in Europe, projects such as Erskine's housing at Byker, Kroll's Medical Dormitories in Louvain La Neuve, deCarlo's university expansion in Urbino and Habraken's Support Structures for housing in the Netherlands, came to embody an alternative community architecture which contrasted strongly with US advocacy, clearly reflecting the designer as well as the community.[8]

Comerio defines the late 1970s as the 'entrepreneurial phase' of community architecture.[9] In an increasingly conservative political climate, public funding for community participation programmes was cut on both sides of the Atlantic. Practice inevitably became less idealistic and began to favour self-reliant economic and community development for local needs. 1980s Britain saw the arrival of the 'neutral tool' of participation, developed initially for use with middle-class Americans, and now used by disadvantaged people and their design and planning facilitators to produce another strain of community architecture.[10] But the supposed neutrality of community architecture has been criticized by some who view this position as a denial of its latent political potential.[11]

Though their work received little mainstream attention, throughout the 1990s, activists, planners and designers continued to collaborate with residents and users. Academician-practitioners developed tools in an attempt to make design and planning participation processes more effective on the ground. In particular, a large body of work was developed using an action research approach;[12] work which continues today. At this time, community participation continues to be supported in the guise of neighbourhood planning, community-based development,[13] and community planning,[14] each of these areas offering a range of methods for including people in decision-making about the development of their environment.

The relatively complex history and evolution of community participation explain the many possible interpretations and connotations of the term today. The threads of this history have been carried into the work of today's community architects, so that those enveloped by this term represent many different beliefs. For some, their work remains a political cause and mechanism for social change. For others the importance of their work lies in the development of an accessible design method able to include more people. Yet others simply see participation as a means to make their designs more responsive to their users.[15] Where does Consensus Design fit into this picture?

Consensus Design

Consensus Design was not consciously built on the historical strands of participation, instead evolving in parallel through the direct experiences of Christopher Day in designing places. Throughout the 1970s and 1980s he worked essentially on his own, only occasionally hearing something about co-design, advocates and community architects. It was not until the 1990s that he began to be asked into what he terms, 'a more mainstream world'. Around this time he began to formalize the method which he had essentially used for years.

Day wasn't driven by a political or social cause,[16] he didn't aim to include more people in the design process or even make his designs more responsive to users. That is, he did not *specifically set out* to achieve any of these aims. Instead, he was driven by a desire to create what he calls 'beautiful places' – environmentally appropriate places of minimal negative impact, which have a positive effect on the health and spirit of their users. It was in striving for this goal that Day arrived at participation.[17] The participatory design method developed by Day was to engage relevant parties by focusing on place.

Of course, that Day should arrive at such a method is a reflection of his values and beliefs. Some of these he shares with other proponents of participation. He believes in the value of local knowledge and experience, knowing this to be as important as that of experts. He therefore believes in demystifying the design process in order to include people, seeing mystification as the expert's means to acquire power over others – something he clearly doesn't support. Where he perhaps differs from many community architects is that he doesn't believe in empowerment, which, as he sees it, means giving users power *over* other parties:

> ... I don't like the idea of power anyway. I don't want someone to be powerful over me and I don't want to be powerful over them. One of the things about [much 1960s, 70s

and 80s] participation was putting the community on top. I wouldn't like the
community on top of me. And many of the techniques were based on a power structure,
albeit a different one and one we would regard as much more, perhaps not equitable,
but much more acceptable. I prefer not to run on a power basis at all.

Underpinning Day's approach is his belief in consensus as an alternative to repre-
sentative democracy which he sees as unfair to the outvoted minority. But Day does
not see his own response as being about political power, in the sense that he does
not aim to empower people. Instead, through the consensus method, he enables people 'to unfold their potential'. This does not mean that the process results in a compromise which satisfies no-one – a common criticism of the consensual stance. Day's
own consensual stance *demands* that all participants are satisfied at every stage.
Consensus is about collaboration and partnership – *equal* value and *equal* power.

   Other design participation methods have also aimed for consensus in decision-
making. Methods such as Community Appraisal, Participatory Strategic Planning,[18]
the Delphi Technique and its relation the Community Consensus Survey, Nominal
Group Process[19] and gaming methods such as ROLE[20] all mention consensus in
their process description.

   But there is a key difference, Day would argue, between the Consensus Design
process and *all* other design participation processes. Where other processes – including others founded on a consensus basis[21] – encourage the expression of individual
ideas and ideas generation through methods such as brainstorming, Day's process
urges participants to instead *dissolve* pre-formed ideas.

   According to Mehrhoff,[22] 'The truth in terms of community consensus is quite frequently a negotiated settlement'. But this is what Day seeks to avoid. In common with
many design participation methods, the consensus process begins with study of place.
The four-layer structure provided, allows study of the qualitative as well as the quantitative; not only the physical, but also layers which give meaning.[23] The themes that
emerge from the place-study stage are crucial ingredients of the design work that follows.

   What Day seeks through the Consensus Design process is architecture that is 'right
for place and circumstance'. Right? Does this mean that there is always a right answer
in his eyes? Day's view on this point is controversial – he does believe that there exists
an archetypal design for each place and circumstance. However, the level at which the
archetype can be defined might exist only at a pre-material and pre-form level:

> ...with two groups of people you would probably get two right answers, but the thing is
> that they would be close to each other in many ways and would probably only diverge at
> the final stages where they find form and material, both are likely to be in the same
> related families of materials, both related to families, or palettes, of form and scale,
> sharp and soft qualities, this sort of thing.

It cannot be denied that Day's hand is apparent in the products of Consensus
Design. He freely admits this, seeing it as his limitation: 'In a sense, it shouldn't be.
It shouldn't be visible, but I haven't got there yet'. But one could argue that this is
simply a reflection of his own knowledge and experience and evidence that his contribution to the process is more than one of technical facilitator.

   Community architecture has been criticized for its avoidance of direct discussion
of style through focus on process, instead inferring that 'a certain vernacular will
emerge effortlessly from the process of collaboration because that is what people

most naturally relate to'.[24] While the emphasis of this book is necessarily on process for the sake of replication by others, the process itself has been shaped primarily through a concern for an appropriate end product. Day does not fall into the trap of equating the process – the means – with the end: it is the end which justifies the means. On the other hand, he does believe that successful and proper engagement with the process will achieve the desired end.

Day describes his role as one of 'leading from the back', only stepping forward when things become difficult. While he dislikes the term 'facilitator' he recognizes this is a part of his role, since he uses a structured process. But facilitation extends further:

> I think it's helping people recognize that they can contribute in a meaningful way. So every individual is of value – is of high value. The group depends on value from everybody.

Day's role is not confined to facilitation: he too is a participant in the Consensus Design process. Just as with every other participant, his knowledge, skills and experience feed into the process. But the process doesn't demand that he, as design professional, be relegated to a neutral technical facilitator – a good thing since he does not think he is very 'technical or facilitatory'. While he avoids making suggestions, instead using questions to help the design to 'condense', he does not ignore the responsibility that comes with the knowledge he has gained through experience of working as and being educated as a design professional:

> … you can draw somebody's attention to things like the daylight will be inadequate, or where will the sun be at this time of day, or won't this space be rather hard acoustically? We don't have to give the answers, indeed you should just ask the right questions.

He makes the other design participants aware of the feasibility and implications of the various design decisions discussed. The knowledge he offers here isn't purely technical, it's multidimensional – both quantitative and qualitative. Drawing the attention of other participants to issues as diverse as spanning capability, the effects of certain materials on human health and how something might make you feel because of its smell, Day enables the design group to make decisions based on the same information that he himself holds, along with the information that other participants offer. According to Day, the Consensus Design process demands this architectural professional input for its success. This input is not defined by information alone; its value lies in an ability to relate spatial thinking to ones 'inner-most feelings'. On this basis, the architect involved in the consensus process 'should be able to bring an insight and with it a means of describing it to other people, so they understand …' thus accelerating understanding of this relationship for other participants.

Achieving consensus relies on Day's agreement in decision-making along with all other participants. His values, therefore, cannot help but influence the process. In fact, if his values proved to be entirely at odds with other participants, then consensus would not be possible. Since all of Day's clients invite him to work with them, he has not experienced such a situation. Perhaps then the process is in a sense idealistic, since it relies on shared values?

Day believes that it is not idealistic. He has used the method in a variety of situations and with a variety of people and sees no reason why it could not be applied to any group design situation. But as it has been pointed out:

it may be relatively easy ... to ... reach consensus, and involve people in developing
programs in neighbourhoods that are integrated or parochial. In these places, people
already share a common view; there is social homogeneity; they speak a common
language; they may be ethically related; and so on. Interventions in these kinds of
neighbourhoods, with the potential to organize, will be in stark contrast to those that
are diffuse, stepping-stones, transitory, or nonneighborhoods.[25]

So, is Day simply optimistic? Only by extending the use of this method will the
answer to this question be found. Enabling others to use and extend the use of the
Consensus Design method is precisely the purpose of this book.

Possible futures

The late 1990s into the 2000s appear to have brought a political climate supportive
of increased participation. From UN conventions[26] to national governmental strategies,[27] participation is seen as an essential ingredient in the creation of sustainable
community. There appears to be a dawning recognition that community participation
should mean something more than consultation – that there needs to be direct and
active involvement of 'community' through true partnership.[28] Social exclusion is a
hot topic for the 2000s; a recognized problem which governments on both sides of
the Atlantic aim to tackle. The British Labour Government, elected in 1997, introduced the Social Exclusion Unit, the first major report of which describes the problem of social exclusion as follows:

> over the last generation, this has become a more divided country. While most areas have
> benefited from rising living standards, the poorest neighbourhoods have tended to
> become more rundown, more prone to crime, and more cutoff from the labour market.
> The national picture conceals pockets of intense deprivation where the problems of
> unemployment and crime are acute and hopelessly tangled up with poor health, housing
> and education. They have become no go areas for some and no exit zones for others. In
> England as a whole the evidence we have suggests there are several thousand
> neighbourhoods and estates whose condition is critical, or soon could be.[29]

This is the climate in which the architecture and planning professions are evolving.
How will the architecture profession respond? An oversimplified view of this
challenge, based on past experience, would see two reactions: one set of architects
embracing participation, their role becoming marginalized to the extent that they are
limited to producing 'surface aesthetic and technical efficiency'[30] and the other set
who defend their ground against the threat of participation and its ability to undermine the architect's autonomy and control.[31] Of course, examples of either extremes
are rare.

Public participation has been recognized at multiple levels as a necessity for a
sustainable world. This participation needs to go beyond the 'pseudo', to achieve
'genuine' participation,[32] allowing for partnership and cooperation. The evidence
suggests that planners and architects cannot ignore these external pressures if they
themselves want to be sustained in their professions. Equally, if architects are to continue to be recognized as a key profession in the development of the built environment, they cannot waive all responsibility in the design process, giving this solely to
'the people'. Design professionals need to be clear about what it is that they offer, or

as Habraken puts it: 'The better we are able to formulate exactly what is our irreplaceable contribution, the more effective we will be ...'[33]

In his conception of Consensus Design, in the principles which underlie this method, Day becomes the type of architect at the centre of Habraken's vision for a new professionalism. One who understands settlement as a natural phenomenon with its own state of health and well-being:

> ... the aim is to nourish something that is alive to make it better, stronger, and beautiful. It is the attitude of a gardener who works to let plants grow ... intervenes in the process to improve it – sometimes makes infrastructure, sometimes weeds and trims, sometimes feeds and stimulates.[34]

Day believes that social relevance *will* ultimately exert major influence on the evolution of architects' practice. He believes this will inspire architectural professionals and the people working with them. The shaping of socially inclusive environments can only be made possible through the active involvement of all kinds of people. If people are to believe that their contribution to society is valued, then they must be shown that they are valued through the environment they use. For Day, this is the most pressing challenge facing architects.

Day does not claim that his own work has specifically strived to tackle social exclusion, but he believes that this will in the end be the cause which cannot be ignored and for which mainstream architectural practice will gradually develop more inclusive design processes. This metamorphosis, which some might argue has already begun,[35] will enrich the role of the architect. At least this is Day's experience.

The challenge will be to allow teamwork – an area in which architecture has traditionally been weak[36] – to supersede individualism. This requires individuals to give-up the idea that one has to give-in to other people. In fact, as Day points out, working as a successful member of a team can only be achieved through individual strength. In the end this is more demanding than working as an individual, but it is also 'more fulfilling to rise above, effectively, your individual narrownesses and work in this way.'

This book is dedicated to Day's own particular method for designing in teams – Consensus Design. This might not be the only way in which to achieve consensus, but it is one with which Day and his clients have achieved great success and fulfilment. This fulfilment he would like others to experience. It is for this reason that this book describes the why and how behind the process in detail and offers project examples to aid the use of this process in any group architectural design situation that you might be a part of.

Rosie Parnell

(All quotations from Christopher Day are extracted from the transcript of an interview carried out in November 2001 by Rosie Parnell.)

Notes

1   The advocate assisted citizens in expressing their views and interests in the technical professional language made necessary by the planning system – hence the term advocacy planning, frequently abbreviated to advocacy.

2   See for example, the case of Sandra Graham in Boston, a public housing

resident, who successfully organized local people to lobby the local authority for neighbourhood improvement money, using evidence compiled by community designers: See Hester R.T. (1990). *Community Design Primer*, Ridge Times Press.

3   Ward, C. (1974). *Tenants Take Over*, Architectural Press.

4   Hain identifies two different perspectives on 1960s and early 1970s participation: first, the 'radical', and second, the 'liberal'. Rather than rejecting the existing political system, the 'liberals' called for changes *within* this system to allow it to work once again. See: Hain P. (1980). *Neighbourhood Participation*, Temple Smith.

5   In: Comerio, M. (1984). op. cit.

6   Critics such as Crawford have argued that in fact 'the already fictional roles of the all-powerful architect and the ideal client' were simply reversed by community architects. See: Crawford, M.C. (1991). Can architects be socially responsible? In *Out of Site: A Social Criticism of Architecture* (D. Ghirado ed.), Bay Press, pp. 27–45.

7   This view is outlined by Hester in his paper: Hester R.T. (1987). Participatory design and environmental justice; pas de deux or time to change partners? *Journal of Architectural and Planning Research*, **4**:4, 289–299.

8   Comerio describes these projects as being seen by many as 'the models for all that was good in community architecture' See: Comerio, M. (1990). Design and empowerment: 20 years of community architecture. In *Participatory Design: Theory and Techniques* (H. Sanoff ed.), Henry Sanoff, North Carolina State University, pp. 49–62.

9   In: Comerio, M. (1984). op. cit.

10 See: Wates N. and Knevitt C. (1987). *Community Architecture: How People Are Creating Their Own Environment*, Penguin Books. Wates and Knevitt describe housing projects ranging from Segal method self-build homes in Lewisham to the refurbishment of local authority housing blocks such as Lea View House, Hackney.

11 According to Till, the political potential of community architecture 'is largely suppressed by recourse to the consensual stance set-up to quell the doubts of left or right.' See: Till J. (1998). Architecture of the impure community. In *Occupying Architecture: Between the Architect and the User* (J. Hill ed.), Routledge, pp. 62–75.

12 At the heart of this work is a desire to reconcile social science with architecture – the social environment with the physical. See for example: Sanoff, H. (2000). *Community Participation Methods in Design and Planning*, Wiley; Mehrhoff, W.A. (1999). *Community Design; a Team Approach to Dynamic Community Systems*, Sage Publications.

13 See for example: Peterman, W. (2000). *Neighborhood Planning and Community-Based Development: The Potential and Limits of Grassroots Action*, Sage Publications; Rubin, H.J. (2000). *Renewing Hope Within Neighborhoods of Despair: The Community-based Development Model*, State University of New York Press.

14 See for example: Kelly, D. and Becker B. (2000). *Community Planning: An Introduction to the Comprehensive Plan*, Island Press; Wates N. (2000). *The Community Planning Handbook*, Earthscan Publications.

15 These different drivers for co-design are identified by Comerio, M. (1984) op. cit.

16 He was always, however, strongly committed to freeing people from dependency, hence, to demystify the building process, he taught building skills to unskilled volunteers for some 20 years.

17 Interestingly, John Habraken, the architect well known for his interest in participation, also claims that he was not primarily driven by the users' interest, but the broader interest of a healthy environment, which he believes is unattainable without the user's intervention. See: Habraken, J.N. (1990). Towards a new professional role. In *Participatory Design: Theory and Techniques* (H. Sanoff ed.), North Carolina State University, pp. 71–5.

18   Lewis J., Unsworth C. and Walker P.,
     Eds (1998). *Twenty-one Techniques of
     Community Participation for the 21ˢᵗ
     Century*. New Economics Foundation.
19   Mehrhoff, W.A. (1999). op, cit.
20   See Sanoff, H. (1991). *Visual Research
     Methods in Design*, Van Nostrand
     Reinhold, p. 176.
21   See also: Mehrhoff, W.A. (1999). op.
     cit., p. 87.
22   Mehrhoff, W.A. (1999). op. cit., p. 80.
23   In a similar way, action research
     recognizes that: 'Combining survey
     research with community visioning
     techniques offers valuable opportunities
     to gain a greater and more accurate
     representation of community opinion,
     overcome static positions, and create a
     deeper sense of community consensus
     on the process' Mehrhoff (1999). op. cit.
24   Till (1998). op. cit., p. 68.
25   Hamdi, N. (1995). *Housing Without
     Houses: Participation, Flexibility,
     Enablement*. Intermediate Technology
     Publications, p. 38.
26   See the UN-ECE Convention on Public
     Participation in Decision-Making and
     Access to Justice in Environmental
     Decision-Making, 1998.
27   For example, the British Labour
     government's Urban Policy White Paper
     2000, sets out a vision which includes:
     'people shaping the future of their
     community, supported by strong and
     truly representative local leaders.' Cited
     in: Schneider R.H and Kitchen T.
     (2001). *Planning for Crime Prevention:
     A Transatlantic Perspective*, Routledge,
     p. 211.
28   See for example, the British Social
     Exclusion Unit's National Strategy
     Action Plan (2001) which aims to
     empower residents and get public,
     private and voluntary organizations to
     work in partnership.
29   Social Exclusion Unit, 1998:9 – Cited in
     Schneider R.H and Kitchen T. (2001).
     op. cit., p. 208.
30   Till J. (1998). op. cit., p. 70.
31   Gutman, R. (1988). *Architectural
     Practice: a Critical View*, Princeton
     Architectural Press, p. 90.
32   Deshler and Sock (1985) identified
     these two levels of participation: cited
     in Sanoff, H. (2000). op. cit.
33   Habraken, J. N. (1986). op. cit.
34   Ibid.
35   See the work of practices such as Fluid,
     Muf and Architype.
36   Reports such as the British Property
     Federation's survey of major clients
     (1997 – cited in Rethinking
     construction: the report of the
     construction task force (Egan Report,
     1998). Department of the Environment,
     Transport and the Regions.) and a study
     by Lawson and Pilling (1996 – cited in
     Nicol D. and Pilling S. (2000).
     Architectural education and the
     profession. In *Changing Architectural
     Education: Towards a New
     Professionalism* (D. Nicol and S.
     Pilling, eds), E&FN Spon, pp.1–26),
     have highlighted teamwork and
     communication skills as specific
     weaknesses in the architectural
     profession.

Acknowledgements

This book is the result of *communal* design, so I must thank the many I have worked with over the years. Particularly, however, I owe a huge debt of gratitude to Margaret Colquhoun. Without what I've learnt from her, there would be no process method and no book. Nor would there have been a book had not Penina Finger encouraged me to write it. Obvious as this way of working seems to me, it was she who recognized how different is this from 'normal' design methods. Amongst many others to whom I owe thanks: Vicky Moller, Aloma Day, Kim Sorvig and Tom Woolley gave invaluable editorial advice; Alison Yates and Lesley Gray managed (despite my disorganization) to get the book together; Katherine MacInnes arranged critical appraisals which greatly helped clarify my thinking. Indeed I realized it *is* useful to think sometimes. And especially, I am grateful to Rosie Parnell for research to complement my non-academic experience, and her discerning editorial clarity – and for being fun to work with (work that isn't fun is boring, hence this book is all about fun work). Most of all, I must thank those many who trusted me, as I have always started every project knowing 'nothing'.

Christopher Day

Dedication
To Heddwen, Aloma, Brynach, Dewi,
Martha, Owain and Michael-Tâl.

PART ONE

Introduction

CHAPTER ONE

Architecture as a social art: a journey

My first contact with architecture was conventional: I studied it. Less conventional was at the same time attending evening classes in sculpture – and as sculpture students in my college spent more time in the pub than in the department, the tutors were quite happy if I came in during the daytime. Soon I was doing sculpture by day, often in the evening as well, and architecture by night. After three years of architecture school, students work a year in an office. I worked in a large municipal one and got so bored that I swore never to work in an office again. (Swearing doesn't seem to work in this sort of way, as I've since discovered.) I then studied sculpture 'legally' for three years. After this, and in need of some kind of part-time work to keep alive, I put together a course on space and form from my combined architecture and sculpture background – and this was the beginning of my architectural teaching side-career.

Fairly early on, I began to realize that architects experienced buildings differently from the way lay people do. I tried to get my students to stop looking at complete building forms – only visible from above – but instead to imagine the journeys through and past their buildings. I was developing *place* consciousness, something I should have had all along, but surprisingly rare in the 1960s.

In those days, I made sculpture, but architecture I only taught. However, 1972 saw me move back to Wales and build a house. The result of this was that neighbours came to me to ask me to design buildings for them. Already, I'd come to realize that I had no right to impose my ideas on those who'd be paying for and living in these buildings. I would, therefore, offer several options (usually about five) for them to choose from. This led to day-long joint design sessions in which I would illustrate whatever my clients said they wanted, but go on from this to show the limitations and also the potentials that arose. I soon found that I was seeking to penetrate through my clients' eclectic collections of 'good ideas' to the mood-picture – the soul – of what they *really* wanted, but couldn't give form to.

It was some years before I fully realized how much *activity* colours the mood of a place; that activity can do more for mood than visual appearance. From then on finding the right places, and moods, for *activities* became increasingly central to my approach to design.

Around the same time, my work began to involve groups, rather than single individuals; and new buildings instead of conversions. This led to walking around with the client group – mostly the actual future occupants – and agreeing together the locations for each activity-mood. We would pace the edges of places 'coloured' by the activities bordering them; also the pathways connecting places, agreeing as we went, the views to enhance or screen, the thresholds to mark. This was the intuitive foundation for what has since become a more conscious method.

In 1990, I was persuaded to be part of a group to research 'spirit of place'. This study group was initiated by Bruce May[1] who proposed a particular method. It was, in fact, an evolution of a method of landscape study developed by Dr Margaret Colquhoun,[2] whom I did not know at that time, but have since worked with closely and frequently – more of her method later.

We would walk a short urban walk such as Burlington Arcade, in London, and the streets at either end of it; or an indoor journey, for instance from street-front, through front door, up stairs, along a corridor arriving in an office. (It was the office of one of our members, but our repeated group walks did attract some curious looks, not least from security personnel.) On the first walk, we observed and noted, with sketches and diagrams, the purely *physical* aspects of the place. On the next walk, we looked at how the space 'breathed' – how its space, light, form-gestures and movements expanded and contracted, accelerated and slowed. We also considered all time-related factors: changing light, traffic, noise and life. This was about sequential experiences: the *time* aspects of the journey. On the next walk, we observed how we *felt* in different parts of the journey. We then asked how, in human terms, the place might describe itself.

For me, this was a new way of looking at things. It didn't seem something I would ever want to apply, nor could I see that I was learning anything from it. I had to concede, however, that it was an interesting process of observation, and it was certainly striking how we always reached consensus. Interesting, but only interesting, until it occurred to me that perhaps we could do the process *backwards*. We now followed each four-stage journey-study with a mirror process. What *should* the place say? What *moods* would support the place's message? What breathing *sequence* of spatial experiences would induce these moods? What *physical* changes would achieve these?

As all our study was done in a posh part of London (Piccadilly and the Royal Fine Art Commission offices), not much cried out for change. Little could I guess that this technique would lead me to places that *really* needed change. Ugly, squalid, outmoded and unloved – places where, at first glance, there was no potential, nor enough money to radically change them. Nonetheless, this method became the basis of a consensus design process I now use for rehabilitating buildings (or rooms, streets or places). Initially, this was just an experimental technique. The importance of the principles on which it was based, I didn't yet fully grasp.

It was some time later that I met Margaret Colquhoun and realized that her place-study techniques and my approach to finding the right place for buildings were really two halves of one whole, waiting to be put together. Her process was one of science: getting to *understand* a place – effectively to understand the *past* that has formed it. Through this we could learn what the place *is* – its 'character' (*genus loci*). In doing so, we begin to recognize what it needs to maximize its health, what it is asking for that design can fulfil. My half was concerned with what *will* be there in the future; the creative realm of art. How the new – usually a building – can best fit into a place. Working with her, I learnt how science and art, understanding and creation, past and future, place and project need each other.

We – always *we*, because this works best as a group process, to even out and moderate the imbalances of individual egos – start by absorbing *first impressions*, in silence and without judgement, inference or analysis. First impressions are easily one-sided; even distorted by what we want to see. Working as a group frees us from this sort of 'perception pollution' making it much easier to see what is *really* there.

Next we observe – exactly and unselectively – just what is *physically* there, again, with no distortion by values, thoughts or ideas.

Though we hadn't been looking for it, this provides evidence for the next stage of study. Tracing the place's *biography*, from distant past to last year and last season. Actual events, like house-construction and factory closure, may have been staccato, but seen as a continuum, we can get a sense of a current of time flowing through the place. Like water abrading rocks, this constantly refines its shape, mood and spirit. Once in this stream of time we get a sense of how future will grow out of past. We can now imagine how the place might change next season, year, decade and further into the future.

Next we focus on our experience of the special 'character' moods of different parts or 'sub-places' and the feelings these induce in us. Lastly, letting all these levels live inside us, we begin to recognize the place's essence – its oneness of matter and spirit – almost as if it were a person. We can then ask how the place would describe itself in human terms.

Dr Colquhoun describes these steps as meeting 'the four layers of landscape':[3]

- The solid objects, physical facts, the 'bedrock' of the place;
- That which is constantly changing, flowing and growing;
- That which lends character to a place, gives its unique 'atmosphere' and appeal – so inducing feeling responses in us;
- And that which is the essence or inner reality of a place.

When we work together, she leads this place-study phase. I follow on with the process of incarnating buildings into this place.

We start by asking what the project is about and hence, to provide a fit home for this, what the place *should* say. Listing the activities the project would generate, what moods – like warm sociability for communal eating – would they bring? Where, from what we now know of the place's moods, would these feel at home?

Now the building plan: what gestures, like inviting, protective or outward-looking, would enhance these moods? What arrangement would confirm the plan-gestures we have 'found'? This leads us to three-dimensional modelling.

What sequential experiences are appropriate as we journey between buildings: enclosed courtyards and portals, wall-confined paths or open greens? And finally: what materials, textures and colours reinforce activity-place moods?

Although the technique has evolved since our first practice workshop in 1991 – described in Chapter 11, and now a real project under construction – we still work with the same principles: consensual group work, future meeting past and the four levels of place. My journey has not so much been one of technique, rather one of moving from being a solitary designer, convinced of my brilliance, to freeing myself from any individually sourced ideas and letting designs slowly condense out of the consensus group process. Now I can't design on my own – or at least, I think I can't and certainly won't. 'My' designs these days are not 'mine', but the product of a group. Different groups with different members, different architects or consultants, must arrive at different forms – but not so different, for we are all listening to a single marriage of the needs of place and of people, of past and future, of the flow of time and the specific, new, situation. Regardless of group constitution, we are listening to *what wants to be there*. The techniques I will describe facilitate impartial holding-back of ideas and form. They help us rise above individual preference and prejudice. It is upon this listening approach that trans-individual, consensus design and 'rightness in place' depend.

Notes

1   Of the Scientific and Medical Network (Northleach, England). Other core members included Axel Ewald of the Life Science Trust and Richard Coleman of the Royal Fine Arts Commission – had I not known, and worked at conferences, with each of them already, I would certainly have felt a professional small-fry.

2   Of the Life-Science Trust (Gifford, Scotland). Her method in turn was based on Dr Jochen Bochemühl's (of the Natural Science Section at the Goetheanum, in Switzerland), the inspiration for which stretches back to Rudolf Steiner and Goethe, before him. See for example: Bockemühl J. (1985). *Towards a Phenomenology of the Etheric World*, Anthroposophic Press; Steiner R. (1989). *Goethean Science* (republication of *Goethe the Scientist*), Mercury Press; Goethe J.W. (1978 edn). *The Metamorphosis of Plants*, Biodynamic Literature.

3   From the Life Science Trust touring exhibition, 1996 (Life Science Trust, Gifford, Scotland).

PART TWO

Consensus Design: Why?

Participants' comments:

My first exposure to Consensus Design was when I was working with Christopher Day designing the proposed ASHA Centre, north London. The process lasted for four days and involved all the parties interested in the end result. I found the procedure novel and interesting. It led to a result which I believe was not pressurized by any one party exerting a major influence on the group. As a result of this, all interested parties felt that they had a stake in creating a successful project. The quality of this positive energy cannot be underestimated.

Lawrence Bloom – Developer, London.

CHAPTER TWO

Why: community design and place

What shapes places?

No one person designed our everyday surroundings. Towns, neighbourhoods, streets, even most houses were rarely designed by architects. Indeed most were never designed at all. They just 'happened'. Some are social and environmental disasters, others so delightful they're highly sought after. Most are somewhere in between.

Anywheresville, London: who designed the home, the street, the town you live in? Most of us live in places which, whether originally 'designed' or just 'built', have evolved over the course of time. Their mood, the way they're lived in, the traffic that flows past and through them, and even bits of their substance, have changed significantly since they were first built. They have, in fact, been shaped by life. *How can design align with life – shaping currents? How can it respond to* people's *life-needs?*

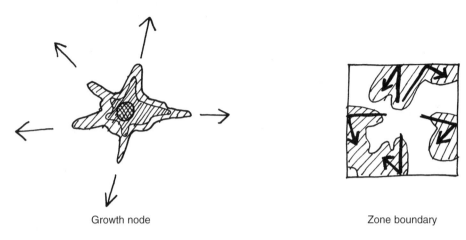

Growth node   Zone boundary

Pressures or planning?

They 'happened' – but not through happenstance. Their form and character result-ed from pressures: economic, social and ecological pressures; cultural, geographic and climatic ones. This gave places built before the era of conscious design an integrity that today we can only struggle to achieve. It also integrated them perfectly with the economy, community, ecology and the whole way of life of their day. This, however, is also why old buildings and places, even attractive ones, aren't matched to life today. We can no longer do things in the old way and expect success, for modern form-giving pressures are different. There were no 14-wheel trucks in the middle-ages; roads can no longer be scaled for horse and carts as they were then. But this is only one example; most form-giving pressures are less visible and more subtle.

What are these pressures? How do we identify them? Respond to them? Integrate them into an inseparable wholeness? Form-giving pressures are easy enough to identify in retrospect – that's the job of culture-historians. But, just as with history, the pattern isn't so easy to see at the time.

Design by the community: why?

We rarely think about the pressures that give form to our environment, but live our daily lives adjusting to them. We know where to find sun or shade, or avoid wind-driven rain, how to take the easiest or most enjoyable route, or economize on energy by combining errands. We go to a shop for its convenience, prefer to sit by a window with a view, agree to meet where it feels secure to wait, pause and rest where something within us feels fed. We know where children play, where teenagers hang-out; which places we treasure, which to avoid. We know a lot of things about the place where we live that outsiders don't know. We may not *know* that we know them, but this unconscious knowledge is revealed by our daily actions.

Not only this: the place where we live is 'our' place – something we identify with at a feeling level. As somewhere laden with memories, associations, hopes, even family history, it imparts layers of meaning no outsider could even guess at. Invariably, there will be bits of the place where we live that we have 'improved'. Whether these improvements are for better or worse, they give us proprietary feelings about the place. Many places also have a communal dimension, which overlays them with a web of relationships that barely leave a visible trail.

This isn't stuff you can learn from a questionnaire. Nor can you see it. You have to get to know places, know their layers: their physical substance, the life that flows through them, their moods and their spirit. The best, probably the only, way to access all this is through the people who already live there. The knowledge they hold is invaluable. Invaluable both for living in places and for *forming* them. But this sort of knowledge isn't normally given credit by professional designers. Even where it is, it isn't readily accessible. It needs dedicated technique to bring this – often unconscious – knowledge to the surface, to enable it to form places – places of integrity, matched to need, in harmony with environmental context, right for climate and culture, economically vigorous. Such places have a vitality and honesty that rational (but un-felt) planning, with all its 'real world' material-only concerns, can never deliver.

Outsiders can help, bringing valuable contributions just *because* they are outsiders, but they can never make design socially relevant, inclusive and respectful without the input of the people who live and work there. Not only do we, the users of a place, know our own requirements and how we like to do things (better than does anybody else), but we also know the place, its climate and the micro-climatic subtleties of every valley and hillside, every street and open space. We never make the (in our view) stupid mistakes outsiders do. Locals don't plant orchards in frost pockets, build where every ten years it floods or buy luxury apartments in fly-range of the dump. Only local 'users' can do what is best for, and – no less importantly – maintain what is done for, users. It's in their interest to act responsibly, and most do. They alone live in the stream of local experience, have to live with the place around them and can't (in most cases) just walk away from it.

This is why it's good for *places* if they're formed by people. For the *people* who live there, the benefits are, of course, self-evident. Many professional designers may dispute this, but their right of dominance over everyone else has, at best, only a thin ethical justification.

What design involvement does for the community

Most places are formed by forces over which we've no control, and indeed can rarely even put our finger on. 'Somehow' places just change. Change isn't necessarily for the worse – but when we're powerless to influence it, it can be worrying, upsetting and resentment-breeding. We feel – and often are – dis-empowered, de-valued, of no consequence.

It's a sad fact that many people live in places that they don't feel connected to. They don't feel their value confirmed by the places where they live and consequently don't themselves value these places. Such places attract abuse – starting with litter, then progressing via graffiti to vandalism and worse. They silently abuse the people who live in and use them. These are places over which residents have no control – or at least *perceive* themselves powerless to do anything about.[1]

Though there are too many housing estates where residents want to move out, don't want their children to grow-up, fear their neighbours, resent their decrepit buildings and blame their landlords, there are also those where participatory-based improvements have reversed attitudes. Lea View House in Hackney, London is one example.[2] Prior to rehabilitation in the 1980s, 90% of the residents of this public sector housing estate wanted to leave. Following intensive architect–resident collaboration, this socially and physically deprived community was turned into a place with positive community spirit. Vandalism, thefts and muggings, formerly common, virtually disappeared; tenants' health improved, communal areas were looked-after and dignity and respect re-established. People now wanted to move *onto* the estate.

This is just one illustration of the way care flourishes once a community feels proprietary about a place. As well as improving physical environment, this encourages social bonding, crime reduction and communal responsibility.[3] However ugly, polluted, environmentally abused, is a place, our relationship to it changes as soon as we're free to alter it. And it changes profoundly once we start *work* on it. It becomes *our* place – something we value. Not only are we empowered to co-shape our own future, but what we value, think, feel and do counts.[4] It is of significant consequence – and so, therefore, are we ourselves.

When we are part of the process our sense of cultural, individual and community worth can blossom – in our own, as well as others' eyes. Places we have shaped ourselves, we feel responsible for. We value and guard them. The Swansea valley restoration project tells a classic story. In the 1960s, thousands of acres of smelter slag and mining waste were re-graded and planted with trees. By the time the local children had enjoyed swinging on them, hardly a tree stood. But more trees were planted, this time by the children themselves. These small children grew into teenagers, then into strong young men and women – and *nobody* was going to damage the trees they had planted. The formerly bare, toxic landscape is now green and forested.

Places that don't respond to our individual actions – because they're too inflexibly controlled, too big, too traffic dominated, too geometrically dominating, of too unalterable materials, give a clear message that the individuals who live and work there don't matter. Fortunately, we can almost always reduce perceived scale, calm – or at least shield from – traffic and, if not *re*shape, moderate aggressive shapes with vegetation or paint.

Once we take control of the re-shaping of a place, we become, by definition, important. But important can also be exposed. If we make stupid, embarrassing mistakes or attract the scorn or ire of neighbours, all our hesitant confidence can be knocked out of us. Success brings even worse problems – as every initiator has found when the time comes to pass the baton to a new generation. Almost without exception, one-person founders, initial prime-movers, are rejected, even expelled by those who follow.

It's different if work is communally founded. In particular, consensus decisions ensure that not only will there be no rejection, no polarized camps, but also that the aggregated knowledge and wisdom of a community will avoid 'stupid mistakes'.

From families to cities, in many 'communities' there are plenty of feuding factions and individual fixed positions. Nonetheless, if the community uses techniques to rise above these limitations and share its experience-based wisdom to make impartial, trans-emotional evaluations, a wealth of unexpected, hitherto unvoiced, insight is unlocked.

This isn't just about social fairness, nor even just making the right decisions. Consensus technique depends upon listening to everybody's contribution. When we are fully *heard*, we are accorded value. By contrast, we all know how value-demeaning it feels *not* to be heard. Many, who formerly felt they had nothing important to say, no right to speak, discover through the consensus process that they have knowledge and insights of value; that they deserve to have confidence in themselves. I've seen this happen time and time again. This is a personal growth process for all those concerned, which transforms the spirit of the community. Indeed, it builds community.[5]

Public meetings can make as many enemies as friends, but consensus-based meetings that take ideas forward, bring people together. Certainly that was my experience when setting up a school. Being a small group (around ten) so dependent on every individual's energies, we couldn't afford less than total will. This made consensual decision-making a practical as well as moral imperative.[6]

Of course, in a lot of places, people may live and work near each other, but these people aren't really *communities*. Neighbourhoods in modern times may have scant social 'glue'. Often their only layer of bond is proximity. People work, shop and holiday elsewhere. They don't work together or for each other; share childcare, hardships, resentments against employers or bus services; nor worship, culture, festivals or very much of anything else.

Shaping the future together, however, is bond forming. When it involves struggle against opposition (as when defending land from a new road) or against invisible, but witheringly potent forces like urban blight, it is especially so.[7] While planning together can bond community, it also can drive it into bitterly opposing camps. Small-townism is rife – and not only in small towns. Common as this is, it's not inevitable. It can easily be avoided through the consensus approach.

But doesn't rescuing a place and community depend on money? Money both solves and creates problems. It can improve physical surroundings, but 'heart' is not to be bought. Physical improvements convey messages of care – but if things are done *for* you, it's paternalistic care. Monetary support for things you're already doing or working towards shows trust, appreciation and external validation. It helps immeasurably, boosts confidence and re-vitalizes almost burnt-out will. Small sums sustain, even accelerate, momentum. However, large sums mean changing gear, which can cause organizations to suddenly lose the identity that drives them. And, in this new gear, they easily become dependent on this money before they realize how prone it is to external politics, and how many strings come with it.[8]

For communities in decline – and too many are – the consensus design process can initiate a renaissance. This won't be artificially dependent on one policy, one source of money, one person. But being self-fuelled, so independent of funders' initiative-inhibiting procedures, whims and policy changes, it will be more robust and inherently socially sustainable. Such a renaissance – and the place qualities it generates – is shaped by living pressures from within the community itself.

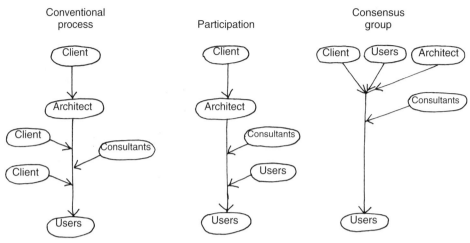

The design process. Who is involved? When? How integrated the result? And how satisfied are the users?

Notes

1   The roots of crime have been much studied. Early place-based crime prevention theories, based on Newman's *Defensible Space* (1973, Collier Books) and Jeffery's principles of crime prevention through environmental design (CPTED) focused primarily on physical design and the principles of territoriality, surveillance, boundary definition, access control and maintenance. Emerging theories take a broader view, including management and community involvement components as well as physical issues. For discussion of all of these theories and their application see Schneider R.H. and Kitchen T. (2002). *Planning for Crime Prevention: A Transatlantic Perspective*, Routledge.

2   Described more fully in *Community Architecture* (Wates N. and Knevitt C. (1987). Penguin Books, pp. 73–6) and *Building Communities: The First International Conference on Community Architecture Planning and Design* (Sneddon J. and Theobald C., eds (1987). Cais Ltd, pp. 28–30). Tenant participation was central to this project's success. The identical estate

next door, housing the same type of people and renovated by the same local authority, but *without* tenant involvement, reverted to a slum within six months of refurbishment.

3   Further examples include Black Road, Macclesfield, co-op schemes in Liverpool (both in Wates N. and Knevitt C., op. cit., pp. 70ff. and pp. 77ff.) The Eldonians, Liverpool (in Sneddon J. and Theobald C. eds, op. cit., pp. 26–28) and Harbordale Florida (in Schneider R.H. and Kitchen T., op. cit., pp. 159ff.).

4   This is one reason I always encourage groups to do at least some of the physical work themselves. Another benefit is that by de-mystifying building, people realize what they are able to do and so cease to be dependent on others. A third reason, at least as important, is that they can start *now*. Waiting for grants and governments can be initiative-stifling.

5   Many others have found that participatory design processes build self-esteem and enhance sense of community, for example: Laurie, Cooper Marcus and Blakely (reported in Hester R.T. (1990). *Community Design Primer*, Ridge Times Press, pp. 10–11)

6   For more about this Steiner school see: Day C. (1990). *Building with Heart*, Green Books; Day C. (1998). *A Haven for Childhood*, Starborn Books.

7   For example, the struggle of South Armour Square residents in Chicago against the building of a new high-profile stadium, which would wipe-out most of their neighbourhood. Although the residents eventually lost their battle, the process of resistance so reinvigorated community involvement they went on to win management of their own neighbourhood. (See Peterman W. (2000). *Neighborhood Planning and Community-Based Development*, Sage Publications, pp. 91ff.)

8   The economic vulnerability of the community can potentially result in subservience to a funder's agenda. To avoid this problem, H.J. Rubin suggests financial 'leveraging'. This essentially starts with a seed fund and builds further funding in stages (Rubin, H.J. (2000). *Renewing Hope Within Neighborhoods of Despair*, State University of New York Press, pp. 66ff. and pp. 176ff.).

CHAPTER THREE

Why not: shouldn't professionals lead design?

There are powerful arguments why professionals know best. Powerful and well rehearsed, for we've heard them for most of a century.

Architects, planners, engineers and surveyors may have made a mess of our world – but not necessarily a worse mess than anyone else. If nothing else, professionals know how to manage processes of design rationally and effectively. They know how to coordinate people and information; also how to arrange decision-making structures and single points of contact for unplanned (but inevitable) emergencies.

Professionals know lots of things, and – at least as importantly – know how to think in the relevant mode. That is their job, and why we employ them. Architects have five years of college training, most of which is needed to develop the ability to think *spatially*. And, because they've worked many years in a specialized field, they have more experience (though some might say also narrower blinkers) than non-architects can hope to have.

The knowledge held by occupants, users, homeowners and entrepreneurs is often limited to experience in a particular set of circumstances – not always relevant to a new building or social situation. A classic example is rural Irish travellers keeping

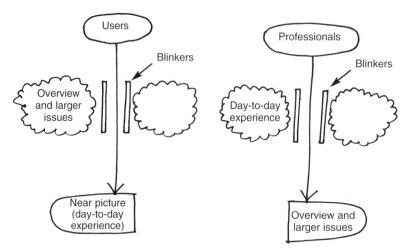

Users of professionals: no one group sees more than half the picture.

horses in the tower-block apartments in which a tidy-minded state has housed them, or ex-country-dwellers keeping a kettle boiling all day on a gas stove as though it were a peat-fired range. These mismatches of behaviour and surroundings result from the assumption that those who subsidize housing have the right to dictate way-of-life. The re-housing is (usually) well intended, but the pattern-of-life requirement unconscious. The decision-makers assume, at best, that everyone is like them; at worst, that they're indisputably right.

While professionals can usually see the big picture, local people tend to have disproportionate priorities – just *because* they are too close to things. Whole sets of buildings have to be located where they won't interfere with a tree someone planted last year (and so could easily be replanted next year), or a shed someone is so proud of having built. Recently, asked to help design an open-air theatre, I found its location had been fixed by proximity to toilets. This was an economic decision. Nothing wrong with that, but I felt it appropriate to ask some questions. What should drive the design? Approach, view, evening light and noise considerations – or toilets? One would influence audience numbers, hence economic viability; the other make small (but not insignificant) savings – greatly easing starting-up. This wasn't a case of one decision being right, the other wrong, but of seeing the larger and longer term picture, not readily visible to those on the spot, blinkered by the enormities of fund-raising.

Architects and designers have concerned themselves with aesthetics and taste for their whole designer life. Even if most of the time spent at work is committed to more mundane things, like complying with regulations, aesthetics and taste is what being a designer is all about.[1] Their taste may be rarefied, idiosyncratic or competitively individualistic, but they regard it as central to their profession.

There can never be any copyright on taste, but as it's fed by what we've experienced, 'public taste' is easily shaped by advertisements, magazines and the media. There are some very deliberate shapers of taste out there, including many architects, with agendas not everyone wishes to share.

To many architects and designers, popular taste is advertiser led, 'kitsch' and unsophisticated; and popular design concerns are short term, narrow in perspective and disproportionately prioritized. That is their view – and lamentably, they're often right. But this doesn't give anyone, not even me as a professional, the *right* to judge another's choice. Even if, for good reasons, I don't like their choice, that doesn't invalidate it.

If I am to find meaningfulness in design, it must accommodate others' wishes, indeed *fulfil* them. It must, of course, *also* satisfy me. Compromise will never achieve both of these aims. To do this, we have to identify what lies at the heart of what every different party wants, bring this out and raise it to a synthesized form.

Can this be achieved through the conventional architect-dominated process? Yes – there is evidence it *can* be. But, more compellingly, the evidence shows that this is rare.[2] So rare, that this is certainly not the *inevitable*, nor even the *probable* outcome.

In every other sphere of life, except perhaps the arts, teams have supplanted individuals. Life, after all, is about interactions: teamwork. Businesses nowadays depend upon it.[3] Amongst architecture firms, research has shown the more participatory are offices, the more effective, both in business and design quality.[4]

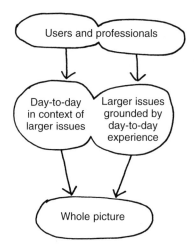

Users and *professionals: local experience* and *overview.*

Tycoons and prima donnas are something of the past: nowadays few of us want to hand over the place where we will live to such egocentric personalities.

The consensus design process is team based. The more socially inclusive this team, the better the chances of satisfying all parties. Meaningful design depends upon synthesized outlooks and inputs from both professionals *and* community.

Notes

1   While many nowadays consider architectural aesthetics purely subjective, it was once seen as a key element in improving people's lives and fostering better behaviour (see: Fisher T. (1996). Three models of future practice. In *Reflections on Architectural Practices in the Nineties* (W.S. Saunders, ed.), Princeton Architectural Press, p 37). This argument is less about *whether aesthetics affect people,* but what the *concept* means – that which is novel and artistic, or that which nourishes soul and spirit (see: Day C. (2002). *Spirit & Place,* Architectural Press).

2   The Royal Institute of British Architects' *Strategic Study of the Profession (Phase 2: Clients and Architects* (1993), RIBA Publications) reports that 'the gap between clients' needs and the service provided by architects is much larger than we could have anticipated ...'. Lawson and Pilling (1996) confirmed that both clients and architects are aware of communication problems: 'much of the frustration that architects and clients experience in design stems ... from a failure [of the architect] to engage with the client' (cited in Nicol D. and Pilling S. (2000). Architectural education and the profession. In *Changing Architectural Education: towards a new professionalism* (D. Nicol and S. Pilling, eds), E&FN Spon, p. 5).

3   Across diverse areas of work, teamwork not only speeds goal achievement, but also increases productivity and quality of output (for examples, see West M. (1994). *Effective Teamwork,* BPS Books, p. 1).

4   See Blau J.R. (1984). *Architects and Firms: A Sociological Perspective on Architectural Practice,* MIT Press.

CHAPTER FOUR

Consensus versus democracy

I have to admit that I am not a democrat. I have yet to be convinced that the right of the majority to impose its will on the minority can be ethically justified.[1] Nor do I believe in debate! I have never found arguing about things ever convinced anybody of opinions they didn't previously hold – nor that it produces speedy decisions.

So how can ethically acceptable decisions ever be reached? The more people involved in anything, the more viewpoints, vested interests, prejudices and other ordinary human failings. If two people have two points of dispute, ten will have a hundred. The chances of getting what everyone wants are – at best – miniscule.

Does this mean we have to compromise? Compromising, to my mind, means abandoning – or at least, de-prioritizing – what you want, or the principles you stand for and your own best means of achieving them. This isn't always such a bad thing. When two sides have positions so far apart that they've been fighting each other, it's not so bad to recognize that peace can be more important than sectarian aspirations. In architecture, however, if two (or more) parties are so opposed they resort to violence, they're hardly likely to get together enough to commission or build a building. This doesn't mean you can't have trans-sectarian building projects, but you don't *have* to have compromise in the environmental sphere. For peace instead of war, compromise is worthwhile. For buildings, compromise is neither necessary nor desirable.

At the core of the dictionary definition of consensus is 'general agreement; collective opinion [Latin = agreement (as consent)]'.[2] Consensus design is about everybody

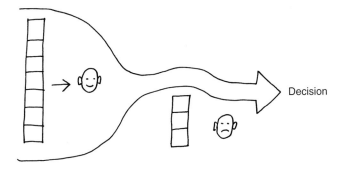

Decision

Voting.

getting – if not what they originally wanted – what, after working together and listening to the whole situation, they have *come to want*. In design, the 'whole situation' includes both buildings, the place where they'll be and the people who will use them. To get to consensus, however, two things must happen: we have to give up rigid past positions and move forward with flexibility. And we have to transcend our own individual-gain outlooks to look at what is best for all. Forward-looking inspiration and holistic consciousness now take the place of past-based narrowness and egotism. Once this is achieved, we, as a community, can agree – and agree willingly – about what is best for *all* of us.

A laudable ethic, but why should *I* do that? What's in it for *me*? Actually, quite a lot – for what improves things for all, invariably improves things for each individual. Peace in Northern Ireland is an example. And the stony road to it is also an example of what happens if the majority – or any other group – attempts to impose its preferences, outlook and values on the minority.

Consensus is not an *automatic* state. We may start with full agreement on major aims, but over details this is rare. Buildings are built out of details. That there will be a hall, office and garden may be easy to agree – but not how large, what shape, materials, proportions, where and how we can enter them, what light and colour qualities … and suchlike things. Yet you can't build buildings without deciding such details.

The old way was to agree to a basic remit (or programme) and authorize someone else (the architect) to get on with it. A more democratic way is to decide a chain of decisions, then vote on each one as it comes up. As I've stated, I don't like voting. I don't like the resentments of those who've been outvoted, the political horse-trading often necessary for voting success, the polarization and debates. I don't believe voting is fair to all – certainly it isn't to the outvoted minority. And I don't believe it's necessary. But how can we achieve consensus if we start out with differences of opinion, background or outlook?

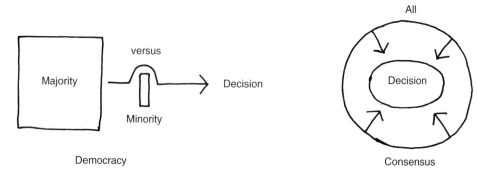

Reaching decisions: democratic or consensual routes.

Obviously, we can only do this if we can step back from the ideas, opinions and strong feelings most people start with. I don't believe we should ignore these – for each person they are completely valid. But their premature form, personalized viewpoints and associations obstruct any coming together. If they're expressed at the wrong time, they easily obstruct agreement, if not lead to argument.

We certainly shouldn't suppress the emotive. Emotion is a very real, if invisible level of life. Without it, we aren't human. Moreover, ignoring how other people feel wouldn't just be disrespectful or even crushing – it would deny, and probably destroy, the motivation somebody comes with – and in so doing assault their whole being.

I know it's important that I listen to, and respect, emotional statements. We can't go forward as a group unless we know these strong feelings. But we can only work constructively if we know where they *come from*, so we can objectify the issues they are knotted into. This opens avenues of dealing with these issues in non-reaction-triggering ways. Unless we can work at a *pre-emotive* level, we'll never be free from reaction and counter reaction. These will bounce us from one pole to the other and never let us get a dispassionate overview.

But even after treading carefully into emotionally mine-free ground, how can we obtain agreement, let alone consensus? What shape, for instance, should a building be?

Are there shapes, colours, moods of light and sound that affect all people – at a pre-thought, pre-conscious level – in more or less the same way? I believe so.[3] But I don't believe I can just tell people that. This would be the 'trust me, I'm an architect' road. And this doesn't have a good reputation.

If we start out by trying to agree these shapes, colours and so on, we aren't likely to get far. Choosing colour schemes has led to many bitter arguments. I like blue, she likes yellow; we could mix them and make green – then neither of us is happy. At the *other* end, however, the less specific, but more fundamental end – we ought to be able to agree the underlying essence of a project.

Indeed, if we can't agree this, which is central to what the project is for, the project is never likely to ever get going – certainly a building won't get built. Once we agree what a project, or room, is *about* then we'll have a fair idea of what *mood* is appropriate. It won't be hard to agree this. If we know the mood we're after, some colours and colour relationships are clearly inappropriate – and others will support this mood. This is about the universal – physiological – effects of colour: its 'soul-quality'.[4] Colours are never isolated. Each always has a context – so is influenced by what we see before and after it. This temporal relationship (our journey sequence) further narrows the colour range that would be appropriate. We haven't necessarily agreed the precise colour, but we're very close to it. More importantly we've aligned ourselves *to what the situation needs*. No longer led by our own preferences – which have nothing to do with the situation – final agreement is now easy.

In my view, this is much fairer, more constructive and more conscious – so more fully involving – than voting. This is why I prefer consensus to democracy.

Which level to start at?

Existing situation: sequence of levels for consensus appraisal.

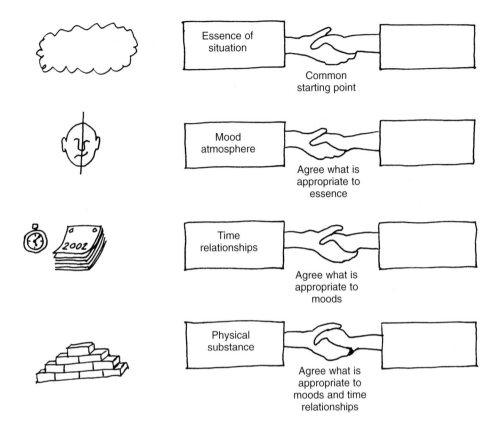

Design stage: sequence of levels for consensus decisions.

Notes

1   This is not to say democracy has never been right! The ancient Athenian step from autocracy to equality of voting amongst the slave-owning upper class was a *huge* step for its time. So also has been the superseding of colonial or fascist authoritarianism by 'one person, one vote'. Moreover, many social infrastructures are unsuited to consensual systems, leaving democracy the best alternative. Nonetheless, while some see its innate confrontational tendency as a debate-sharpening asset, I distrust – and dislike – confrontational, power-based, decision-making.

2   The definition is broader, and includes 'majority view' (*Concise Oxford Dictionary*, 9th edn, Oxford University Press). I use the word, however, in the 'agreement' sense.

3   This is not to ignore the effect of culture on environmental perception. While the links between colour and emotion are culturally influenced, colour also has trans-cultural effects, influencing for instance, blood-pressure (see, for example: Cassidy T. (1997). *Environmental Psychology*. Psychology Press; Bayes K. (1970). *The Therapeutic Effect of Environment on Emotionally Disturbed and Mentally Handicapped and Mentally Subnormal Children*, Unwin Brothers Ltd).

4   Cultural and personal factors are also involved, but group working balances these out. Universal factors are both stronger and shared by all. (See: Day C. (1990). *Places of the Soul*, Thorsons; and Day C. (2002). *Spirit & Place*, Architectural Press.)

CHAPTER FIVE

Community & players

Surviving change

Places change. The history of most towns is one of organic change – mostly small changes, but a continuous abundance of them. Until recently, nearly all were generated by local circumstance, only occasionally interspersed with larger changes originating from external sources. The coming of the railways, building of by-passes, motorways or edge-of-town supermarkets brought sudden social, economic and physical re-patterning. Such changes are often outside the absorptive capacity of the organic continuum – just as buildings or activities that change the face of a town or district can also be. Communities (nimbies excepted) may crave employment generators, but if these are too large they're socially and environmentally dislocating.

Humans are adaptable, but only so adaptable. Change is exciting if you're young and feel confined by a claustrophobic present or are optimistic about a new future unfolding. But it's frightening if you're trying to hang-on to the threads of a fast-disappearing world, a way of life, a memory-laden past, an appreciation (even if just a nostalgic one) of how things *were*.

It's a fact of life that communities, industries and places grow or decline. Sometimes growth and decline work subtle, organic changes to places; sometimes major. Will these be traumatic or beneficial? Can the direction and process be managed? And by whom?

There is a growing appreciation that healthy change depends upon a lot more than government or council planning and entrepreneurial finance. Successful planning must involve a diversity of interested parties: the 'players' and the 'community' who live or work in a place. Involvement means more than just sounding off concerns at public meetings. But the players who hope to see advantages and a community that fears change can easily have polar positions; one tending towards exploitive imposition, the other towards ossifying nostalgia.

Players and community see things differently, but, except where aims are totally antithetical – like nuclear waste dump and living community – confrontation rarely serves either party.

Between the well-worked-out strategies of players, and disparate, but emotively laden ideas of community, between the needs of the community as a whole and of the place where all this will happen, we need to somehow find common ground. One route is to clarify the 80% of hopes and fears most people agree on, and argue and compromise through the remaining 20%.[1] Another is to step back to the level before

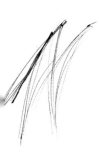

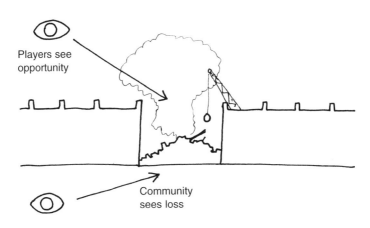

Players see
opportunity

Community
sees loss

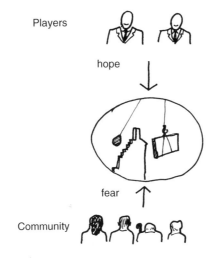

Players

hope

fear

Community

formed ideas in order to achieve consensus. As this seems a better way to deal with that 20%, it is the route I practise.

Community and non-community

We can't go very far in reconciling players and community, without knowing what we mean by 'community'.[2] Nowadays, lots of people haven't even spoken to their neighbours.[3] There is no communality about such a 'community'. Indeed, it has few claims to the word, for *meaningful* community has many layers, overlapping bonds and a resilient web of multiple relationships. Nonetheless, when big changes are imminent to a neighbourhood, all will be affected by them. In this sense all the strangers who live near each other are in one way a 'community'.

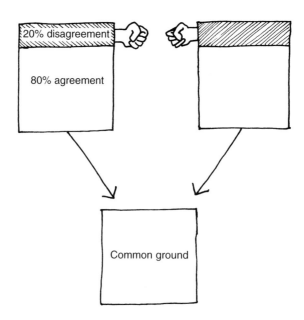

Mediation skills.

Community – like place – is essentially formed by the past. That's why new towns take a generation (or more) to socially 'settle down'. You know – and trust – people because you have *met* them, *got to know* them, *heard* things about them – all past tense. And much the same for places.

Social places don't necessarily stay social. The Welsh mining valleys are linear settlements and many villages are just long single streets. A generation ago, nearly every man walked past neighbours' doors to work. With the pits now closed, there's no camaraderie at work – indeed no work – and streets nowadays are for driving on. Past forms, even social forms, don't necessarily suit contemporary life.

Nor do communities stay the same people. Populations shift faster and faster. Half a century ago many country people spent most of their lives in the same parish, and had never travelled beyond the market town. Now you're lucky if you can even find work so close. Most industrial towns have immigrant populations – and increasing numbers of asylum seekers from all over the world. In London (as of 1999) 93 languages are spoken. Immigrants bring their own religions, cultural patterns, food and sometimes clothing. Global influence also brings new food and clothing trends. Where were hamburger and pizza restaurants before World War II?

This isn't *fixed* community. Global personal mobility has brought globalist currents into parochial societies often before they're ready to recognize their own narrowness. This brings a fantastic richness – but also an identity threat for those who look to the past for their identity. The twenty-first century is, in this respect, very much a 'new world'. But there can never be social harmony while a scattering of mutually mistrustful sub-groups are aggressively defensive about how they're superiorly different. Social harmony depends on a framework where diversity can be seen as enrichment.

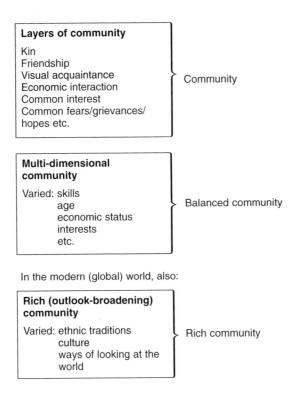

```
┌─────────────────────────────┐
│ Layers of community         │
│                             │
│ Kin                         │
│ Friendship                  │ ⎫
│ Visual acquaintance         │ ⎬  Community
│ Economic interaction        │ ⎭
│ Common interest             │
│ Common fears/grievances/    │
│ hopes etc.                  │
└─────────────────────────────┘

┌─────────────────────────────┐
│ Multi-dimensional           │
│ community                   │
│                             │
│ Varied: skills              │ ⎫
│         age                 │ ⎬  Balanced community
│         economic status     │ ⎭
│         interests           │
│         etc.                │
└─────────────────────────────┘

In the modern (global) world, also:

┌─────────────────────────────┐
│ Rich (outlook-broadening)   │
│ community                   │
│                             │ ⎫
│ Varied: ethnic traditions   │ ⎬  Rich community
│         culture             │ ⎭
│         ways of looking at the │
│         world               │
└─────────────────────────────┘
```

This framework is a cornerstone of community. One of its key supports is *place*. Both community and place evolve, sometimes faster than we might choose, but retain some sort of stability through a *sense of continuum*. Continuum is fragile – too large a change and it's submerged. It depends on confidence in a place's durability – knowing what is there, what to expect. It also depends on memory – with all the values it layers upon places.

Being past-formed, community and place are threatened by change. Not surprisingly, communities are typically *fearful of change*. Especially if they haven't asked for it. But places *will* change. Often, as old formative patterns decline and new ones emerge, this change will come in large steps, financed and influenced by external sources. How can the conflict between fears of change and its inevitability be resolved?

Players

The 'players' are those who have a vested interest in change. They see the future as an opportunity; something to be shaped more by their individual aspirations than by the stream of continuity (what is there and what was there). They look forward to change, for change – if so directed – can unlock the potentials latent in a place. For many players, development – change – is all about *hope*.

These hopes, however, are already substantially shaped. Each player tends to have specific, often selfish, gains in mind and ideas about how to achieve these. Sound as

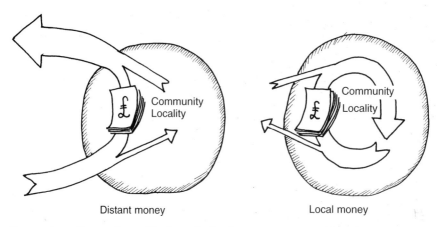

Distant money   Local money

Finance from distant players bleeds profits back to its source. Local finance tends to cycle through local-contact networks

these ideas may be, one person's idea for progress rarely suits everybody else. So how can individually held aspirations be deflected to the service of the community as a whole?

Players, community and non-community

Nowadays we recognize how essential is the participation of all involved in any planning for change.[4] There is, however, plenty of conflict potential: fear versus hopes; the commonly valued versus the individualized, egoistically conceived; the rigidity of the past versus the endlessly unfolding future; community versus players.

What separates these groups? What unites them? What can transcend the separateness? Bring socially introspective and exclusive parts into a whole? Transform diversity from a fragmenting to a healthy influence? Must hopes and fears, past and future, individual and community, the stable and the growing, be incompatible?

Players and community have different agenda, seek different things, but both need each other for an 'easy ride'. Moreover, there is one incontrovertible fact to put any apparent conflicts into perspective: the place *will* change. The new can either be planted *into*, or *onto* the old – so resolution is in everybody's best interests.

If new is to grow out of, not be imposed upon, old, its advocates need to know the old. To *complement* a place, changes need to build upon its strengths and remedy its imbalances. Changes that don't benefit places leave wounds. Resentment, lack of local support and ecological mis-fit can lead to over-dependence on distant conditions, hence economic fragility. So players, as much as community, benefit by knowing it in depth before doing anything. Likewise, both parties need to fully understand the proposed initiative and its implications. Only then will they be ready to consider how each can, at least, avoid compromising the other; at best, fulfil each other's needs.

Communities that can harness the positive processes of change already at work, can *grow*.[5] Whatever the injection of externally sourced money – which inevitably means externally attached strings – such communities can grow *organically* in a way that suits them. This is quite different from imposed changes that characterize the divisive supremacy of one set of narrow ideas over another. This is growth for place, for economy *and* for people. Working with economically responsive, socially consolidating and environmentally enriching tendencies can encourage jobs, sociability and place quality. All of which help non-communities to grow into communities.

Notes

1   Amongst techniques, see: H.J. Rubin's 'organic theory of development'. This guide for developmental activists aims to reconcile the apparently contradictory goals of players and community (Rubin H.J. (2000). *Renewing Hope Within Neighborhoods of Despair*, State University of New York Press, pp. 133–).

2   For discussion of what is meant by community (and in some cases neighbourhood) see: Peterman W. (1999). *Neighborhood Planning and Community-Based Development*, Sage Publications. pp. 10–22; Mehrhoff W.A. (1999). *Community Design: A Team Approach to Dynamic Community Systems*, Sage Publications, pp.15–26; Ward C. (1993). *New Town, Home Town*, Calouste Gulbekian Foundation, p. 19.

3   A MORI poll published in December 1999 showed that 10% of people in Great Britain hadn't spoken to any of their neighbours in the past week – 26% had spoken to only one or two people. (*Caring Society 1989 – 1999*, MORI)

4   Indeed, in 1998, 35 countries and the European Community signed the UN/ECE Convention on Access to Information, Public Participation in Decision-Making and Access to Justice in Environmental Matters. This convention recognizes that, to be effective, sustainable development depends on full and active public involvement in decision-making at all levels.

5   This is illustrated by a case study in *Renewing Hope in Neighborhoods of Despair* (op. cit., pp. 221–222), in which the Harlem community was initially very negative in its response to the city's plans to build a huge sports facility. Helped by a developmental activist, they were able to turn initial fears about potential gentrification into a plan for revitalization of the historic district, developing the Blues district as an entertainment attraction – a product for export. This created jobs and wealth for the area as well as supporting cultural identity.

CHAPTER SIX

Design process for sustainability

Recent decades have seen a huge increase in ecological awareness. Sustainability has become an everyday word, and energy-efficient and low carbon dioxide-causing design is now part of everyday good practice. But what does consensus design have to do with sustainability?

Lamentably – and worryingly – little human action is sustainable. 'Sustainability' isn't just a euphemism for 'ecological'. For something to be sustainable, it must *continue*. And, as nearly every stable ecosystem in today's world is held in balance by a partnership of humanity and nature, this continuance depends upon people. Hence – as Agenda 21 recognizes – human value cannot be sidelined.[1]

Consensus design has obvious *social* benefits, but these days we are waking up to the need for all development to be sustainable in ecological as well as social and economic terms. Ecological, social and economic design are all specialist areas. So specialist that we still – after some 30 years of 'ecological' architecture, 80 of 'social' and many more of economy-led – can't get them quite right. Few would dispute the ethical desirability of socially inclusive design. But what do 'ordinary' people know about ecology? Shouldn't the desperate need for specialist knowledge override any wishy-washy ideals about social inclusion? Isn't sustainability more important than consensus?

Consider the old, pre-industrial, way of building. It had to be more or less sustainable, otherwise people, society and a relatively stable ecology would not have survived for perhaps 10 000 years of building. We can't say the same for the latter half of the twentieth century – a period of hitherto unimaginable environmental exploitation and desecration. One central difference between pre-industrial people and us today is that they worked in harmony with, and with respect for, nature. This wasn't necessarily a loving respect, but to disregard nature's energies meant trouble, often death. Relationship to nature was based on a combination of awe and pragmatic necessity. Nature was strong. You could work *with* her and survive, even flourish, or oppose her and founder. The power of modern technology – and the attitude that came with it – changed this. We now can, and routinely do, *overcome* nature. Overcoming is scarcely a recipe for harmony.

We may choose to respect nature, respect other people, but we have to *learn* how to work in harmony with them. And there's a lot to learn – perhaps more than we can ever fully achieve. The consensus design process, however, raises *consciousness of our relationships* with our natural and social environment: place and people. It is out of these conscious relationships that design for development and the buildings themselves, condense. They don't have to have sustainability aspects grafted on to them – these are already there.

Proprietary stewardship

All buildings bear environmental costs. The largest part of their energy (and CO_2) costs is due to heating and cooling. Design can minimize this. But, as these are costs of *use*, energy-conscious design is easily overridden by energy-unconscious use. Smokers keeping windows wide open in cold weather, for instance, negate all the effort put into energy saving, just as televisions on constant standby undo the electricity savings from low-energy bulbs.

Things, including buildings, looked after, work better and use less energy as well as lasting longer. This is a matter of attitude: things loved and understood are usually cared for, whereas someone *else's* treasure, on the other hand, is often just an un-asked for liability. This is one of the problems of rented buildings. Even here, however, the more people are involved in design,[2] the better able, and the more willing, they tend to be about responsible use.

It's easy to dismiss the attitude of users as outside the sustainable design sphere. Their attitude, however, is crucial to its success. The unfortunate fact is that many places devalue people – with predictable cyclic effect; those people don't value that place. Nor is there any shortage of buildings that place little value on the life of nature, and on the place already there. To their designers the place is just a 'site' – an area upon which to build a building; and after its desecration by the construction process, they just plant trees, shrubs and grass. (If you can't think what else to plant, then just grass – acres of it.)

Think 'site' – somewhere to put a building – or think 'place' – somewhere to do things.

Consensus design reconnects people with place. Moreover, the buildings that result from this process revere both people and place, the life of nature and of human activities. The beauty that emerges arises from the unlocked potentials of place, people and situation. It's not just added. It is integral, just as the trees, shrubs and even perhaps grass are.

The multi-layer connection that, through the consensus process, the design group has with a place makes for designs that subsequent generations of users can connect with more deeply than just through immediate sensorial delight. Somewhere where I can lie in a deckchair in the sun might be pleasant, but after a while I get a niggling sense of inadequate meaning in the place. I only have one level of connection to it: a suntan but empty boredom. Progressive layers of connection, built upon each other, enrich this meaning – and nourish us thereby.

In contrast there are places where every message conflicts: visually attractive but noisy (from traffic or air-conditioning fans), restful and comfortable, but smelling of new plastic – so claustrophobic. Others are secure and luxurious but socially insulated, even defended islands. These sort of things happen when design is not holistic, not a process open to the wholeness of the situation, no more than a single level and, at that, solely visual in concern. Clearly that is not a sustainable approach.

No 'ecological' places for people will be sustainable unless people *want* to live there, want to maintain them, imprint them with care. We tend to care for things to which we feel connected, and not for ones where we don't. The more levels of connection, the deeper is our relationship.

The deepened connection and multi-level practicability gained through the four-level consensus process gives users a sense of ownership. This in turn fosters responsibility, and a relationship of growing attachment developing into proprietary care – the foundation of *stewardship*. All of this is built on a foundation of respect, even reverence. Respect for what is already there, for what wants to be there, for the people involved. Respect for place demands that we become as conscious of what it *can't* accept as what it can. Beauty cannot be built on disrespect – that's what makes for ugliness, whether visual, acoustic, racist or socially exploitative. Nor can stewardship.

Development within time-continuum

At the centrepoint of the consensus process is the time-continuum stage. We look *backwards* to see how a place has been formed: its journey to the present. Then we look *forwards* to where the place is going: its journey into the future. Once you see something in a long time perspective, this overcomes most tendencies to shortsightedness. Shortsightedness is a classic problem of unsustainable architecture. In particular, it is shortsightedness about environmental impacts that makes conventional architecture so non-ecological. No concern for where things come from and go to, no worries about obsolescence when styles change, nor about harmonizing with surroundings, or about maturing place.

Buildings themselves have significant costs embodied in their materials and construction. Inappropriate buildings need frequent re-vamping; some get demolished within 30 years. Such buildings may not have seemed inappropriate when built; some were the height of fashion. But, unaligned to the current of time, they rapidly became unsuited to changing circumstances. Others were never really what their occupants wanted.

Once we concern ourselves with time-continuum, our relationship to future consequences becomes conscious, no longer either a 'problem' or an issue easy to ignore. The better buildings are matched to people and place, the better they will be cared for, and the more tolerant the occupants will be of any shortcomings. The better their alignment to time-currents, the longer will be their relevance. For both reasons, they tend to last longer. The longer they last, the lower their economic and environmental costs.[3]

Even if we're wrong about how we picture the future developing, we're unlikely to be as far wrong as if we had never considered it. Indeed, because we start out focused on the *relationships* of things, people, forces and processes and the moods and spirit of places, we can reasonably expect to be quite close. It is this *relationship focus* that is essential to any *really* sustainable building. The gadgets – from solar panels to composting toilets – are only bits and pieces. Essential, but not in themselves enough for wholeness and harmony.

Elemental sustainabilities

Since Aristotle, we've been familiar with the concept that our world is made up of four elemental constituents.[4] These four elements make comprehensive, meaningful and also convenient categories for reviewing ecological impacts: mineral resources and pollutants, water, air quality and energy. But the elements are more than just earth-sourced minerals, water, air and fire. They're also qualities of life and soul, and they are manifest as layers of our being – and the being of all living places and living situations (see Chapter 7).[5]

The four-layer consensus design process, in working through the physical, time-based, emotional and individual layers of *place* also connects us to the currents of the substantive, the fluid, the expressive and the inspirational: elements within our own selves as well as within society, situations and places. The more we are awake to the resonance in our own selves, the more consciously are we aware of what elemental imbalances or emphases do to places.

Elemental balance, as in forest or farmland, is about dynamic, ecological stability, namely *life-vigour*. Elemental emphasis, as in mountains, crashing waves or burning desert, is about raw power – the *source* from which modern living so disconnects us. We need both balance and emphasis, to physically sustain life and also as food for the soul. Unfortunately, there's not a lot of either in everyday life. Because this lack is mostly unconscious, we are normally only aware that something is missing in life. Some turn to risk-rich adventure (sometimes safer cyber-adventure), sensory stimulus, chemical stimulants or protective social cliques to fill this void. Others just find life boring, insecure or overpowering. The more, however, we can bring these issues to consciousness the better we can resolve them in our surroundings – with therapeutic resonance in our soul.

The consensus process gives a multi-dimensionality to elemental issues which can raise their meaning beyond the merely physical. We recognize sunlight as not *just* for thermal energy but also to warm the soul. Likewise material is not just something to recycle, but is anchoring and rooting; water not just to conserve and clean but also to enliven us through its fluid mobility and rhythmical motion; and air not just an issue of pollution, but, particularly through sound and scent, an agent of emotional connection between, for instance, indoors and outdoors.

This gives deepening of meaning to the otherwise physically bound relationships of ecology. Also to the strong feelings we have about environmental issues; it enlivens the often archivistically dry matters of heritage and history; it makes tangible the sometimes romantic, mystical, approach to 'spirit-of-place'. It also clarifies what we, as humans, can contribute to places. Without this *understanding* it's easy to view people as only destroyers of place, ecological balance and planet – for there is certainly enough evidence to support this view. With such holistic understanding, however, we can work as *contributors* to nature, to places, to society – this brings us nearer to the real, the holistic, meaning of the word 'economy'.[6]

But don't specialists know more than lay-people about ecology and how to design in an ecologically responsible manner? Of course – otherwise they wouldn't be specialists! Few communities have such skills among their members, so such people are invaluable. Without a consensus-based, multi-layer *approach*, however, ecological design can serve the ethically dedicated, but though its admonitory strictures may convince others of its necessity for human survival, it doesn't necessarily have any great appeal. Indeed, imposed 'ecological' design is easily resented.

Once, however, we can connect material necessity with soul nourishment, the needs of nature with our own, and the needs of place with the needs of our activities there, sustainable design ceases to be an add-on extra. It becomes the obvious, even inevitable, way to do things. That is what the consensus design process is about.

Notes

1   Agenda 21, signed by 179 nations at the UN Conference on *Environment and Development* in Rio de Janeiro in 1992, calls for each community to formulate its own Local Agenda 21, through dialogue between local authorities, citizens, local organizations, and private enterprises. 'Through consultation and consensus-building, local authorities would learn from citizens and from local, civic, community, business and industrial organizations and acquire the information needed for formulating the best strategies' (Agenda 21, Chapter 28, sec 1.3).

2   And, management, improvements and maintenance.

3   Providing, of course, they're not high consumers of energy in their operation and maintenance.

4   Oriental tradition recognizes five: wood (living matter) in China, spirit (or breath) in India are fifth elements. These differentiations stem from their ingrained world outlooks. Mine, however, is European, so four I know, the fifth I only *think*. (See, for instance: Puri B.B. (1995). *Vedic Architecture and the Art of Living*, Vastu Gyan; and any book on *Feng-Shui*.)

5   For greater detail, see: Day C. (2002) *Spirit & Place*. Architectural Press.

6   Economy: '**1 a** the wealth and resources of a community ... [... from Greek *oikonomia* 'household management', from *oikos* 'house' + *nemo* 'manage']' (*The Concise Oxford Dictionary*, 9th edn (1995) Oxford University Press).

PART THREE

Consensus Design: How?

Participant's comments:

In the design process led by Christopher Day we all learned to listen to the place in such a selfless manner that our initial and therefore shallow preconceptions were held back. Having listened to the moods and the feelings of areas of the place we imagined how the place had been over 100 years ago and traced a probable path of change up to the present day and 50 years into the future. By undertaking this simple but fascinating analysis in groups the 'common sense' of our combined understanding began to emerge. Once we knew the site a bit better we began to allow the complex series of buildings required by the client to settle in their appropriate place on the site and by modelling it as a group an incarnation emerged with such sensitivity it already felt like it belonged.

Ben Bolgar – Architect, London (ASHA project)

CHAPTER SEVEN

The principles behind
the process

The techniques described in this book aren't just pragmatic. A structure of understanding, outlook, even philosophy, underlies them. If you're only interested in practical applications, skip this chapter (for the present). But don't regard it as irrelevant, for practical technique is like technology. Modern technology, as everyone knows, works: but it's no longer fully bound to what science now knows.[1] To *develop*, it requires re-appraisal in the light of modern scientific discoveries. So when you've successfully used these techniques two or three times, please read – or re-read – this chapter.

Ideas and aspirations

Community decision-making is nothing new. Even community planning, a fashion movement for the media in the 1970s and 1980s, still continues, albeit without much publicity. There are a number of well-established techniques for community decision-making.[2] Each of these methods has unique strengths. Some, by their apparently undemanding structure, leave people free to express their deep-felt concerns, and assure them that they have been heard and taken seriously. Some put the community in the driving seat. Others round out professionalism into a holistic, multi-faceted approach. Some focus on emotive issues, others on practical matters, but in an emotionally strong process.

   Most community design techniques are ideas based in one form or other. From the inevitable plethora of ideas that emerge, it takes considerable skill from design leaders to reconcile (apparent) differences and find common themes. Mediation skills may be valuable in nearly every situation, but they don't come easily. There are people who can extract the essence of what each conflicting party wants, present it as a non-threatening case, and show how its acceptance is to mutual benefit. I have high respect for those who can do this. I can't. Fortunately, I never need to, because the consensus process is built on a different approach.

   Of many possible routes to reach consensus in community design, this book focuses on *one* particular technique. Having evolved this over three decades of working with building users, I know it works. As the case-studies show, it doesn't have a rigid form, but, being principle based, has a clear structure. Unlike most other community design processes, this technique is not ideas based. Indeed it deliberately does *not* start with ideas. In an ideas-led world, why doesn't it? How does this non-ideas process work?

Virtually every project starts with ideas – usually lots of them, mostly sound and well thought-out. It's natural, for many people have been worrying and thinking about issues for a long time. Everybody involved has at least one suggestion for improving the place. But 'improving' according to their own viewpoint, hence criteria. Naturally enough, these differ and compete. This doesn't help agreement, doesn't help the place, doesn't help things to go forward. Moreover, there are often strong feelings and personal-worth issues bound to these ideas. Emotive values are potentially explosive. It takes special skills to put lids back on when they blow off.

This is why I like to start at a pre-idea level: the only level at which agreement comes easily. This will get us where we want to go quicker, more equitably and with richer multi-dimensionality than any idea debating, synthesizing or bargaining.

We always therefore, start safely: communally looking at what is there, *now:* the physical description. It's something which, even though we each see different things, we can all agree on.

But places aren't fixed things. They're slowly changing *frameworks* through which life flows. No still photograph or flying visit describes a place in any meaningful depth. We need to know it in a *time context*. Getting to know the biography of a place is always interesting, but this has more value than just raising interest. Places have more depth when we understand their history – much of which is also family history for the people who live there, hence emotionally laden. And, even more importantly, we begin to see the *reasons* they have taken the form and character they – and their people – have. Most important of all, we start to enter into the stream of time so that the future is no longer a list of options to choose among, but a current to harness.

When we consider the moods of a place, concealed values start to emerge. Many are built on memories, others on different perceptions. Children experience, value, and focus upon, places differently than adults. Adults all too often forget to look, and easily *think* too much to uninhibitedly *feel*. Sometimes also, childhood perceptions, treasures, horrors and fears can colour adult response.[3] What disciplinarian torments – or, for others, carefree happy memories – even just seeing a picture of an old school can bring up. As both outsider and adult, I can never imagine these feelings.

Though quite opposing facets may first come to mind, everyone knows the spirit of a community. Also the spirit of the place that is home to it. Some may focus on what is of value. Others on shortcomings. But – quaintness or impracticality, friendliness or nosiness – we are all talking of one place, albeit with several sides, so it's not impossible to find a single description – like humanly warm – even if qualified by conditions (like: sometimes claustrophobically so). Despite the polarities of players and community, of small-townist factions and clans, of the myriad of competing, often conflicting ideas, this much, so far, can be agreed on.

The problem now is to extend this consensus into a plan for the future. But before any plan, what should the place where the new will happen *'say'*, be about? It can, of course, say anything, but unless this is a development of what it now says – a metamorphosis, shaped by hope, of what already *is* – it won't feel at home there. This

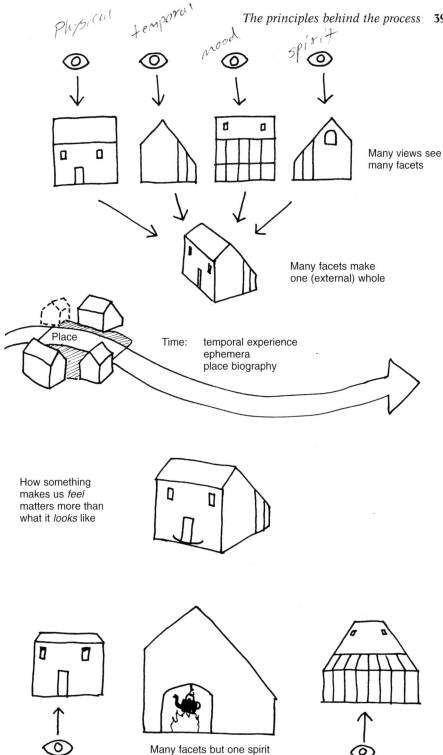

Places build meaning through their four layers: physical, temporal, mood and spirit.

is about relating the essence, the spirit, of a project to the essence of a place, its 'spirit-of-place'. This gives a frame for all future discussions, plans and actions. Anything outside this frame will undermine the spirit we're working towards. Anything within it will support these.

We start the design-stage, therefore, with communally generating a phrase that encompasses the aspirations of all involved; a phrase to encapsulate the essence of what we hope to achieve, or 'spirit-of-project' (the spirit-of-future-place), nourishing for the whole community.

Usually, people whom circumstances have brought together can agree on some issues of principle. Republicans and Loyalists in Belfast don't need to speak to each other to agree that peace is something they all hope for. About practical details, however, they could hardly be further apart. Similarly, on a housing estate, some may want fun for children, others tranquillity for the elderly. As adventure playgrounds and tranquil gardens – namely, as *physical manifestations* – these may be dramatically opposed.

But as 'spirit-of-place' nourishing both young and old, for the whole community, they need not be. It's not hard to find a phrase that encompasses both aspirations. After all, both parties want a socially sustainable – which means multi-generational – community. It *is*, however, hard to find physical forms that satisfy both – if we go straight to this stage. If instead, however, we hold back and let the spirit at the heart of things slowly condense into form, we can find the forms appropriate to all. It is this 'spirit-of-place' that lies at the heart of the consensus design process.

Spirit-of-place

We live in, and on, a material world. A planet with land and vegetation, buildings and rooms, furniture, bits, pieces and all manner of things. But even the most atheistic amongst us refer to the 'spirit' of a place and 'places of spirit'. What does this 'spirit' mean? Does it have any bearing on daily life? Can it be designed into a place? And, if so, is this possibility compromised or enhanced by consensus process?

By any definition, spirit is not material. The material can cradle, enclose or focus the spirit of a place, but this spirit is fed by, amongst other things, the values, thoughts, emotions and actions of people who live in, work in and use the place. Castles can be as old as, and as visually dramatic as, cathedrals – but they don't have the same spirit (and indeed, one cathedral can have a very different spirit from another because the motives behind their building and the secular power they exert-

Even buildings which hardly show can alter the mood of a place immeasurably.

ed varied greatly). Military bunkers can look like the landscape; nuclear power-stations like breweries; toxic waste-dumps like quarries. But they emanate totally different auras. Use – and the attitudes, values and feelings that go with use – influences, builds or alters the spirit-of-place. In turn, spirit-of-place influences us: our behaviour, attitudes and moods. There are places in which we don't think twice about dropping litter, pushing and shoving, shouting, even swearing. Others where we feel constrained, courteous, respectful, even reverent.

At the heart of every project lies its (usually unvoiced) inspiration, its spirit. Homes aren't about roofs, but the spirit under them. It is spirit-of-place that affects us in places. Yet we only meet them through their substance – for our five physical senses are only attuned to *physical* things like chemical composition, weight, pressure and light.[4] And, although they change all the time, we only see what's there *now*.

Can spirit be designed into places? Design can make places upliftingly beautiful – but this only sets the scene. It's the people who use a place that breed its spirit. And, as spirit is so bound up with the community of 'users' (those who actually use the place), it is they who influence what direction this spirit takes. This is a practical reason for participatory design to add to the ethical ones.

Not all users start out honest about their interaction with each other and the place; many have their own undeclared agendas. One of the purposes of the consensus design process is to rise above this all too human level to reach the level of truth that resounds in, serves the interests of, and is fulfilling for, all involved. This is about social cohesion and communal vision; personal empowerment, self-esteem and inner growth. But it's also about design that is right for place, ecological context and contextual continuity. Neither is more important; the human and environmental benefits result from each other. Can we really do all this? From my experience: yes.

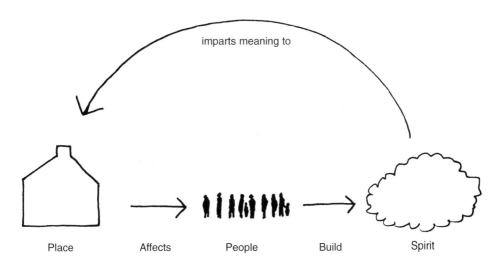

| Place | Affects | People | Build | Spirit |

Places are material, but it's their spirit that matters to us – and this is influenced by how, and why, people use them.

Science and art: understanding and creating

We meet places and things – like people – through our senses. But to *understand* them, we must uncover principles – like organizing patterns – that underlie this sense-accessible surface. This is what responsible science is about: understanding the depths.[5]

Science requires objectivity in place of subjectivity. To explain things, scientists need evidence, so they're interested in what *has* happened. To prove things, they need repeated experiments, giving predictable, repeatable results. The scientific approach, therefore, tends to conformity, sameness.[6]

When this approach is applied to buildings, it makes sense to repeat the most rationally functional designs. But as repetition implies mass-production, focus easily shifts from best suited to most economically produced. And even with the best-suited designs, relevance declines as time goes on. Factory-built houses can be attuned to the exact needs of a model family. But not only are *real* model families rare, we live so differently from only a few decades ago that it's likely life will be different again a few years hence.

Art, on the other hand, focuses on creating things – how to use what's there to make something new, something *as yet unmade*. Pursuit of novelty can easily override fulfilment of archetypal soul needs, so individualistic designs don't necessarily even feed those individuals they're designed for. Moreover, innovation and soul-expression commonly lead to individualistic personal expression – the more novel, the better. Of course, sometimes there are good reasons why something has *not* been done before. Nor do all of us want to be victim to someone else's whim.

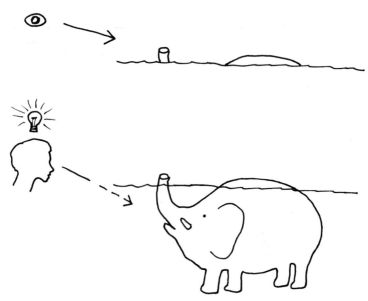

Understanding means penetrating beyond what we see.

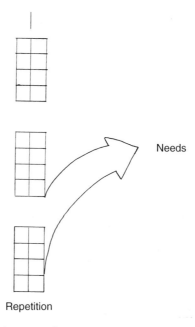

Repetition means sameness, but needs change as time progresses.

Although common, this is narrow, *unbalanced*, polarized science and art. A more holistic, complete science and art can touch every soul. Understanding is about the *past-formed present*. Creation is about *where we go from here*. Just as the present – life – only exists in the tension between past and future, the fixed unalterable and the ever-flexible unknown, so do the findings of the scientist ask for creative development, and the innovations of the artist need a foundation of understanding. *Life*, after all, is neither about unvarying repetition, nor the endlessly novel. It always involves the interaction of universal principles with individualizing context. Neither

Place and idea, past and future. How can they meet, not fight?

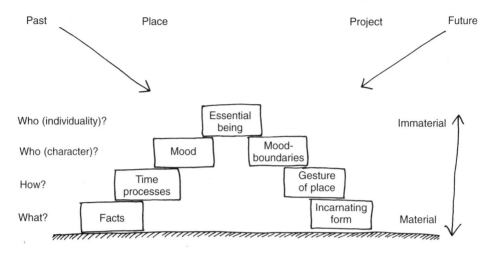

Incarnating project out of place-study.[7]

science nor art are ever complete in themselves. Though conventionally so separate, they need each other to become whole. Narrow materialistic science and individual-istic, ego-promoting art don't have much to meet about. To transcend their poten-tially insular polarities and meaningfully complement each other, the scientific must be holistic, listening to the whole situation, and the artistic: *trans*-individual, listen-ing to what the situation *asks for*.

Science depends upon observation but, unless we make early assumptions about what is irrelevant and use mono-function instruments to exclude it, every person who observes sees different things. Seeing is not objective. However much visual information arrives at the eye, it isn't *information* to us until we recognize and *iden-tify* something. We are bound by what we know and by what we can give names to.[8] Everything else is visual 'noise'.[9] This is why group observation is so valuable. It gives a broader, even if culturally bound, picture than any individual can.

Intuitively, we take in everything, every layer of a place – but with the sort of imprecision that dreams and old memories have. I can vividly remember a town I vis-ited 30 years ago – but I can't draw it, even though drawing is my trade. It's a mood picture, better described with adjectives than with a pencil. We glimpse its essence, or spirit, but can't anchor it in form and matter.

If sense-bound, our experience of places would be limited to the surface – bark and wall, not tree and home. But these are *superficial* manifestations, not the essence of things. Sight – the most *informational* of all our senses – is the most surface-bound. To reach the essence of anything we have to see and to listen *beyond* the senses; pen-etrate beyond observation.

Scientifically – that is, with a Goethean scientific approach – we can work towards understanding the forces, physical and spiritual, temporal and atmospheric, that make a place.[10] Goethean science doesn't start with a hypothesis, but with detached, broad observation. The observer notes every sensory experience, the feelings induced and temporal context. Out of this whole 'picture' the essence of what is being studied, hence how it 'works' becomes clear. From narcotic treatment to social structures, this has very practical results. Understanding the essence of a plant suggests its medical applications; the essence of a colour, its therapeutic potential. This approach underpins the techniques this book describes. Getting to know a place at a structural level enables us to align design, use and management with the forces, active or latent, there. By sensing the flow of time through places, how their moods evolve and how what they 'say' influences what people do, how they value, use and re-shape them, we can begin to understand the effects our buildings, or other interventions, will set in train.

As scientific rigour brings stabilizing balance to art, the sciences need consciousness-stretching creativity to advance with meaning. An understanding of essence, or spirit, brings *wholeness* to scientific understanding, and raises the artistic-creative phase above the sense-bound and individual-limited. It feeds and is fed by the currents at the very heart of the place – or thing, or situation. This is why the consensus design process has two phases: scientific observation, with artistic sensitivity; and (artistic) creation through a scientifically rigorous condensation process.

Levels of place: beneath the surface

To the ancient Greeks, the whole world was composed of four elements:

- Earth: the substance of which our world is built.
- Water: fundamental to all life, the fluid transporter and exchanger of all substance.
- Air: the bearer of sound and smell, of communication and emotion.
- Fire/warmth: the energizer of all movement.

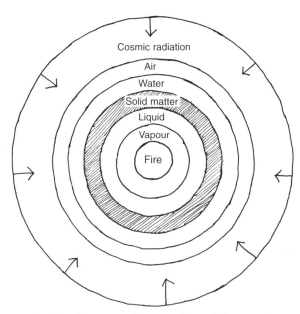

Our planet: we live on the edge of matter in the zone where all elements interpenetrate each other. Outside this zone, there is no life.

Viewing these elements as principles, not chemical ingredients, these potent archetypes are as relevant as ever. In my experience, every problem, personal, social or ecological, has four levels to it:

(handwritten margin note: 4 elements of problem)

- a material level
- a continuity level
- an emotional level
- an underlying root; its essence, spirit.

Nothing is ever properly resolved without addressing underlying root causes. Nor can we achieve anything without material action. Continuity is essential to the social and ecological 'fit' of any solution and to harmonious evolution, while the emotional aspect is essential to acceptance.

Is our world just matter – a lifeless lump of substance? For those who believe it's more than that – from Gaia to deity, from multi-realmed nature to pantheistic spirits – parallels with the layers of human being are inescapable:

(handwritten margin note: 4 elements of being)

- we have physical bodies
- we are alive: have been shaped by our biographies, reveal our nature by our movements
- we live in an atmosphere of feelings and moods
- at the heart of each of us lies a unique, individual, human spirit.[11]

To meet someone, we absorb a first impression, then gradually get to know them more deeply than by mere appearances. The world is not only what we see. Sight can even obscure its real being. When you look closely at somebody's face, it's hard to concentrate on what they're saying. When you listen to the sound of their words, how they pronounce them, it's hard to also listen to what they mean. Yet when, on the phone, we hear words without seeing a face, and even more when we read printed words without hearing tone of voice, many layers of meaning are lost.

We tend to put our energies so much into what we do, and take places so much for granted, that we rarely really consciously know them. Before working with them, therefore, we need to get to know them. Places have the same levels of being as people:

(handwritten margin note: 4 elements)

- First, the material, physical and sense-accessible, facts – unclouded by value judgement or speculative theory. This is the 'earth' of a place.
- Then the process by which it has become: the flowing history of the place, its 'water' quality.
- Then how it reveals its essential being through its different moods, to which our emotions respond: its 'air' quality.
- And finally the essence – the individual identity of the place. Its genus loci or spirit-of-place: the 'fire' at its heart.

Everything we see and touch in our surroundings is material. Everything that touches us is spiritual. Spirit-of-place, though tangible, has no material substance – although we experience it via the material to which it is bound. To know a place objectively, we can only start with things beyond dispute: physical facts, then progress up the ladder of apparent intangibility – from matter to spirit. To study a place, building, situation – or anything else – we therefore progress carefully from the

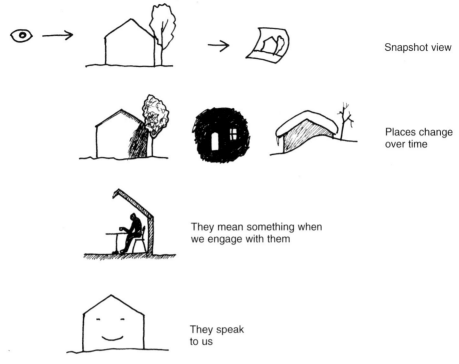

Snapshot view

Places change
over time

They mean something when
we engage with them

They speak
to us

We don't really know a place unless we know it through all its layers.

material to the life and time related, then to the realm of induced feelings and finally to the spirit at its heart.

Walls and roof, ground and trees. Such bits and pieces make up the tangible
aspects of places. That isn't all that places are, but it is all that, initially, we can easily agree on. Only the material facts are 'solid'. Although in Eastern terms, these are
'Maya', illusion, it is only through meeting these fully that we can come to know
what stands behind them.

Material substance isn't fixed. What lasts unchangingly forever? Even the longest-
lived plastics discolour, scar and break. Not only in sub-atomic physics is our world
one of constant change. We don't really know places if we don't know them in relationship to time – our time, as we journey through them – and their time, as they
form, age, mature, metamorphose and fade. Single snap-shots never tell a whole
story.

Nor do we know places unless we engage with them. Statistics only tell dry stories. Being there, we can breathe their ambience. We can feel them. Feel their moods
and how they affect us. That's why novelists have to visit their settings, also why so
many people travel for pleasure. But these are still only outer moods. Until we use,
do things, in places and they become a barely conscious background, we haven't really engaged. You can't do this in a one-day visit, but you can listen acutely to how you
feel in places. This gives a finer, deeper, sense than does the novelist's accumulation
of sensory experiences.

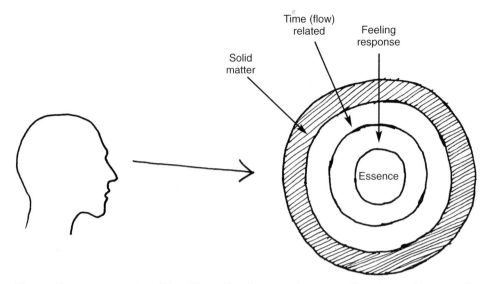

The world we experience is solid and limited to the present moment. To understand it, we make memory associations, so link it with time-flow. Things gain meaning from how they affect us and how this makes us feel. There is something about people, places and situations that is individual, their unique essence.

We aren't wholly there in a place unless we're open to its spirit. But this spirit, though easy to intuit, is elusive to anchor. Different people will describe it differently. Spirit is central to what places are about, to why they are, to how they affect us and to how we can complement or compromise them. For the spirit (of a place, thing or situation) influences our moods and feelings. These are never fixed, but develop and change over time. Time also works on matter – even the apparently immobile and permanent. This is the magic of process: creative process, consensus design process, or any other process.

Notes

1   While technology used to be considered merely applied science, we now regard them as distinctly different but interdependent, often overlapping (See *Encyclopedia Encarta*, World English Edition (2001), developed for Microsoft by Bloomsbury Publishing plc.)

2   For summaries of a range of techniques see: Wates N. (2000). *The Community Planning Handbook*. Earthscan Publications; New Economics Foundation and UK Community Participation Network (1998). *Participation Works!: 21 Techniques of Community Participation for the 21st Century*.

3   See, for instance: Bachelard G. (1964). *The Poetics of Space*. Onion Press; and Cooper-Marcus C. (1995). *The House as Mirror of the Self: Exploring the Deeper Meaning of Home*. Conari Press.

4   The idea of the five senses (sight, hearing, touch, taste, smell) refers only to certain of the body's sensory receptors that respond to stimuli from *outside* the body. In fact we have many other senses that inform us of our internal and external environment.

Such subtle senses, like those of life, warmth, movement and individuality, can tell us more about the 'essence' of things than sight – which is about appearance from a single viewpoint. Sight is exceedingly important, but, on its own, only skin deep (see for instance: Aeppli W. (1993). *The Care and Development of the Human Senses*. Steiner School Fellowship Publications; and Steiner R. (1975). *The twelve senses and the seven life-processes*, in *The Golden Blade*. Rudolf Steiner Press).

5   The root of the word 'science' is the Latin verb, *scire*, 'to know'.

6   An insight I owe to Dr Margaret Colquhoun.

7   After Dr Colquhoun

8   Hence the importance, early in creation myths, given to *naming* things.

9   Things we see without understanding can alarm or give pleasure but they have no conscious precision.

10   Goethean science, named after its founder, Johann Wolfgang von Goethe (1749–1832), is an approach to knowing the underlying 'essence' of things through their material manifestations. H.B. Nisbet (1972) describes this as an intuitive or 'right brain' complement to the traditional rationalistic 'left brain' science (*Goethe and the Scientific Tradition*. Institute of Germanic Studies). This, however, is no simple intuition, but that won by rigorous, detached, broad-band observation. A good example of Goethean science in practice is Bockemühl J. (1992). *Awakening to Landscape*, Allgemeine Anthroposophische Gesellschaft.

11   I owe my first contact with this insight to lectures on Steiner's way of looking at the world by Francis Edmunds in Emerson College, Sussex. These layers of our being have great significance on how places affect us. In *Spirit & Place* (2002, Architectural Press), I describe in detail how places designed with these insights can work on us beneficially and even therapeutically.

CHAPTER EIGHT

How in practice: place-study

Place and project

Every project initiative exudes a spirit. If it is building based, this colours the spirit and mood of its building(s). Every building that houses an initiative influences its spirit and mood. Every building is, or will be, built in a particular *place*. If project and place are to be in harmony, they need to be saying at least compatible things. All too often, they aren't. Initiatives shouldn't have to change – but buildings and places can. To bring initiative and place into harmony, it is *place* we need to work on.

A 'place' may comprise buildings, attractive landscape, or it may be 'nothing' – desecrated land with temporary structures. However unappealing, even the ugliest place has much potential. We may get glimpses of this potential, but never a whole picture until we know the place at all its levels. Only then are we ready to incarnate new buildings or modify those already there.

Many places are seriously mismatched to use. Some are ugly, aggressive, squalid and uncared for; others were formed in another time, with other attitudes, values and expectations. In my work, I commonly encounter two sorts of situation:

- An initiative has an existing building (like a school) or a place (like a meeting-courtyard) that isn't right for it. The spirit-of-place is incompatible with what the initiative stands for. This is about *correcting mis-match*. Small changes can bring large effect here.
- An initiative seeks to build or develop something new. 'Development' involves changes to a pre-formed place. Our job is to ensure that these will complement, not compromise any positive spirit the place may have.

One situation is about modifying existing spirit-of-place, so that it speaks of what is *now* happening there, not what *was* there. The other is about bringing new, future-inspired, ideas into harmony with the past-formed; allowing the new to grow along with the stream of time; the marriage of what *will be* with what *was*. In both situations the consensus design process has two essential stages: place-study (Chapter 8) and design incarnation. For new building developments, the design stage is two-part. Firstly overall place design (Chapter 9), then the more detailed design of individual buildings (Chapter 10).

These several situations require different forms of consensus design process. Nonetheless, there is one basic structure to each stage. This comprises four layers:

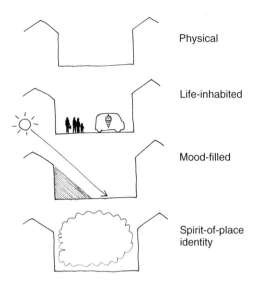

The four layers of place: basis for the consensus design process

- physical substance
- everything time and life related
- moods and the feelings induced in us
- individuality, spirit.

Working with place

Whether we're trying to redeem unsatisfactory places by modifying what's there, or developing land by building something entirely new, we'll need to match new needs to existing places. Match won't be whole unless it is multi-layer: in spirit and mood, as well as practical functionality. This won't happen if we approach places just thinking how we can *use* them; only by working *with* them.

Surprisingly many projects start without a 'site'. 'We want a centre, headquarters, house, factory ... .' But until there's a place to put a building, there is no project. 'Site' is an exploitive term – it has come to mean somewhere we can do whatever we want. Unfortunately, we can. Machinery power and money can change the face of the Earth, if not the Earth itself. But a 'site' is also a place in its own right. Some eyes see nothing – as when the British government found nuclear test sites in the 'uninhabitable' Australian desert.[1] Others – like the aborigines who lived there – saw these as sacred landscapes, part of their identity. Even if ugly, abused, infertile, toxic, every 'site' is still a place. Even if it needs major change to heal and remediate, it deserves at least some respect. From my experience, small changes can have big effect and major change is yet to be proven necessary.

Nature is a self-healer. Natural processes can remediate anywhere. But they are slow, so we often need to initiate and accelerate them. All this has economic consequences. Sometimes you don't need to spend money; nature will do it. Sometimes time is so expensive it's cheaper to pay to accelerate things.

Alignment with extant and latent processes isn't just about saving money. It's about respect for what's already there – the place where the new will be built, or which will itself be modified. With this approach, the new tends naturally towards harmony with the old.

No place to be developed is ever virgin land. It has been worked on by the forces and processes of nature and by people. Even Antarctica has been altered by human-induced climate change. Place-study uncovers this historical imprint. Every place, attractive or ugly, already speaks to us. Whatever we're going to do will alter how it speaks. Unless we can harmoniously develop the *present* spirit-of-place, the new will just be something alien. It won't fit in spirit. Everyone who uses it will feel this disharmony. It will also manifest itself visually and ecologically – which, in turn, has social and economic implications. As the consensus design process is about *match*: past and future, project, people and place, it begins, therefore, with a study of place. But what place? Sometimes our area of study can be small, only a *part* of our 'site'. At others we need to widen it to include the *surrounding* area.

Processes of change: visible and invisible

Change is central to life. Things that don't change aren't alive. But there is a difference between nature's developmental processes and human-directed, thought-based changes. Plants grow and die. Species supersede each other. Livestock graze plants. These processes, developmental and annually cyclical, govern how *nature* changes countryside. Change is continuous and visually consequential – you can (usually) see what's coming. But landscape isn't just nature-formed. It is also, to a lesser or greater extent human-managed or influenced – even if without intent. Invisible factors, like regional economy, grant-policies and agricultural practice, are also at work. These can cause major changes; some sudden like forest-felling and hedgerow uprooting, others slower like abandoned fields reverting to forest. Generally, however, countryside *evolves* slowly. Cities are different. While deterioration may be slow, continuous and barely noticeable, most changes occur in steps – some small, some overwhelmingly big. Changes in ownership and use, demolition, renovation and new construction occur almost overnight. They *occur* overnight, but the processes that bring them into being have been working below the surface for some time. Blight, gentrification, re-invigor-ation and rising property value don't happen at random. They are caused.

To study nature-shaped time-continuum in the countryside, we need only look at what *has* happened to extrapolate what *will* happen. While human-directed changes also occur, most – though not all – are related to 'natural' developmental processes. Even forest-felling is (usually) related to tree maturity.

In the city, however, we only see *manifestations*. What pressures bring urban spirit, moods, processes and forms into being? These often originate off-site, like nearby economic vigour causing traffic and housing demand. Some aspects of the same pressure (like traffic) can reduce property value, others (like housing demand) increase it. The result is manifested in building and place quality, upkeep and replacement or renovation. It is, therefore, often *surrounding-area biography* that tells us most about place-continuum.

In urban projects, the site itself will often be completely re-shaped. As appropriateness of the new will depend in large part on alignment with contextual currents, it is these we need to focus on.

Britain is full of declining market towns. Historic, visually attractive, but with many shops boarded-up (or selling antiques[4]). That's what we *see*, but it is biography that really tells the story. As usual, it is adjacent areas that have driven change: closure of docks, railways, cattlemarkets and industries; opening of ring-road businesses, urban-edge supermarkets and out-of-town offices. These don't just re-direct moneyflow, they also change patterns of movement in time, space and quality. Many high streets nowadays are populated by shoppers by day, young drinkers in the evening and are ghostly empty at night. Three layers of age, activity and mood that

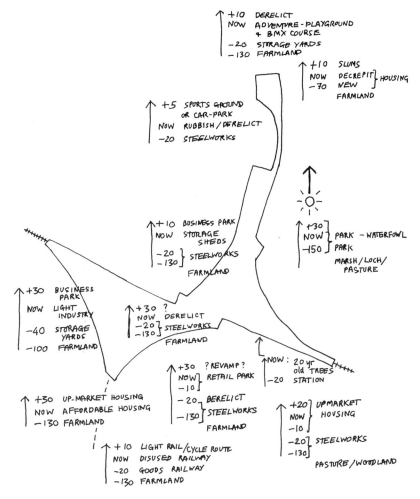

Surrounding-area biography: past through present to future.

have nothing to do with each other. Extrapolating this flow of change into the future can paint a depressingly bleak picture. That's no bad thing. It's a wake-up call – still just in time.

When studying place biography, we need to be aware not only of the place itself, but also of off-site pressures from neighbouring activities to regional socio-economics. The quality of some places depends on their views – namely *surroundings*. Others are visually confined to their own physical boundaries. In all cases, however, invisible pressures will influence their development – in spirit and mood as well as appearance. In such ways, a region's biography can influence and thus become part of a place's biography.

Place-study

To know the underlying essence of a place, we study its four layers (physical, time and life related, moods and spirit) separately. It takes some effort to disentangle these layers. A war-memorial, for instance might be materially, a statue with name plaques. Historically it records a community's trauma, fading with the passage of time. Its mood, once grief-laden (and still so for an ageing generation) may now be sociable and relaxed: a teenage hangout. Its *whole* meaning only becomes fully clear when we've worked through all the layers. But first, we need to get a sense – both factual and intuitive – of *context*

Orientation and first impressions

Initially, a brief orientation can help us to 'land'. Where are we geographically? Where's North? Winter and summer sunrise and sunset? The sea? What's the underlying geology, soil, climate, latitude, longitude and altitude? The ownership history?

Because we can only experience *first* impressions once, we always precede the four-layer study with a silent walk towards, *around*, or to and *through*, our place. While a single structure underlies the consensus design process, places to be redeemed and ones to be developed differ in scale and intent-focus. Hence in some stages what we do is common to both, in others it differs.

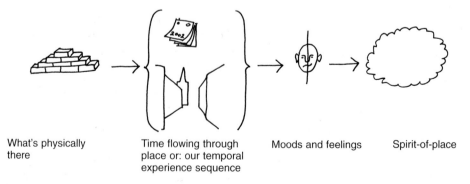

What's physically   Time flowing through   Moods and feelings   Spirit-of-place
there   place or: our temporal
                         experience sequence

Place-study progresses sequentially through the four layers of place.

Will the project be shaped by:

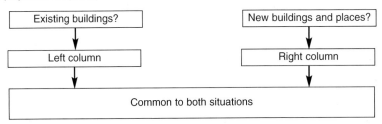

Redeeming places

For an already-formed place, we try to identify a 'key' approach journey, the one that normally introduces us to the place. For an existing building, the approach sequence is critical. It has a major influence on how we experience the building. A range of journeys would give a more rounded picture, but most groups can only spare a day, so there just isn't time. Our study journey starts at the point just prior to where we become aware of the building's presence, like the corner from which we first see it. We finish at a 'key' destination, which might be a reception office, day-room or problem classroom. Only people who know the place can choose this route.[2]

Developing places

With an undeveloped 'site' there is, as yet, rarely any destination to journey to, so the key destination might instead be the deepest inner, private, sometimes secret, recesses of the site. Along the way, we try to relate 'sub-places' in a more or less meaningful sequence. For a large development, there may not be time for the whole group to walk everywhere. Unfortunate, but often unavoidable. Our walk, therefore, may have to be around the boundaries. From this overview we can identify those areas that might be affected by any development (which includes roads, minor elements and activities, as well as buildings). These we can string together to make our 'journey'.

Often everybody but me knows the place – and route – well, so I'm the only one to get first-impressions, but I encourage others to look with new eyes by assuming another role: a child arriving at school, a patient to hospital, or an employee to an office, or even just someone walking instead of driving.

This first-impression walk we do in silence; no judgements, interpretations or ideas for improvement. We just *absorb*. This may sound simple, but even to walk in silence is hard, let alone refraining from thinking. We then meet together and share what we've experienced – our vague, but pertinent, sensation of the being of the place.

Example: La Palma, Therapy Centre: first impressions

After a short briefing meeting, we started by 'walking the bounds' insofar as thorns, cactus and dry stone walls allowed us. We shared our first impressions: idyllic – but inaccessible – sea views; dry, thorny, but not unwelcoming; complicated topography and field patterns. An abandoned landscape, its potential waiting to be redeemed.

As we review our first-impressions, the distinct parts of our journey, like gateway, path, front-door, lobby become obvious. If there are no existing buildings we instead identify the 'sub-places' of which the overall place is made up. Sub-places are areas of identifiable mood, with enough sense of unity and mood-boundary to know when you're in, or out of, them. They vary in size. As there's rarely enough time for us all to study everything in sufficient depth, we need to group the sub-places and distinct areas into 'parts-of-journey' (like approach, entry, ground-floor, upper floor, or next to the road, behind the trees, along the fence). We decide who (ideally three to six people) will study each journey-part. We relate these sub-places in a journey sequence which, for consistency, we utilize for each stage of place-study.

La Palma, Therapy Centre: sub-places

The place divided easily into several sub-places: entrance track; former homestead area; the complicated fields and slopes below this; and the long parallel terraces beyond it, ending at a ravine. We each took one to study.

We need to now agree where to gather (usually the end destination) and when. So quick mental arithmetic. When do we want lunch? How many stages of the process (usually eight more – and at least another day – if we design buildings)? How long per stage? How long to walk to and from gathering point? How long for several people to describe each stage? What verbosity, inefficiency, slippage and coffee-break extension factors to allow? Sample timetables in Chapter 26, based on the differing time-demands of each stage, show how I do it. Silence is no longer *essential*, but chatting, flirting and thinking-out-loud to your colleagues do weaken concentration.

We now commence the more structured process. We will study, in turn and with self-disciplined focus: the physical place, flow of journey experience or of place-biography, and the moods of its constituent parts. After observing each level, we meet to share observations before continuing to the next level. Only after doing this, can we 'hear' its essence.

Physical substance

We start by observing the place's physical 'body' in exacting detail. This is the same for all kinds and scales of project, although timekeeping tends to be easier for small projects.

We observe just what *is* there, *now*. Not what has been (like flowers, now past), nor what will be (like when building works are completed).

It's hard not to make assumptions. Purely *physically*, an elephant-headed statue is just that. We need cultural familiarity to recognize it as a statue of Ganesh; and spiritual attunement to sense its deity. Fortunately, the four-layer process will work through these aspects from physical outer to spiritual presence. But within this physical layer of place-study, a door is not a 'front door', rather, a 'large door with a trodden path to it'. Likewise, we must be careful to distinguish fact from value, so not 'nice' but 'variegated ochre' brickwork.

All group members determinedly discipline themselves to just unemotive, undisputed, *physical* observation. This may sound dull, even boring. It isn't. So many things we never see unless we really look – little things like where paving is broken, grass trodden and paint chipped. In due course these seemingly inconsequential observances will reveal much about the place and its processes, how it is used, and causes and effects that we would otherwise have missed.

It also sounds easy – but nor is it this. To stay disciplined is tremendously demanding. Even I keep wandering into interpretations and ideas. It's important we hold these back. Appealing as they are, they're still premature. And premature ideas will blind us to the place as it is, and blinker our ability to recognize what is asking to be – which we have yet to uncover.

To conclude this layer of activity, we meet to share our observations, each group presenting them in turn, in journey sequence. Again, we avoid any value-permeated adjectives or analogies. Instead of 'squalid institution-like' corridors, they are 'rubbish-filled, repetitive-doored, fluorescent-lit'. We also refrain from speculating on reasons, history, future or improvements. So ground isn't damp '*because* it's shady', but 'damp *and* shady'; a wall isn't 'about to fall down', it is 'leaning 15 degrees'; a courtyard wouldn't be 'busy if lined with shop-fronts' – it's just how it is now. Opinions, values and suggestions often creep in here, so I often have to ask participants to re-phrase their observations in objective terms. The result is a purely physical description of the place using words and diagrams – a mono-dimensional picture. But we're not yet ready to draw any unbiased inferences.

La Palma, Therapy Centre: physical description

From a steeply descending asphalt road, entry was by a dirt track, bulldozed across a ditch and through a stone wall. This track rose steeply then levelled out. To the left, apart from one new house, was wiry dry grass, then steeply sloping scrub and cactus to a broad sea view (but two miles away and inaccessible beneath cliffs). To the right, topped by dark avocado trees, was a stone terrace wall sinking from head- to waist-height as we ascended.

We then came to a high, dark, stone wall with a sharply jutting corner, 20 feet (6 m) high, barring our way. Another track came down from the right, turning us to the left. Dropping downhill to cross a water channel and pipes, we then pivoted around the 60° corner. The path now rose between figs and shrubs to a plateau with camping caravan, shade canopy, tables, chairs and other paraphernalia of life. Behind low stonewalls stood an old cottage, slightly ruined. Below were slopes and terraces. Field walls and walled tracks cascaded downhill, undergrowth obscuring all connections between one enclosure and another. The view now opened up as narrow parallel terraces ran for some 400 metres until they met a cliff-sided ravine. All to the left, spread an expansive sea view above polythene-shrouded banana farms.

Time and life related

Next, we set these material 'facts' in a time context. Either the experience sequence as we journey through a place, or the time continuum into which our work will be set, dependent on circumstance. Movement is a priority sense for survival. Flies don't recognize a fly-swat – but its movement, they do! Biography explains so much about how a person is, and how they will respond and act. Likewise, it helps us understand places: their ecological, and especially, their social dimension.

Whether we're planning new buildings, or simply altering an existing place, both sequential experience and place biography are relevant. However, with existing places that we'll only slightly alter, *the journey through them* has a major impact on how we experience them. Conversely, with new developments, it is time *working on place* that has established an ongoing current of change. Interventions (like buildings) aligned with this will fit harmoniously. Ones that aren't, won't.

Depending on our focus, therefore, we either study sequential experience or place biography. Had we the time we could study both, but normally only one is of determining significance. Only occasionally is it fruitful to do both.

Time/life stage

Sequential experience

As we repeat our key journey, we now consider experience *sequence*. Journey elements – like paths and gateways, passages and stairs – are agents of mood. The sequence in which we meet things is significant. Hollywood films have happy *endings*; happy beginnings don't have the same effect. In particular, we look at how the space 'breathes' – how it expands and contracts, evolves or contrasts, flows or jerks. Are our movements sharp, abrupt or fluid? And what space and form gestures do we encounter? How do these resonate in us? What gestures – cramping, expanding, uplifting, burdening and so on – do they induce? We also observe life-vigour around us: the flow, speed and movement qualities of others like people or traffic.

When we breathe, we don't jerk from full lung to empty, but move rhythmically from one state to the other. Like a pendulum, the further we move toward one pole (full lungs), the more power-

Place biography

Looking firstly at the evidence, but also assisted by documented history (like geological maps, old maps, paintings and photos), if available, we uncover the place's 'biography'. How was it last season, last year, a decade, generation, century ago? In historical, pre-historical and geological times?

When we look closely, there is a surprising amount of evidence. Although we may know nothing of a place's history, we can perhaps see recently cracked paving, five-year-old trees in unmaintained gutters, sterile demolition-refuse soil, 1980s temporary buildings, 30-year-old trees, industrial revolution buildings, medieval street meanders, pre-development names, and water, ice and volcanic shaped topography. From its condition, we can guess how long ago a tree stump was felled, then count its rings. Buildings reveal their age through subtleties of style and components; hedgerows through their diversity of species.[3] Both towns and countryside can be accurately read this way.

ful the draw of the other pole (empty lungs). Unlike a pendulum, which is bound by the laws of gravity, momentum and friction, we can accelerate and expand this movement, also modulate it and enrich it with sound. External factors (like heat and air pressure) influence this, so do (for humans) internal ones, like mood and intent. So sometimes we pant, sometimes sing. This makes breathing a *living* oscillation.

Just like our own breathing, how experience sequences 'breathe' affects our moods. Not all spatial experiences breathe comfortably. Some jolt, slam, slap in the face or collapse. But they all *move*. These movement qualities resound in us. So do frozen movements – gestures.

Shapes, forms and spaces, and our own bodily or eye movement, all convey gestures. When we walk a journey, the sequences of expanding or contracting, and vertical, longitudinal or transverse space, fluidity and abruptness, hard and soft acoustic, light and dark, welcoming or unfriendly texture, all breathe and gesture. These gestures can lead us on, expand our attentions, jerk or exhort us upright, even heavenward – or crush and compress us. They have inductive effects on our posture as well as mood. By anthropomorphizing, caricaturing and bodily gesturing these spatial and form gestures, we can become more aware of them.

The energies they release, channel, intensify, block or disrupt, affect our own life-energies. In Feng-shui, these energies are called 'chi'. Movement has many qualities: speed, fluidity, abruptness, forcefulness, three or two dimensionality, rhythms and complexity. These also we describe, gesture and draw as, all together, we re-walk the journey.

This gives us a picture of how the place has developed over time, bringing it to how it is *today*.

But how will it be in the future? For the journey from the past to the present doesn't stop today. Indeed it never stops – even the most concrete of places change over the years.

So now we ask: if we leave things as they are, how will the place be next season, year, decade, generation, at the end of its buildings' life (say 60–100 years), when its trees are mature (several hundred years for oaks, up to 2000 for sequoias)?

In cities, it may well be changes already visible *around* the site that will dominate how things change *within* it. Changes of use, ownership, occupation and property value; changes in roads and traffic or employment, shopping or recreation 'magnets' may have greater impact than growth-rate of trees or clogging ground-drainage.

La Palma, Therapy Centre: biography

The whole island was one huge extinct volcano, with lava-scoured ravines. Agriculture – and Christianity – only arrived with Spanish invasion. Even 50 years ago, this area would have been densely settled, large families in all the now ruined cottages, and even the ravine cave-dwellings; fruit trees, vegetable and arable crops, sheep, goats and hens – and lots of children everywhere. Since then extensive banana plantations, nowadays plastic-shrouded, took over. Small farms difficult to absorb into the plantations were abandoned, reverting to thorns and cacti. This is how we now saw it.

What would the place be like in a few decades? Walls would crumble under root action and field boundaries

*La Palma, Therapy Centre:
sequential experience*

Next, we looked at the movements, gestures and breathing sequences of this journey. The roadway arrowed downhill. But the entryway, abruptly at right angles and steeply rising, was quite disconnected. The track, almost wrapped by wall and avocado-tree shade to the right, breathed out to the left and distant sea horizon. It then collided with the rebuffing wall. Then, descending, crossed another track and swung around the jutting corner. This emanated a powerful and disquieting energy – a feng shui 'poison arrow' – a point to hurry past. Now rising between walls, trackways opened left to fields, and right to the ruined building. Arriving on the plateau, the space now breathed out to sky and view in all directions. Through a weak banana-tree boundary, long terraces, stepped up to the right, sea view to the left, led to the ravine stop.

Again we meet and share our findings, as before and in the same sequence. While the physical, however, is usually best described in words and diagrams, time and life are about movement, so often require our own movements and gestures to communicate the flow of events.

Even if we study places at untypical times, with thorough physical observation, the evidence of rush-hours or dead-at-night syndrome is visible. Life-activity, sound, light, scent and suchlike ephemera are fundamental to mood – our next stage of study.

disappear in impenetrable scrub. We would see a landscape as inaccessible as the distant sea, with its history and any human continuity upon which we could build, buried from view.

Attempting, even guessing, these questions gives us a sense of where the place is 'going'. But next we can ask how it would develop if we make small interventions like removing a gate, building a path or wall, closing a road or shop. We can postulate bigger and bigger interventions, even ridiculously vandalous ones. This gives us a sense of the sorts of things the place can and cannot accept. Normally it's best however, *not* to include any project ideas. These could all too easily lead on to design. We aren't ready for that yet.

This whole stage of future evolution, I don't usually tell people about until we do it. I don't want them thinking about it prematurely, so forming thoughts before these are ready to emerge on their own. But of course, I have to include it in this description.

As the group puts together the sequential evidence from the past, and extrapolates this into the future, a time-stream begins to become visible. A time-stream whose patterns, flavours and repetitions give it a distinctive quality. This leads us towards an experience of the character or mood of the place.

One of the purposes of place-study is to understand the formative currents that have shaped place and community, economy and attitudes, up to the present. This will make it easier to match *future* activity and location in a way that improves place, strengthens society and reinforces economic viability – namely an *economically,* as well as environmentally and socially, sustainable way.

Moods and the feelings they induce

A place's mood atmosphere can make us feel relaxed or tense, soporific or energized, aggressive or peaceful, secure or vulnerable. We now identify the moods of each different journey-part through, in or around our place, and how these moods make us feel. Moods may be confined to a particular mood zone or – as when we ascend a staircase where different views, light and activities open off each landing – they may evolve almost step by step.

Some places seem neutral; we don't notice any effect. But everywhere has some sort of atmosphere, even if negative or dull. Silent, empty places that are usually full and noisy can have a disquieting mood; they're asking for activity. Beneath this reverberates an echo of their usual busyness. So the mood we observe in an empty sports stadium, a 4 a.m. town centre or a weekend factory yard, is a shadow of its active mood.

La Palma, Therapy Centre: moods

The entry, hot, dry and disconnected, offered no hint of invitation, though after some 50 metres the expansive sea view opened the soul. The uncomfortably confronting volcanic-rock wall, its corner's energy exacerbating the direction of the cross-track, made a real division. The now rising track became bright and airy with an 'arriving' mood. On the plateau, open and breeze-cooled, car, caravan, tent and the old house with its social focus echoes, made this the heart of the place. Sea views and sheltering retaining walls made the long terraces somewhere to soak up peacefulness, even meditate. The ravine edge felt an especially retreat-like place.

We can record the feelings evoked in us with notes on drawings. Or even better – as colours are so mood-linked – we can make coloured 'mood maps'. As before, we meet and share our findings, building this time a whole-site or whole-journey 'mood-map' to layer on the 'experience-breathing' or 'time picture' map, already overlaid on the physical record map. When we add, and constantly rebuild inwardly, the physical clues and temporal rhythms of use, the whole (fluctuating) mood-picture emerges.

Spirit-of-place

We have now brought to consciousness three experience layers. The first was tangible *physical* phenomena, the only things we actually see, touch, smell and hear. The second located us within the flow of *time* (without which, despite its invisibility, nothing has life). And the third level was our inner *soul* experience. Though induced by the place, this is not materially present at all.

It is the sum, and relationship, of these layers that establish spirit-of-place. We're now ready, as a group, to ask: were this place to describe itself in human terms, what

multidimensional viewpoint = consensus design

would it say it is – what would it stand for? What values and attitudes does it embody? What is its message? In other words: What is the spirit of this place? Its subliminal messages like 'I am dumped, abused', I'm a forgotten jewel' or 'I welcome and care for you' affect how we behave. If possible, I spring this on the others. If fore-warned, they may have started thinking about it too soon – so forcing a hypothesis rather than let the place's being resound.

How can we possibly agree on something as amorphous as spirit-of-place? Our intuitive first-impressions were individual, subjective, fluffy and divergent. But now, after sharing a trans-personal, listening-focused and perception-sharpening process, our eyes are no longer clouded by personal subjectivity. Just as opposite viewpoints tend to lead to dispute, *whole, multi-dimensional* viewpoints tend to generate con-sensus – a principle underlying all aspects of consensus design.

While there may be several suggested phrases, all will be close to each other. We try to refine these into a single, or at most two or three, sentences, phrases, even sin-gle words. The discipline of the four-layer process has given us an impartiality that makes consensus easy. This is what the place, as it is now, says. And it says it to *everyone* involved, albeit subliminally. This spirit-of-place, and the subliminal mes-sage it emanates, is central to how the place affects us – to our well-being, moods and behaviour.

What the place says is much more important than how it looks. If they are to touch us, *mean* anything, it is what architecture, placemaking, homemaking, are all about, even though we rarely think about this consciously.

La Palma, Therapy Centre: spirit-of-place

Now the question: what did the place, as a whole, say? It was certainly beautiful, but sliding into depopulated despair. An island of thorns surrounded by chemical-intensive monoculture, it was neither healthily wild nor symbiotic. Nature was reclaiming it, but by scrub and cactus making everything inaccessible. It asked for new life to give meaning to its beauty, and human life to re-connect and make accessible its intricate parts. It pleaded to be redeemed not from, but *with* nature.

What a place says more important than how it looks KS

La Palma, Therapy Centre: summary of place-study

First impressions: abandoned
Sub-places:
1. Entrance and track.
2. 'Cross-roads' by jutting wall.
3. Rocky ledges and ascending track.
4. Plateau.
5. Terraces.
6. Ravine edge.

Physical description:
1. Ascending dirt track through drystone wall. Avocado terrace above, to right. Downsloping dry grass to left.
2. Water pipes and channel. 6 meter wall with 60° corner displaces track downhill to left. Another track enters from right.
3. Track curves up between stone walls. Fig trees to right, rocky ledges to left.
4. Plateau with camping caravan. Sea views to left, ruined cottage to right.
5. Three parallel terraces. Sea views to left, terrace wall to right.
6. Transverse ravine, rock-soded, sloping seaward to left.

Journey flow:
1. Abrupt, then closed, dark to right, open, expansive to left.
2. Multi-directional at crossroads, aggressive thrust of corner.
3. Confined track swoops right; confused (overgrown) hints of openings, left.
4. Track opens to expansive views, enclosed to (landward) rear.
5. Leads forward, breathes out to left.
6. View expands in (almost) all directions.

Biography – past:
Volcano.
Agriculture.
Rural depopulation.
Present: scrub overgrowing fields.
Future: man-made landscape reverting to nature.

Moods of place:
1. Unexpected, unwelcoming, then dry, open, exposed, then sea-focused, sun-trap but relieved by avocado-orchard shade.
2. Unsettling.
3. Open, domestic, arrival.
4. Airy, open, quiet.
5. Tranquil.

Spirit-of-place: 'abandoned', 'ambiguous', 'siesta.'

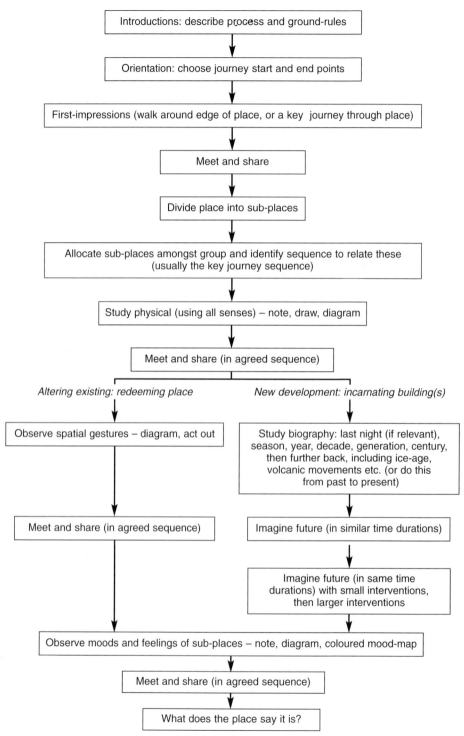

Introductions: describe process and ground-rules

↓

Orientation: choose journey start and end points

↓

First-impressions (walk around edge of place, or a key journey through place)

↓

Meet and share

↓

Divide place into sub-places

↓

Allocate sub-places amongst group and identify sequence to relate these (usually the key journey sequence)

↓

Study physical (using all senses) – note, draw, diagram

↓

Meet and share (in agreed sequence)

Altering existing: redeeming place

Observe spatial gestures – diagram, act out

↓

Meet and share (in agreed sequence)

New development: incarnating building(s)

Study biography: last night (if relevant), season, year, decade, generation, century, then further back, including ice-age, volcanic movements etc. (or do this from past to present)

↓

Imagine future (in similar time durations)

↓

Imagine future (in same time durations) with small interventions, then larger interventions

Observe moods and feelings of sub-places – note, diagram, coloured mood-map

↓

Meet and share (in agreed sequence)

↓

What does the place say it is?

Summary of place-study stage.

An important side-benefit of place-study is that it <u>frees</u> us <u>from the pre-formed</u> <u>ideas we've brought with us</u>. It's obvious that, however good they once seemed, we would have to strain to fit them with what we now know.

We live in a time-scarce age. This process takes time, indeed time is crucial to the process. Usually the most influential people: executives, chairpersons and the like, are the busiest. They naturally want to leave place-study to someone else, read the executive summary and just focus on the design. I discourage this, for the design process is not an *accidental* mirror of the place-study process. It addresses, answers, builds upon, what we've learnt of the place – an experience-based, living knowledge, not an abstract, read knowledge. It builds layer by layer. Missing the place-study phase leaves nothing to build on.

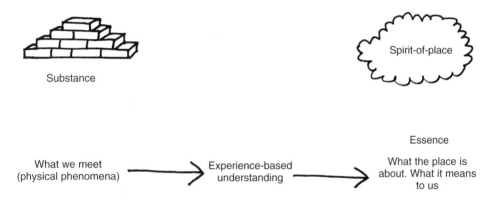

Reorganizing the spirit *of a place through its* material *substance.*

Notes

1   The USA, USSR, China and France have done the same thing in Nevada, Khazakstan, Siberia, Tibet and Oceania.

2   Where the journey is through an existing building, this invariably starts with the entrance people are used to using. On at least two occasions, however, by the end of the day we've found a better one. This doesn't mean a day wasted – we've learnt much and have been able to see beyond our habit-blinkers to find the 'right' entrance.

3   In Britain, roughly one new species of hedge-tree per 100 years. Most hedges date from the Enclosure Acts; a few, particularly along parish boundaries are much older. Strip fields are often Saxon, tiny ones, Celtic – but these are only crude generalizations, needing other supporting observations.

4   Most people buy more groceries than antiques. When shops offer the reverse ratio, it shows something is seriously out of balance.

CHAPTER NINE

How in practice: outline design

Matching project to place

Projects can start surprisingly loosely. I've been approached by people who wanted to build an eco-town. They had a site, but only the loosest idea of what the town would be about. Things may start this way, but they don't have much prospect of reality until we know what's going to happen there. And we can't design anything until we know what spatial needs these activities have. Budgetary limitations come in here. These fix the size of what we're dealing with. We need this level of reality-contact before we start.

Places are *already* here. They're about the *now*. Everything that's here now is, by definition, *past-formed*. Any proposed project, on the other hand, hasn't *yet* happened. It's still an idea. It lies solely in the future. Future ideas need to be grounded in the past – just as past-formed rigidities need to be enlivened by future inspiration. We can't ignore either past or future without building disharmony into the very substance of a place.

By mirroring the place-study process we can bring hopes and visions, still in the future, down to earth, in *this* place, for *this* time. This allows the spirit, the essence, of a project to manifest itself in *appropriate* substance. The buildings and places that result support both the spirit underlying the initiative and its practical needs.

The design stage starts, therefore, with the *spirit at the heart of the initiative, or project* – sometimes very different from that of the place. We then descend, in turn, through:

• the *moods* which support this
• the *temporal relationships* (and life) to support these moods
• the *physical* means to achieve these.

How we do this varies according to circumstance.

Even though attuning spirit-of-place to spirit-of-project is our concern, the place's physical composition must, perforce, be our starting point. The starting point for place-study – and, for design, the end point. After all, the only things we can actually do to places are to alter them materially. Hence understanding the spiritual requires observation of the material, and spiritual objectives can only be achieved through material action.

It's not easy to meaningfully flip from material to spiritual and back again. But once we involve ourselves with those layers of place, project and people that lie

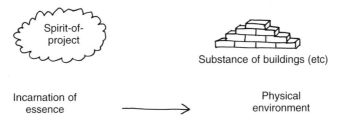

Condensing spirit-of-project into material form.

between, the progression flows smoothly. The design process, therefore, works through all four layers of being. And, because its core purpose is the spirit of project and place – about which people committed to them naturally agree – consensus isn't wrung out of compromise, but while not inevitable, is a natural tendency.

Spirit-of-project

The design phase opens with a review of our place-study concluding with what we've agreed the place currently says. Actual design starts with the obvious – and fundamental – question: *what should the place say?* Or, in other words, what is the spirit of the project? This, above all others, is the one issue fundamental to the spirit, viability, sustainability, and success of the project. As before, there'll be a few suggestions, different in words and emphasis, but, as everyone working in a project shares a sense of what it's about, these are fundamentally in the same direction. It's easy, therefore, to agree and condense these into a phrase or two.

We do this – encapsulating the spirit-of-project in words – whether we're altering something existing or building new. From this point on, the processes diverge. One is about refinding match between new needs and old buildings (or places). The other about incarnating new buildings into a past-formed place in so harmonious a way that everything feels like it *should be, and always has been,* there.

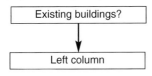
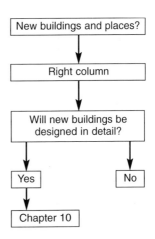

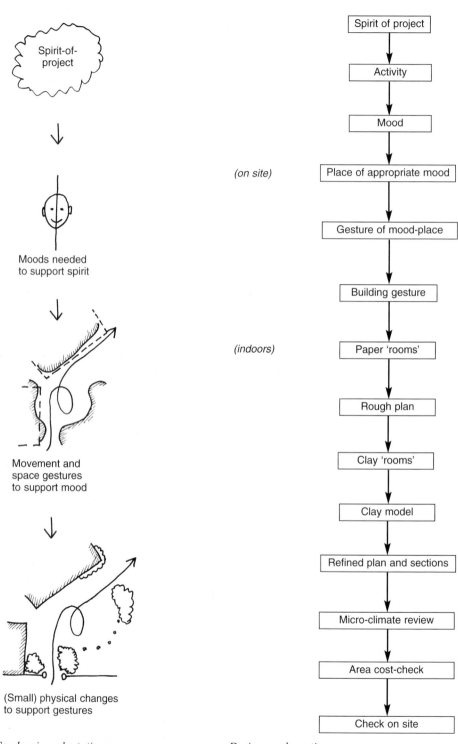

Spirit-of-project

Moods needed
to support spirit

Movement and
space gestures
to support mood

(Small) physical changes
to support gestures

	Spirit of project
	Activity
	Mood
(on site)	Place of appropriate mood
	Gesture of mood-place
	Building gesture
(indoors)	Paper 'rooms'
	Rough plan
	Clay 'rooms'
	Clay model
	Refined plan and sections
	Micro-climate review
	Area cost-check
	Check on site

Condensing adaptations.   *Design condensation.*

La Palma, Therapy Centre: spirit-of-project

What about the therapy centre? What should that say? What spirit should stand at its heart? Certainly this should be about de-stressing, perhaps also about spirit renewal and uplifting. 'Be at peace with yourself' was the phrase that came up.

Mood of place

Redeeming places

If altering an existing place, we, all of us together, re-walk the key journey asking: what *moods of place* would support this message? This enables us to agree a mood-sequence for the journey as it *needs* to be. *How* we achieve these moods is still premature to consider – indeed we still need to hold back from ideas or anything that's too formed. This approach is like painting out of colour. The colour sets the mood, out of which only subsequently are we ready to condense forms. If we drew first, then coloured-in, the colour-mood may somewhat enrich the picture, but never would the pictorial be a subservient vehicle for the mood. Mood would be secondary.

La Palma, Therapy Centre: mood of place

What moods would 'be at peace with yourself' imply for the arrival journey? The entry would need to greet and the approach welcome. Next, should come a sociable meeting space – the destination for day courses. Then, more private, the residential social core, at once sociable and peaceful. The terraces beyond with their soul-bathing sea-views asked to remain tranquil; the ravine, remote and wild.

New development: incarnating buildings

Spirit-of-place is non-material. Its first step towards materialization is through *activity*: what people – and machines (including vehicles), animals, even vegetative processes (like sewage works) *do*. So, if developing a new place, it is *activities* that we focus on first – for activities *generate* moods.

We consider each activity associated with the development in turn. Every one brings a mood – it 'colours' a place. This applies whether it occurs in the open, like a boatyard, or behind closed doors like a factory farm. Knowing the place as we do, we can easily (so far in my experience!) agree where each activity mood would reinforce, complement or perhaps even heal, a mood of place; and where it would compromise, even destroy it.

We next identify the *boundaries* of activity-coloured zones. These are *places*, not, at this stage, *buildings*. We now focus in on those places to be bounded, perhaps partly enclosed, by buildings – the buildings in which mood-feeding (but usually invisible) activities take place. Where should these 'activity-places' be? What are their boundaries? On an open site, we can mark these out with pegs and string. (I recommend bamboos at least waist high and orange twine. Green or grey string is too camouflaged.) This we can now record on tracing-paper over our site-plan.

To what extent should these boundaries be hard (like buildings) or soft (like bushes, earth mounding or water)? We now have the plan gestures of buildings, or at least one side of them, agreed. This refines our drawn plans.

Marking-out a building on site. Is it right here? Or should the plans be adjusted?

Time and life related

To *re-match* *spirit-of-place* *with* *spirit-of-initiative*, thereby redeeming an unsatis-factory place, we focus again upon the key *journey:* our flow *through the place.* If, on the other hand, our concern is with *overall development*, we look at the *whole* place and the current of time *flowing through it*.

Journey sequence

How can the *movement qualities* of our journey be altered to support the moods we seek to support the intend-ed spirit-of-place? What spatial breath-ing, induced posture and movement, and space and form gestures? What fluidity (or abruptness), force, gentle-ness, speed and rhythms of movement? Again, we all repeat the journey in one group, asking this question at each sub-place and threshold. As with this stage of place-study, we use many means of description; bodily gestures and movements often being most evocative. We do, however, need some record, so also need some words, dia-grams and sketches.

What if someone, carried away by the artiness of all this, makes gestures or sketches someone else feels don't fit? If this were to happen (it hasn't yet), I would return to our decisions at the previous level: what would best serve this mood? Whenever individual-istic 'contributions' threaten to de-rail consensus – at any stage in the process – I always use this 'back-step'. Always I have found the group then re-finds consensus.

La Palma, Therapy Centre: flow through the place

What would these moods mean for the flow, gestures and breathing of space, along this route? To greet, the entrance would need a journey-

---

Flow relationships

Knowing the moods we need to support the spirit-of-place and of project, what spatial sequences, gestures and quali-ties of movement would support them? What relationships should places have to each other? Should there be walls and gateways or should they flow into one another? Should places be con-cealed from each other, unexpectedly reveal themselves, or evolve smoothly one from the other? Are there principal views and directions – events to the side suddenly drawing our attention – or is everything equally accessible, visible and equal in hierarchy?

These decisions about temporal rela-tionships further modify our plans requiring us to adjust the strings and pegs. They also harden up the gestures of the building edges.

marker, a portal. To invite – unlike the present abrupt, unmarked turn – it would need to flow out of the road, gently drawing-in both eye and physical movement. Then gently lead you on. The threshold between day-participant and residential realm would also need delineation. To socially focus, the heart would require greater enclosure, but without sacrificing view. The tranquil land beyond would need a third, softer, threshold.

Physical

Knowing what time-relationships, movements, gestures and spatial, or temporal, sequences would support the moods necessary to support the spirit-of-project, what does this mean practically?

What we will do physically varies from arranging, shaping and choosing materials for the buildings or outdoor places we've already decided on, to small, inexpensive alterations to what is already there.

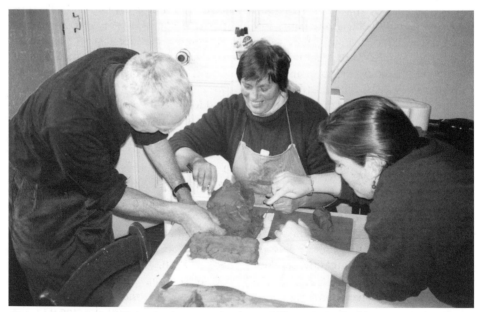

Clay modelling for building extensions: starting by modelling existing buildings.

Clay modelling for building extensions.

With 'redeeming' initiatives, the changes that typically suggest themselves are relatively small, like shaping ceilings or using colour to define different areas and the quality of transition between them. Or changes to paths, like softening abrupt turns into fluid ones, using paving patterns or material to prioritize a route, or shifting approach angle so that the entry greets you, rather than just happening to be there if you turn aside for it. Sometimes we have been brought to re-consider the entrance location or even the whole route, but not often; minor changes are more common. Even just altering paving to delineate thresholds and distinguish between directional paths and places to be still in, can significantly strengthen places and routes. Beyond legibility and connection between place and purpose, such small details can individualize and give appropriate quality to every part of the space.

When it comes to designing new buildings and interventions there are usually more decisions to make. What has to fit into the buildings? Paper 'buildings' of the correct area and probable proportions can help here. Building depth is usually fixed by daylight or cross-ventilation limits. Will our buildings be one or more storeys? If we don't know, we can make long single storey ones and fold them to represent two or more storeys. These we lay onto the plan gestures, tearing and distorting the paper as required. This is the first step to a layout plan, which we can now – very loosely – draw.

At this stage it's wise to do a crude area check on each building to ensure everything fits – both rooms into buildings and buildings in the space available. Often, however, rooms opening off, or looking onto, a place so colour its mood, it's the dimension of this gesture-face that's the limiting one. We

Every time I've worked with the consensus process to 'redeem' places, we've found that the alterations we decide upon are few, minor and consequently easily affordable – but with major effect.

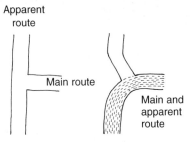

Small alterations can transform experience of space.

Although we've only changed a few things, we haven't just remedied a list of faults. Our physical changes are to support a flow of experience – which is to support particular moods. These in turn support the spirit-of-project we're seeking to establish. That's the only reason we've changed anything. And that's why changes are so few. And why, even though few, they make so much difference to the spirit of the place.

La Palma, Therapy Centre: physical changes

An inviting entry would need a more gentle curve and slope off the road. Plant edged and better paved, it could be marked by a bougainvillea archway. A water cascade and avenue of shade trees could soothingly draw you in. If the path then pivoted around the hall, terraces and balconies would bring you to face the fantastic views. An arc of shrubs at the base of the arrow-corner would soften its excessive energy. By displacing the path, this would increase its swing up to the social heart, now a courtyard.

Distorting a length of paper 'building'.

can now draw a revised plan and proceed to develop things further.

For a large-scale project or one involving many buildings, we need only to know the principle masses at this stage. These we make as clay volumes to place on a tracing of our most recent plan – a tracing (or print), because it will quickly be destroyed as soon as we put clay on it. I prefer clay to Plastacine. Though it dries out and cracks, it's much more malleable, so more effectively frees the imagination.

Relationships between buildings, spaces and routes between them become clearer at this stage and ask to be refined. Again we re-adjust the pegs and strings, and revise the clay model and layout plan.

People can be shy to start modelling. I like, therefore, to get everybody to help model existing buildings and features. This breaks the ice. After that, inhibitions about design modelling melt easily (photograph: Penina Finger).

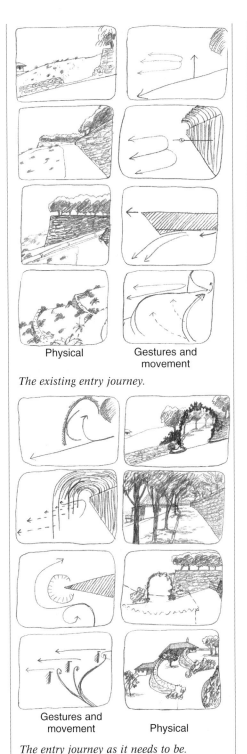

Physical   Gestures and
                  movement

The existing entry journey.

Gestures and
movement   Physical

The entry journey as it needs to be.

Clay modelling group: large and small.

Since our decisions are founded on a deep understanding of place and initiative, and their relationship to each other, it takes little extra time and effort to achieve consensus on details – often even contentious ones. Things, like colour, material, precise shape or size are no longer matters of individual preference to dispute, but servants of aims we have already agreed – hence, in turn, are easy to agree. Consequently, we can achieve a lot for a little in just one day.

But, however detailed, all we have is a design of the *final* development. This, in reality, may never be realized. Most projects are phased. Phasing sequence is, therefore, the next thing we need to address.

Growing places

Few developments happen all at once. This is usually for cash-flow reasons, but there are many other good reasons why it's better for projects to 'grow' than spring fully-formed into being. Projects which *grow* are more cohesive socially, less trauma for spirit of place, better in evolutionary adaptation to new circumstances and give continual opportunities to incorporate feedback lessons.

So what will be the first building, the first change to what's already there? Experience teaches us that, regardless of grand plans, the first one or two buildings may also be the last. Continued money flow cannot be relied upon. Even with money, everything can take much longer than we anticipate. Hence early buildings must be able to stand on their own, socially, economically, ecologically and in the improvements they bring to the place.

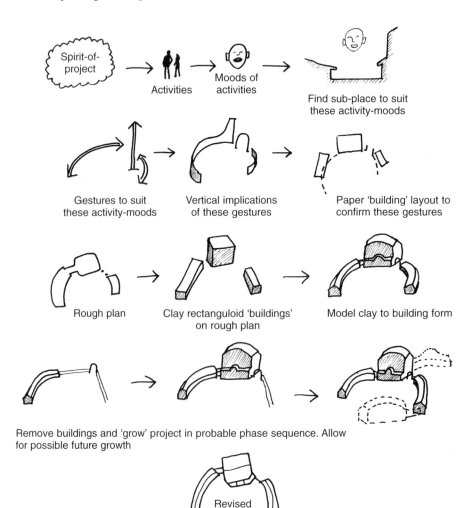

Growing places.

With just one building on it, the place needs to seem perfect and complete. But when there are two buildings, even more perfect and complete! Again for three buildings – and so on. After ensuring they're fully recorded, we need to remove later phase buildings from our layout, so we can sequentially 'grow' the project, one phase at a time. At each stage we need to review what we now understand of the time-continuum. What pressures of change are already in process? What latent – or overt – foci of activity are already there? What nodes of growth energy, like entry points, cross-roads, meeting places? What building will start to generate activities and confirm – or re-direct – this pattern of change? Will the place feel perfect and 'complete' at each stage?

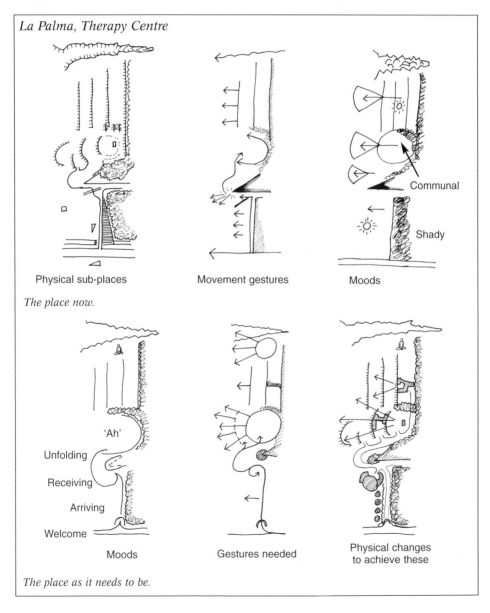

La Palma, Therapy Centre

Physical sub-places   Movement gestures   Moods

Communal

Shady

The place now.

'Ah'

Unfolding

Receiving

Arriving

Welcome

Moods   Gestures needed   Physical changes to achieve these

The place as it needs to be.

Through this growth-strategy we can review the design. With every additional building, the place changes. Its human presence, new-to-old and man-made-to-natural ratios, activity-energy, shade, acoustics and view, also our journey to, past and from it all change. It will alter some sub-place moods and even what the place, as a whole, is saying. For this growth to be, not just a series of impositions, but shaped by the forces of the place and its life, each phase needs to build upon the mood and the spirit of the former.

By means of this four-layer review, we're getting to know the formative-energies that, in the era before paper-based design, would have shaped how places developed. Nowadays, we don't let places shape themselves. We *design* them. But unless we can access a place's formative energies, our designs will be only on the surface, predominately visual, and suitable only to this one moment of time. Indeed, such designs can actually be counter to places' natural, organic, form-giving forces. If, on the other hand,

---

La Palma, Therapy Centre: summary of outline design stage

Spirit-of-project: 'be at peace with yourself', 'be yourself'

Activities:
a. Arrival – locate at 1.
b. Socializing – locate at 4.
c. Courses – locate at 2.
d. Residential: guests – locate at 3.
e. Residential: owners – locate at 5 (upper terrace only).
f. Meditation – locate at 6.

Activity-moods:
1. (a) Inviting, 'don't hesitate', then peaceful, friendly, beautiful, encouraging.
2. (c) Leave the everyday. Choice: activities to learn from each other or enter retreat.
3. (d) Quiet, but also sociable (with children and eating together). A place of renewal, to orient yourself.
4. (b) Heart, life, feels good to give as well as take, participate. Socially focused but outward-looking.
5. (e) A place to retreat into, but also invite friends and neighbours.
6. (f) Tranquil, a place of meditation, a place to *be*; 'the world is at your feet' – to feel closeness to God, universe and beauty of the world.

Flow:
1. Sweep into portal, then compressed to lead up slope.

2. Eddy to hall and view or swing around corner.
3. Slip sideways to guest houses or swing up to social heart
4. Breathe out into expansive views.
5. Invite astride upper terrace.
6. Expand into 300° views.

Physical:
1. Portal: hibiscus archway, then water cascade and tree avenue alongside track.
2. 'Place' instead of crossroads. Vine archway and shrubs to absorb energy of sharp corner.
3. Guest houses around promontory, on ledge below view-line from social area.
4. Courtyard with low sitting walls.
5. Owner's house closing upper terrace.
6. Untouched

Growth sequence:
Entry journey, guest-house 1 and social courtyard.
Guest house 2 then 3.
Hall.
Owner's house.

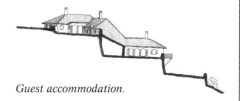

Guest accommodation.

Redeeming place. Short process (6 hours) example: school

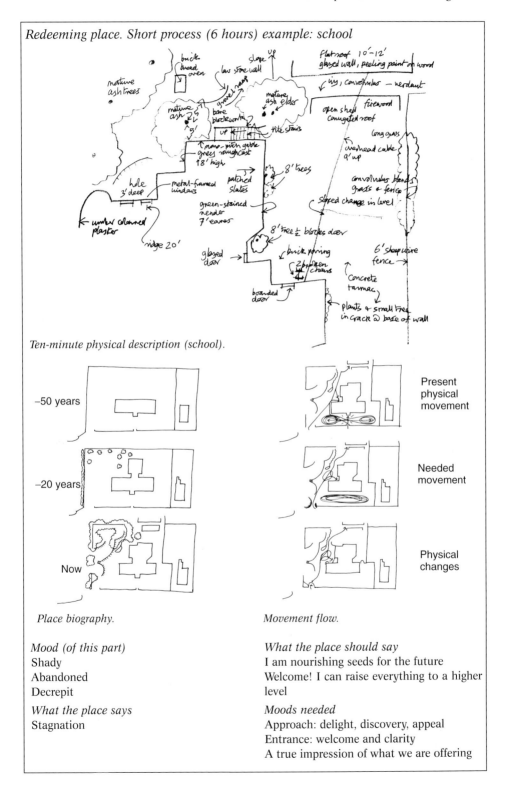

Ten-minute physical description (school).

Place biography.

Movement flow.

Present physical movement

Needed movement

Physical changes

Mood (of this part)
Shady
Abandoned
Decrepit

What the place says
Stagnation

What the place should say
I am nourishing seeds for the future
Welcome! I can raise everything to a higher level

Moods needed
Approach: delight, discovery, appeal
Entrance: welcome and clarity
A true impression of what we are offering

we can connect with these, what we do will both be *socially* viable (which is often critical for economic viability) and *ecologically* appropriate. It will feel as right, as though it had always been there – seamless and inevitable. This is development, not as place destruction, but as place *improvement*. Something worth building.

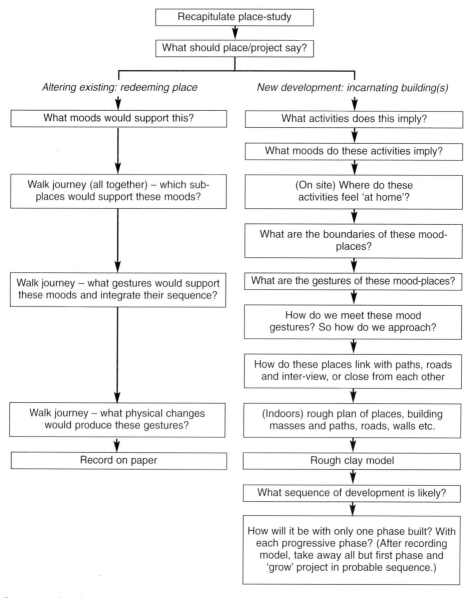

| Recapitulate place-study |
| What should place/project say? |

Altering existing: redeeming place

- What moods would support this?
- Walk journey (all together) – which sub-places would support these moods?
- Walk journey – what gestures would support these moods and integrate their sequence?
- Walk journey – what physical changes would produce these gestures?
- Record on paper

New development: incarnating building(s)

- What activities does this imply?
- What moods do these activities imply?
- (On site) Where do these activities feel 'at home'?
- What are the boundaries of these mood-places?
- What are the gestures of these mood-places?
- How do we meet these mood gestures? So how do we approach?
- How do these places link with paths, roads and inter-view, or close from each other
- (Indoors) rough plan of places, building masses and paths, roads, walls etc.
- Rough clay model
- What sequence of development is likely?
- How will it be with only one phase built? With each progressive phase? (After recording model, take away all but first phase and 'grow' project in probable sequence.)

Summary of outline design stage.

CHAPTER TEN

How in practice: consensual building design

Building and place

Once we're satisfied with both the overall layout and how it grows toward completion, we can focus on one building at a time. We normally start with the first to be built, but occasionally it has to be either the building the project is all about or the most demanding one.

Building a building is a big step. It will physically establish something that will change the place *forever*. It'll bring new energies, change the space and create a changed context for anything that may follow. Foundation-stone ceremonies recognize this significance. We start, therefore, by briefly re-capitulating the process we've been through as this has led us to this building choice, location and form. This refreshes our connections with its *reasons* for being.

From our site layout and its growth projection, we know – both short term and long term – how we'll approach and enter this building. We can therefore walk an approach journey and go through the four layers of the place-study process described in Chapter 8. Much condensed, we can complete this in a couple of hours – more if there's been a long gap since the layout process, or new people are involved. This tells us the message, moods, movements and gestures, and scale and materials appropriate to the place our building will create, to the building exterior and to the approach journey.

Rough design

We know (or anyway, we should by now!) the floor areas required for the principal activities within our building. For these we cut room areas out of paper (card is better; it doesn't blow off the table when someone opens the door). These are rectangular, in what we guess are the approximate optimum proportions. Shape isn't critical at this point; it'll change many times. Rooms that can be on other levels than the principal (usually ground) floor are coloured or distinctively marked. It's also handy to have their area as well as function written on them. Principal rooms are enough. Stairs, halls and small things will fit in as we go along.

Most room-to-room relationships are obvious, like kitchens near eating, but some need discussion. Should a quiet-room, for instance, be immediately accessible, removed enough to require a deliberate journey, or in another building? Arranging the paper rooms in the relationships that they need to be in, we can lay out building plans to create the plan gestures we've agreed and marked on site. This we do on a topographic plan enlarged from the site-survey. Probable future buildings can be dotted (in pencil, for easy alteration). But as these aren't there yet, our design must work well both without, and with, them.

Rectangles put neatly together make rectangular layouts – so it's vital to remember that the agreed plan *gesture* must remain paramount. This is too important to compromise, for it has condensed from mood-of-place needs, themselves servants of spirit-of-place. Rectangular as are our card 'rooms', the rooms we're designing become freer in shape as they overlap and fill in gaps. We now have a revised plan at principal level.

We need, of course, to check that plans at other, less demanding, levels can coordinate with this principal level. The plan we've now come to is unlikely to exactly conform to our string-marked layout, but should be very close to it. It's time now to re-mark and review the revised layout on the ground. And, from this, back to the plan again. By now room areas have stretched, shrunk and changed shape several times. Buildings easily grow at this stage, so it's worthwhile measuring the approximate overall floor area. Is this close to our original brief? If it's larger, what, in terms of estimated cost per square metre/foot, does this add to the cost of the building? Is this acceptable, or must we reduce the building size? We now have a basic sketch plan. It's very rough, but captures the essence of what we'll finally arrive at.

At this point, we should imagine walking through, and being in the buildings, the places around them, and the entry and journey experiences to and between them. This, and the cost review, cannot be too frequently repeated. The excitement and momentum of the group design process can easily by-pass such reality-checks.

Moving into three dimensions

But what we've designed is only a plan. It tells us about sequential relationships on the ground plane, and where people will do things, move around and gather; also where our movement and vision is bounded. Little more. It says nothing of the *experience* of any building, nor of the *places* that it will bound and influence. We need to three-dimensionalize this plan to spatially understand how the whole place will be. We therefore make a tracing (or photocopy) of our sketch plan on which to build a model.

We start by making clay room volumes and placing these on the traced plan. These, like the room footprints, are rectanguloid, though unlikely to stay that way for long. At this stage, I work at a scale that keeps each building around 12 inches (300 mm) in plan size. Four pairs of hands can work on this and it's quick to alter form. Spread-out buildings (or groups of buildings) can cover a larger area. I try to get everyone to make at least one room. This overcomes the first inhibition to modelling with clay.

First, of course, the clay has to be squeezed to fit the plan. But it also has to be coordinated as form. And this brings up questions as to what vertical and three-dimensional gestures are appropriate. This isn't about 'I like', or even what *we* like. Always we must ask, what is *appropriate*? What supports the mood appropriate to activity, situation and place? How can we strengthen those moods upon which what the place says depends?

Even in simple and conventional buildings there are many choices: which way round should roofs be, what slopes, where should the ridges be? But this soon progresses to other questions. Should eaves and ridge be level, or even straight? Should level changes, dormers and abutments be stepped, sloped or curvilinear? These three-dimensional questions can only be fully visualized in three dimensions. As they're still questions, not fixed answers, they need a fluidly manipulable medium: clay.

By asking questions – and following them up with 'show me ...' – I can get most people to put their hands to the model. Otherwise, there's a risk that they tell me, I interpret, and – because it's impressive to see *anything* given form – they are content. If *I* do it, however, they won't *stay* content. This is another reason I want it to be 'our', not 'my' model, and eventually, design.

Building form is bound up with construction and materials. We can't decide on one without the others. What materials are appropriate to the moods we're seeking to establish? What construction does this imply? And, therefore, what building forms?

Once we see things in three dimensions, all sorts of possibilities become apparent. So also do limitations, like one building blocking another's view. Just squeeze and cut the clay and we can open up a window of view. These sort of changes require us to check their implications on the drawn plans – and on the ground.

Not uncommonly, clay modelling has led us to new forms, superseding the original plans. So it's the *model* we need to record. An organic or fluidly formed model can be easy to see and understand, but not to accurately *record*! There are, however, some techniques that don't depend on expensive cameras or software. If it's on a glass base-plate, you can lay it over the site-plan and, using dividers, measure and triangulate from site-plan features. Additionally, you can place it over a grid and measure off this. Or you can span the glass between two tables, stick tracing-paper underneath and draw from below. Awkward and uncomfortable, but effective – especially if someone above can point out what is what. Or even put it on the photocopier. This, however, won't distinguish between clay model and clay mess around the edges. If you have more glass, lay this (on spacing blocks) over the model, draw on it in felt-tip pen and then trace or photo-copy this onto paper. You can also photograph from a distance above (like from an upstairs window) and project the slide (or mounted negative) onto paper, adjusting distance until the scale is right (assuming you remembered to lay a scale beside the model!). This, however, means delays while photos are developed, so often isn't practical.

Additionally, of course, I sketch from several angles and take photographs. It's important to photograph the same day you make the model as, when clay dries, the thinner bits dry first. Being paler, in photographs these look like they're catching light, so confuse three-dimensional modelling. Photographs, therefore, always need to be backed up with sketches.

Using the model

Developing clay model and drawn plans now go hand in hand. At this stage, the plans need section drawings to show vertical relationships across buildings and

Holding a clay model (a future building) against its background (present landscape). From this, we can draw the building in its setting.

places. When more or less finalized, we can hold up the model against its background to see – and sketch – how the building will appear.

With clay models we can also simulate sun and shade, using a desk-lamp. Before these solar checks, what are the critical places and times of day and year? Spring sun in playgrounds for morning break and gardens after school? Shade in the summer? Are windows and conservatories for solar heating still unshaded in winter? In hot climates, what about shading and reflection? Often we only have to adjust the angle of small parts of buildings, or their roof shapes, to gain sun or shade at the times of day and year needed. The flexibility of clay models makes this so easy. View lines are likewise easy to check. Just lay a straight-edge along the view you're checking. If it

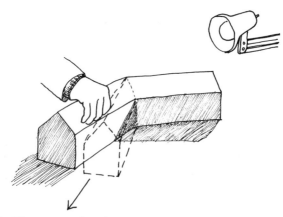

Clay models are flexible, easy to adjust for sun, shade or view.

has to bend over an obstruction, there isn't a view! We can also more easily see noise paths and wind channelling risks – and how to shield against these – than if we're just looking at plans. Also frost pockets, and how to divert cold-air rivers and drain 'lakes'. We can even, to some extent, visualize – and therefore avoid – potential wind turbulence. Blown candle smoke shows this better. Once again, we revise the clay model, paper plans and site strings and, if much has changed, again do a walk-through and cost check.

Organizing diagrams

Larger buildings tend to have more complex demands, like ventilation (hopefully natural) and acoustics – not to mention structure. Even heat distribution and cooling increase in complication with size.

This is the time for specialists to help us. It would have been better had they been part of the whole process, but their time is expensive! With them, we can develop organizing diagrams, like heating, cooling and ventilation sections, pedestrian and traffic flow plans and the like. The demands of these diagrams then need to be integrated into the evolving design: clay, paper and site pegs and strings. Again it's time to check for walk-through and cost.

Detail design

It's time now to enlarge the scale of the drawings. (I do this on a photo-copier.) Many spaces will now be clearly the wrong size and need revising. Usually small spaces are too big, but oddments like cupboards and storage aren't yet there, so things more or less balance out. Doors, windows, vertical dimensions in relation to eye-level and human scale, and changes of ground level become issues to consider at this scale.

We're now ready to make a rough card model. This shows internal spaces, also how the building will be structured and constructed. Rough, so we feel no inhibitions about cutting bits off, and taping, pinning or sticking other bits on. Without this freedom, it wouldn't be a design tool, but a presentation model. Presentation models fix things our design isn't yet ready to fix. I use cardboard boxes cut with kitchen scissors.

I've done a few projects with the whole group right through this stage, but few groups can spare so much time. More commonly I'm left to do this on my own. If (as is ideal) we're working near the site, users can drop in frequently. In one project, I had an (unofficial) rota of co-designers, so I was always making, and revising, the model with one or other (or several) users. Each person helping, and each review session, brings up new issues, for only now can we really see things spatially. So there's lots of cutting bits off and sticking bits on.

From this card-model, we can draw more definitive, but still freehand, plans, sections, elevations, and many, many sketches. I particularly sketch problem areas and awkward junctions. The successful bits, I'm not worried about. Yet again, we need

Though the whole group of teachers (and doctor) designed this special-needs school up to clay model stage, this wasn't possible for the card model. Instead, individual teachers came whenever they had free periods. Consequently the fine-tuning cutting-off and sticking-on moved back and forth until we had something everybody was happy with.

to imagine walking through, living, using and being in the building and the places around it. Again we must check the overall floor area as a cost check.

We now have the building agreed, indeed designed, by all, very substantially as it will finally be. This is as far as I've ever gone with user-group design, though, during construction, I've also developed buildings with the people working on them.

Some issues feel abstract when decided on paper. How, for instance, should this ceiling meet this wall? How awakening or soothing should this window shape be? Towards what should this lowermost step face? To make soul-moving decisions, you need to *experience* these. By tacking up scraps of plaster-board, or holding up batons for each other to view, you can really see how things might be. Such on-site design involvement gives an experiential basis to discussions and the reasons behind our decisions.[1]

There's much more architectural work still to do, mostly about construction, performance, regulations and cost. Some may force design changes, which the group should then review, but it's rare this involves anything very significant. Never, in my experience, have these changes been major.

Unavoidably, because people can't spare the time, there's always quite a lot of work for professionals on their own. I also do this. In the process, I also keep finding minor things I can (in my opinion) improve. Nonetheless, the basic form and space, appearance and user-experience have been decided by consensual group process. What we end up with may not be *exactly* what the group decided early on, but it's around 90% the same. More whenever the user-group can give more time. Had everyone the time, 100% would be no problem.

Although – as with all design – lots of time goes into adjustments and fine-tuning, this main design stage is a fast – and exhilarating – process. Not surprising, as we're all pulling in the same direction. How different from the architect proposing, the client criticizing and eventually everybody compromising.

Design development

Where	What we do	Output
	Recapitulate 'growth into the future' process	
	(With consultants, if appropriate) identify organizing issues develop organizing diagrams	Organizing diagrams
On site	Brief 'key journey' process (as in Chapter 9)	
	Confirm plan gestures and peg these out	Record plan diagrams
	Confirm approach – and (probably) entrance	
Indoors	Lay out paper 'rooms'	
	Draw rough plan (remembering gesture and approach)	Very rough plan
On site	Check this on site	
Indoors	'Walk-through' plan	
	Check floor area re: cost	
	Sectional implications of the organizing diagrams	Section diagrams
	Lay out clay 'rooms' (on tracing plan)	
	Model clay	Rough clay model
	Form implications of materials	
	Draw revised plan and sections	Rough plan and sections
On site	Check this on site	
Indoors	'Walk-through' plan	
	Check floor area re: cost	
	Check micro-climate	Improved clay model
	Draw revised plan and sections	More refined plan and sections
	Enlarge drawings	
	Tighten-up dimensions	
On site	Check this on site	
Indoors	'Walk-through' plan	
	Check floor area re: cost	
	Revise plans and sections	
	Appearance implications of materials	
	Draw elevations	Initial scheme design drawings
	Make and revise card model to determine internal spaces, construction and structure, environmental performance etc.	Rough card model
	Revise drawings	Confirmed scheme design drawings
	Neaten-up card model	Presentation model and drawings for communication to others

Lay paper 'rooms' over plan gesture (already found, see Chapter 9)

Rough plan

Clay rectanguloid 'rooms' on rough plan

Model clay to building form

Revised plan (and sections)

Assess (and revise) clay model for sun, wind, view and noise

Incarnating building form.

Note

1   More about on-site-design by the workforce in: Day C. (1990). *Building with Heart*, Green Books.

PART FOUR

Process development:
two projects

Participant's comments:

Going through this process was for me a completely new kind of education: on my feet, learning to use my eyes, becoming comfortable with my voice, and newly understanding what participation means, with both people and place. I learned about landscape, and the house, and design, but also significantly, I learned about how I learn, and how I see. And that stays with me, and keeps changing ...

... I began to notice how there are always connections happening all around: that when we build, we are building into an already living process. That each project is much bigger than just 'our project', the story is bigger than our story, so listening and experiencing the place in as many ways as possible is not only important, but enriching!

Heather Thoma – USA (Music Centre project, England)

CHAPTER ELEVEN

From experimental method to built project: Goethean Science Centre, Scotland

Two stages: one process

In 1991, Margaret Colquhoun and I met for the first time. We had both heard about each other's methods and had much to discuss. We agreed that her approach – studying a place *up until* the present – was really only half a process, as was mine – developing a place, which means changing it *from how it now is*. We decided, therefore, to try working together, her phase of study leading into mine of design – and with a structure whereby the design process would mirror the study process. We chose a hypothetical project: a Goethean Science Centre, and a place, about 60 acres (28 hectares) of woods, grassland and marsh in Southeast Scotland. We completely underestimated the power of this process to bring a vague dream of a possibility into reality.

The evening of my arrival, we – a group of six – silently walked the boundaries of the land, then met to share our first impressions. From these, we made first-impression mood-maps. This gave us something to sleep on. Next morning we started in earnest. Parts of the land were obviously impossible to build on: too wet, steep, wooded or remote, so we focused our study on the accessible 40 acres (20 hectares). Again in silence, we walked a loop from the entry gateway, taking in this whole area. This enabled us to identify 'sub places'. Each of us then chose one to study.

We first observed everything physical, from the length, shape and colour of grass to the shape of land and trees, then met to build a combined 'physical picture'. The sub-places differed very markedly from each other, from rabbit-shorn sandy turf to succulent, thick waterside vegetation, from a bowl of impenetrably thick young birches to a windswept dome of grass. Surprising diversity – landscape, vegetation, vista and mood often changing beyond recognition in as little as 50 metres. From memory – not always accurate, but always a good editor of memorability – we drew maps.

Next, we looked at the biography of the place, from volcanic upthrusts through glaciation and glacial deposits to more recent centuries: the woodland and its partial clearing for pasture; planted, managed and self-established woodland; the agricultural declines around 1900, the 1920s and 1960s; the evidence of tree felling, and

First impressions map.

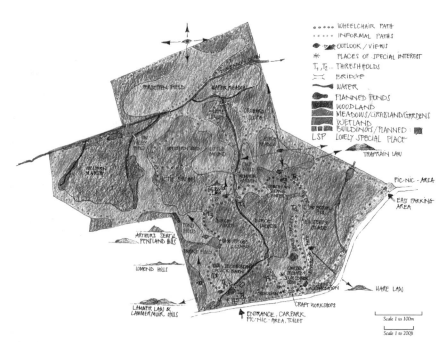

Threshold, route and exploration map and the routes we walked: around and through.

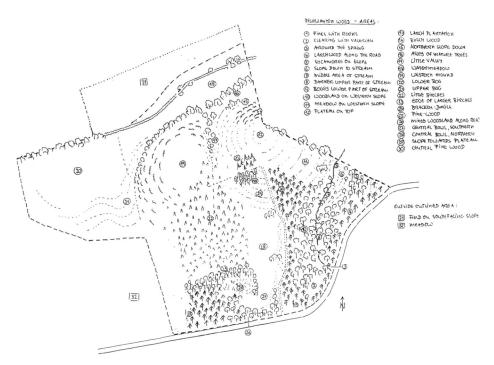

PISHWANTON WOOD - AREAS:

① PINES WITH ROOKS
② CLEARING WITH VALERIAN
③ AROUND THE SPRING
④ LARCHWOOD ALONG THE ROAD
⑤ SYCAMORES ON SLOPE
⑥ SLOPE DOWN TO STREAM
⑦ MIDDLE AREA OF STREAM
⑧ DARKER UPPER PART OF STREAM
⑨ BOGGY LOWER PART OF STREAM
⑩ WOODLAND ON WESTERN SLOPE
⑪ MEADOW ON WESTERN SLOPE
⑫ PLATEAU ON TOP

⑬ LARCH PLANTATION
⑭ BIRCH WOOD
⑮ NORTHERN SLOPE DOWN
⑯ ALLEY OF MATURE TREES
⑰ LITTLE VALLEY
⑱ WATERMEADOW
⑲ WESTERN MOUND
⑳ LOWER BOG
㉑ UPPER BOG
㉒ LITTLE BIRCHES
㉓ EDGE OF LARGER BIRCHES
㉔ BRACKEN JUNGLE
㉕ PINE-WOOD
㉖ MIXED WOODLAND ALONG ROAD
㉗ CENTRAL BOWL, SOUTHERN
㉘ CENTRAL BOWL, NORTHERN
㉙ SLOPE TOWARDS PLATEAU
㉚ CENTRAL PINE WOOD

OUTSIDE CULTURED AREA:

[31] FIELD ON SOUTH FACING SLOPE
[32] MEADOW

Physical description (1991) drawn from memory.

dying and blown-over trees; the successions of pioneer vegetation. More recently, horses grazing had opened up views and created spaces.

This led us to ask how the place would change over the next few years, decades, even a century, if we made no interventions. Within a few years the birch-wood would grow above eye-level, drastically altering our spatial experience. (And, indeed, it has done so!) Self-sown trees would establish downwind of the woodland blocks while wind-damage would eat away at the upwind edge.

And if we made the smallest of interventions? Reduced livestock would let tree limbs grow down, grass and bracken grow up, changing the spatial enclosures and blocking the axes of view. Removing fences or locking gates would set similar or reverse processes in train. And what about more significant – even unappealing – interventions? What would vehicle-accessible tracks do? Or using the place as an equestrian centre[1] – or for clay-pigeon shooting?[2] What would it be like with all the trees felled or the wetland drained? What would a car park, caravan park or chalet development do?

We began to get a sense of what the place could or couldn't bear and how far-reaching can be the consequences of apparently insignificant changes. And perhaps most importantly, we started to experience – not just know in our heads – that the place wasn't standing unchangingly still, nor could it ever.

Physical description: views within site.

View from site.

Place biography through maps: 1855 (upper left), 1908 (upper right) and 1991 (bottom).

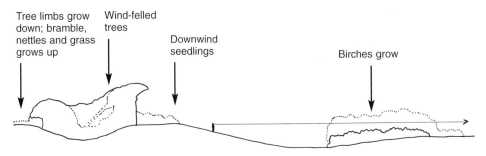

Woodland changes in 10 years.

Next, we observed the moods of each sub-place, drawing mood maps and identifying their elemental qualities and polarities. The wooded valley was damp, warm, and soporific. The hilltop cool, windswept, open to the sky, bracing and awakening. The roadside pine plantation dark, brooding and, it felt, forgotten. The marsh, though wet underfoot, open, sunny, bright and warm. The ridge footpath and the meadow bowl beside it a balance of all four elements. Sharing these observations concluded the individual study phase. From now on we always worked together.

Without realizing where this might lead, I had begun to refer to the footpath ridge as the 'spine' connecting the principal areas in our study. To this others added other organs: the airy marsh as lungs; the wooded valley as a digestive realm; the bald hilltop as a cerebral head; the meadow bowl, sheltered, warm, but with long views and reconciling and uniting all elements; and all the places and moods around it – a heart.

This anthropomorphizing of the place gave us a sense of the activity-moods each part emanated – and asked to have fulfilled. But what was the place as a whole actually saying? If these several organs made one being, one human being, how would it describe itself in human terms?

Despite many attractive parts, the original wood, and the mixed landscape it had since become, had suffered. It felt, not assaulted, but abused by neglect and lack of

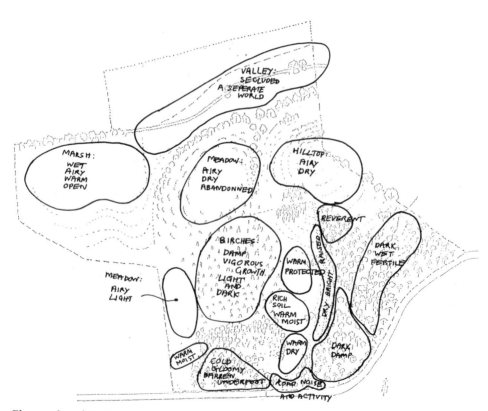

Elemental qualities map.

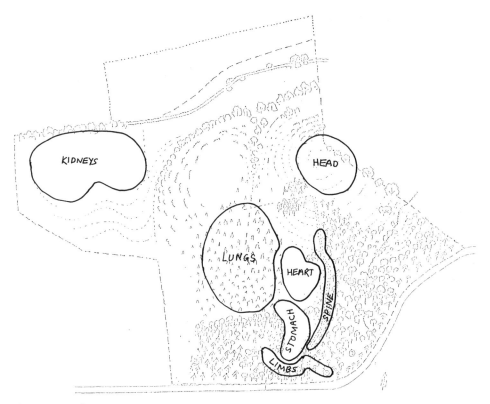

Place as organism.

care. Forgotten, sad, asking to be cared for. In its words, 'I am sad, forgotten, dying – I need help, redemption, new life'.

Next day, our experiences matured by sleep, we briefly re-capitulated the process we'd been through and the place's message. Then asked: what is a Goethean Science Centre all about? How could we describe the spirit that stands at its heart?

Central to Goethean Science is the principle of open, unbiased listening – of letting truth become apparent rather than forcing it or creating hypotheses to test. An attitude of reverence. Most certainly this place was asking to be heard, to be acted upon, to be healed. Fine as a general approach, but what did this mean for what we would have to do? How could this 'airy-fairy' intention translate into actual practicalities?

First we asked: what *activity* realms would a Goethean Science Centre entail? These we listed: laboratory study, educational, social (including eating together), practical working, herb and vegetable gardens, agriculture with animals and farmstead, an art room, places for some people to stay and others to live.

Then we asked: what mood qualities and elemental tendencies would these emanate, and what moods-of-place would best suit them?

Involving cerebral work, the laboratory needed light, openness to the heavens, and a peaceful location at the end of, not somewhere along, a path or track. The herb and vegetable gardens would be the centre of the working realm, the activity heart, linked with everything else. The farmstead, by contrast, could be a bit more independent. Wherever it was, its scale of influence through animal grazing and field care would spread throughout much of the land, but its buildings would provide a nucleus of warmth and activity, even in winter or at night.

Once we had identified these moods, the general localities of the specific-function buildings just fell into place. I don't remember even needing to discuss them, so obvious were the locations: the cerebral laboratory at the 'head'. The herb garden in the 'heart', dining on the edge of the 'stomach' (the access point for the 'digestive tract'), workshops for the hands at the edge between the material outer world (the bounding road) and the heart. (These also, like protective hands, would shield the heart from the road, intermittently noisy with quarry lorries.) The spine to link everything, hands (workshop) at one end, head the other, stomach and heart in between and the farmstead to one side. Along this spine could grow an art room and perhaps at future dates, other buildings for other, as yet un-thought-of, functions.

So the general locations of activities were identified – but where *exactly* should buildings be? We considered the places 'coloured' by activities: How extensive was each of these places? Did they have boundaries and if so, where? These we could now point to and pace out. Which of these boundaries should be the faces of build-

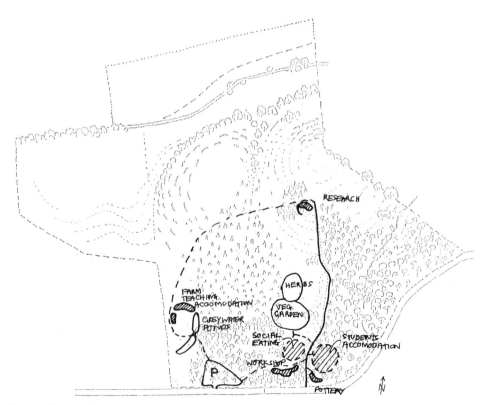

Layout plan: activities.

ings? These buildings would house activities, so generating 'fields' 'colouring' the places they bounded. Now we could be more specific. We didn't always exactly agree – but the largest of these disagreements was four metres. A four-metre disagreement in a 20-hectare site, however, meant we had over 99.5% agreement – which seemed to me acceptable enough not to need a day to argue it out.

These 'building faces' we could peg and string out. For economy, we used what we had: aged bamboos – weathered grey – and green twine. Colours I would not recommend for visibility in or near woodland! More discussions and adjustments, then we had agreed building faces.

To record these as drawings, we used fairly basic means: compass bearings, pacing and measuring to identifiable features on our plan. Fortunately, however, accuracy wasn't too critical because the project would be phased. Precision would grow as we repeated the process for each building phase. We could now draw building faces onto a 1:500 (approx. 1 inch:40 feet) plan (on a table improvised from a door on trestles in the middle of the site).

For most buildings, the back either edged another area or related to physical features like boundary road, woodland edge, or steepening slope. This fixed the rear face – which we also pegged, strung and drew. We now had a plan with the front, back and even some ends of all buildings. Plans drawn as the edges of outdoor places, however, don't necessarily make much sense for indoor organization, nor for building form. These certainly didn't. From the interior planning point of view, they were crazy, meaningless, unworkable shapes.

Development plan 1991.

Site model on site.

It was time, therefore, to look at the *forms* of the buildings. On a tracing of our 'crazy' plan we built clay buildings. Immediately, the jutting-out and cut-in lines, the over-broad and too-narrow, began to make sense as *forms*. We then had to ask which rooms of which volumes should be where – which led to modifying these forms and hence plans. This in turn took us back to the strings and pegs. And for a while, we altered clay model, strings and pegs and rough plans, one after the other.

We then needed to ask questions about how the places would relate to each other. Should there be paths or courtyards connecting them? Should they be screened from one another? Should there be portals, pivot points of entry or view? These decisions affected secondary elements – like fences, shrubs, steps and pathways – and the buildings themselves: their entry points and their enfolding, protective or open gestures. Fortunately, being clay, the models were easy to modify. Yet again, we re-adjusted our strings and pegs.

But we couldn't stop here. Easy as it now was to see the development (about eight buildings) complete, it would be unlikely to work out like this. Money tends to come in streams – or dribbles – rarely in massive lumps; enough only for one building at a time. Which would be built first? And which next? What if they were never all built? We took away our clay buildings (after suitably recording where they were) and replaced them one at a time, 'growing' the development.

Did the place as a whole feel 'right' at every stage? But even more 'right' with every new increment? What did we need to do to ensure that the half-built development felt complete, whole and resolved? Even when there were only two or three buildings, or even just one?

This had little effect on the design of the buildings themselves, but more on their relationship with other elements: trees, shrubs, woodland, hillside. And even more, it affected paths, tracks and courtyards, hence enclosures and ground surfaces.

Now we had model buildings that made sense as rough plans and were already marked out on the ground. But what moods should they have? What should be gentle, what assertive? What sociable, what tranquil, what robust and down-to-earth, what sacred and inspiring?

This brought up questions of vertical gestures and scale. (Vertical dimensions don't show much on small models. Half a metre above or below eye level makes a huge difference, but on a 1:500 scale model, it's only a millimetre – so better sketched.) Should buildings stand erect or hug the low landscape? How softly should they be cloaked with vegetation, extend into hedgerows, merge into trees – or how hard, firm, decisive and 'man-made' should they be?

We now drew eye-level views of the models, then set them in their landscape context. The landscape was alive in colour, but not the grey clay models. To en-mood these 'buildings' meant thinking about colour. Then came questions of texture, materials, details – what would reinforce the moods appropriate to each *place* and building? Suddenly, we had pictures of buildings in the landscape we were now standing in. These began to feel as though they *should* be there, were there in spirit already.

The project began to feel 'real' – something that *wanted* to happen. And indeed from that moment on the project *did* become real. Decisions were made to buy the site and in due course real buildings began to grow there. It now *is* a Goethean Science Centre, albeit fledgling.

The first building takes shape.

Reflections

What was it that had transformed our research exercise into a real project? Partly of course the enthusiasm that *consensus* unlocks from a group of people. Partly also the process we had gone through. Through impartial study we had ascended from the sense-accessible physical qualities of the place through its finer layers to its underlying essence. We had found its *spirit* from its *material substance*. And then we had allowed the *physical substance* of buildings – their forms and materials – to condense out of *spirit* at their heart. And we'd done this by trans-individual, ego-free group work. The ascent from matter to spirit and the descent of spirit into matter mirrored each other. The place was already there as physical reality. The reality of the 'new place' – the future place – that we had incarnated as an exercise seemed hardly less real.

We hadn't always done things the best way, but we had managed to draw towards reality that which was waiting to be – wanting to happen. A biased, wishful view? Perhaps – but we *all* felt like this, and the project *is* happening, is coming into being.

Notes

1   There was planning permission for this.
2   As on a neighbouring farm.

CHAPTER TWELVE

Socially shaped process: eco-village, Sweden

Although the Scottish project (Chapter 11) has since grown into real buildings, it was initially an experiment into developing a new method of place-study and design. I'd learnt a lot, but didn't quite know how to apply it to a 'real' situation. The main thing I'd learnt was confidence in consensual design. I'd practiced this for years, but never before with such formal intention. When, therefore, in 1992 I was invited to design an ecological 'village' – actually a plot of land on the edge of an expanding city – I said I wouldn't *design* it, but work with the group to design it *together*.

We did this in a series of sessions, half-day and whole-day. Prior to the co-design work, we started off with my introducing myself by showing slides. Through questions, comments and discussion, I was able to bring out both ecological and human environmental issues.

Next followed a one-day issues workshop. In the morning, we discussed how environment affects us, and how we can live more responsibly to our environment. We covered a range of issues, from healthy building, and the effects form and space, texture and material, light and warmth have on us, to the design implications of a more ecological life-style. Everything (well, nearly everything!) from the possibility of solar heating with low, brief sun, thermal zoning with insulating shutters and snow and wood-pile insulation, to composting and greywater in a sub-Arctic climate. In the afternoon, we focused on creating 'place' with clay. We worked through the process of 'growing place', starting with a single building, adding others and also trees, shrubs and fences. We went on to examine how low-angled sun (an adjustable angle lamp) would shine into this place at different times of day and year. We then considered what space, light, noise and social implications would do to the *mood* of the places we had made. This day was to sensitize everyone to issues of place and micro-climatic implications.

From now on, all our sessions were focused on the project. Building is expensive, moving home disruptive; this whole thing would be a major event in everyone's life. So what did each person hope for? What did they want from this project? What physical amenities, what environmental qualities, what lifestyle? What activities would occur here? From this, I was able to find a 'palette' of activities that would need locations; also the environmental qualities associated with them. This took one evening.

In the next half-day session, the design stage started. We walked around the site, noting the physical characteristics, vegetation qualities and moods of each part. We then asked: what *activities* belong *where*? And then, following on from activity zones, where should the actual *buildings* be? How far could they extend? We walked around, gesturing and pacing their maximum extent and even positions on the ground. We then tore up pieces of paper into 1:200 scaled house rectangles and placed them on the plan. They blew away. We tried again, weighting them down with pine-cones and stones. (I vowed to use heavier card next time.) We next walked around, checking what this meant on the actual land: Were there important trees to protect? Were spaces between buildings the right size? Did orientations need adjustment for sun, view, shelter and privacy? When everyone was satisfied, I drew around the house outlines and we now had a draft layout – a sort of horseshoe open to the south. Climatically and socially protective, for warmth, wind and noise shielding, sociability, informal child-supervision and security.

For the fourth half-day session, we met indoors and started with the draft layout we had agreed on site. This responded to what was there *now*, what we could see, hear and smell – but not to what *would* come. The city council had plans to build new estates, including high-rise buildings; also playing fields, cycleways and roads, including one carrying by-pass traffic. These would alter some things significantly: walking routes to bus-stops, shops and playing field; cycling routes; noise from the by-pass road; views dominated by high buildings. There would be neighbours across two streets and on the third, an estate of more anonymous multi-story tenants. In the light of these factors, we modified the plan. We now had an agreed layout.

Placing (and weighting down!) paper houses on the site plan, on site.

Clay model, the result of many hands.

The fifth session (the third of design) lasted all day. I brought along a tracing of the layout, and also clay which I cut into house-sized volumes. I gave a piece to each family and asked: which house location do you want? and what do you want the house to look like? My plan was to find out what everyone wanted, indeed have them make it. I imagined this would be easy. It wasn't.

I hadn't accounted for the inhibitions people feel about doing something artistic in public. The clay rectanguloids became worms, ribbons, balls, pinch-shapes – all the forms you can squeeze clay into. But not houses. Nobody dared make a fool of themselves. So I had to. I took a twelfth lump (for a house that wouldn't exist) and made the ugliest house I could (not actually such an easy thing to do) and plonked it in the worst location I could imagine (where no building existed on our plan). As I had hoped, someone said 'you can't do that!' So I said ' what would you do?' – and she showed me. Transparent, but it worked. In no time at all, everybody was making, and placing, their houses.

But there was another problem: few, if any, had played with clay since childhood. They were re-discovering its fun, so the houses that appeared were exotic, some rich with fantasy. And these from a group, of whom many had asked for a locally traditional house (Västerbottonshus) – so I wasn't entirely sure that these were what they wanted to live in, nor could afford to build. I had to remind their sculptors that what they modelled would be built; did they really want to live in a mini-Goetheanum, Hänsel and Gretel house or pagoda? I asked this question, and the more exotic houses became more realistic.

So now there were 11 houses and a community building, but not a *community*. We needed linking elements: car-ports, storerooms, landform, trees and so on, to bring that which was separate into a communal wholeness.

We could now use a table-lamp to simulate the spring sun (the most critical time for solar heating and amenity) – and also look at the wind and noise-shielding capacity of buildings, earth mounding and trees along the eastern and northern boundaries. To avoid social insularity, we now needed to consider the *external*, cross-street social implications as well as the internal, cross-garden ones. We decided to apply for 'play-street' designation for the two quieter bounding roads. This had implications for the position and character of entry points through the building shield to the green-space heart. Such considerations modified the design slightly.

Early on, many families had asked that their homes could expand to match the demands of growing families – and contract as children left home. Expansion could of course be upwards or outwards, so we had to allow space for this. It could also be that houses expanded into attached store-rooms, and store-rooms into car-ports. Contraction meant dividing houses into home and apartment (one or other being disabled-accessible). The model made it easy to see how to do this, along with the new entrances, private outdoor places and privacy for windows, this would require.

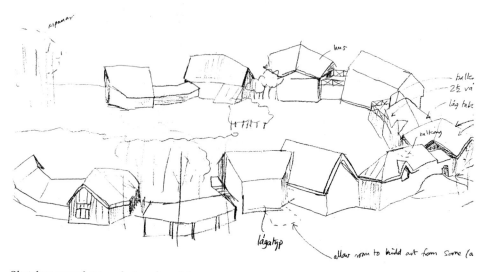

Sketch to record group-designed model.

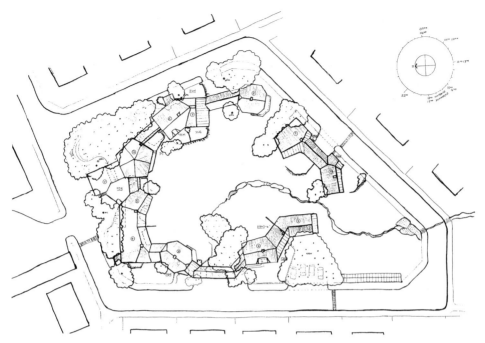

Finalized plans.

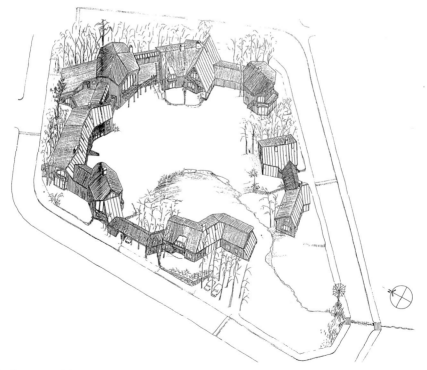

Finalized axonometric.

This completed the *group* exercise. I recorded the model by tracing the building edges, sketching and photographing; then drew up the layout more accurately. Back in my office in Wales I re-made the model from these records, making slight modifications to protect particular trees (belatedly surveyed) and to conform to fire regulations. But for this fine-tuning and neatened-up drawing, virtually the whole design had been consensually formed in the equivalent of two days co-design and one evening discussion. The next step was to go over the design of each house with the family concerned. A day's work per family. We designed the first of these, but then recession hit Sweden and the project folded.

Reflections

Although we worked with all the layers of place in this project (matter, time, mood and spirit-of-place), these weren't holistically related. I hadn't yet learnt how these flow *inevitably* out of each other. From now on I would use the more structured method that I describe in this book (Chapters 8–10). All in all, however, much in my present way of working has evolved from what I learnt here.

PART FIVE

Making it work

Participant's comments:

From my university I came with a feeling of disillusion regarding ecological, social and spiritual themes. I came to see the consensus design process as a powerful method to meet these issues. It is an inclusive process. On a group basis we communicated and agreed upon common observations. Thereby we got a very good sense of the mood of the place, the genus loci.

The challenge I experienced was to learn how to communicate in this open, group-based way, holding back arguments and personal ideas to form. The gift was to see the design emerge from the meeting of place and need, with the group more as bystanders than creators.

Martin Voss-Jensen – Student, Denmark/Germany

CHAPTER THIRTEEN

Leadership and teamship

Leadership: a new model

History is all about leaders. Leaders changed the world. Or we might say, dominated and destroyed it. History, of course, is about the past. We have new hopes for the future. Nowadays we don't want the world destroyed, nor ourselves dominated. We still want to get things done, but we prefer to act through *cooperation*.

Unfortunately, committees have a reputation for procrastination, compromise and horse-trading. Authoritarian leaders and hierarchies of power are more effective at getting things done. That's how generals justify seizing power in chaotic or corrupt democracies. But their popularity (if ever there was any) doesn't last. Practically (not to mention ethically) fascism is not for our time. I've met no-one who disputes this, yet I meet a surprising number of people who, only partly in jest, advocate 'benevolent dictatorship' in their particular field. Even the nicest dictators, however, don't remain benevolent for long.

Fortunately, what has become known as the 'tyrant paradigm' is now passing into history. The 'Gaia paradigm' – cooperation based – is emerging in its stead. So do we still need leaders, managers, directors and the like?

Ideally not, but, when things are less ideal, we sometimes do. But, in my opinion, not the old style of leader, but someone who will *carry* a project, help it over humps, stick with it in difficult times, and take initiative or responsibility. More a 'facilitator' than a 'leader'.

In my own case, when I'm asked to take on a design, I like to have my leadership role confirmed. This gives me sufficient respect so I can lead quietly from the rear. Once I have this authority, I can lay out the process and its rules. Thereafter I hope never to need to invoke it – and very rarely have I ever needed to. (Indeed, I can only remember one occasion.)

This authority makes it much easier to curb the power aspirations of would-be leaders (Genus tyrannicus) and others, less concerned with power but more with just doing what they want to do.

I have had experience of attempted lead-stealing, combined with slander. All this was behind my back, and so skilfully played that I thought, and accepted, that my client was transferring the lead role. Until he too realized what was happening and sacked the other person. I've also had experience of the doing-one's-own-thing syndrome. One person always timed his work to miss briefing meetings; another built his own alternative path alongside a three-quarter finished one – a 'battle of the paths'! Lead-stealing is rare, own-thing-doing more common, but in both cases the mere fact that I am (notionally) in charge ensures that I'm treated at least as equal. And from this basis of equality we can reach cooperative decisions. I *do* have the power to override others, but as I've worked a lot with volunteers – who only volunteer because they feel they're making a contribution – I've learnt to think twice before using it.

As far as possible I try always to lead by *not* leading, other than focusing process direction and momentum. I only step in when consensus cannot be reached – which is rare. As importantly, I try to delicately step *back* whenever I recognize there is someone better equipped to make decisions in their specialist areas. This requires alertness: does their talk exceed their abilities? Am I too enamoured of control or unwilling to admit my weaknesses?

Few of us know more about everything than anybody else. So I work on the principle of transitional, or rotating, leadership. This was developed in World War II for bomber crews: for take-off, the pilot is in charge; for routine flying, the co-pilot; approaching target, the navigator; returning from target, the rear-gunner; routing home, the navigator; landing, the pilot. A management model since adopted in the business world. This is teamwork by dispersed leadership, appointed not by seniority, but according to the needs of circumstance for knowledge, skill or experience. This works very well but it isn't consensus.

I prefer, where possible, teamwork: teams that work as one. Teams can be: as strong as their strongest member – a common sports-team model; as weak as their weakest member – the chain-link model; or resiliently interwoven – the spider's web model. This last team works not as a serial of leaders, nor as a support body, but as one. How can you set up such a team?

My experience is founded on volunteer building sites. Just like consensus groups, I haven't chosen them, but I have put them together. Lots of people, men, women and children, working together to build a wall, many of them inexperienced, unskilled, perhaps not strong enough to lift blocks. Why assemble a team like this? On volunteer projects, these are the sort of people who come. And they all want to build – not just make tea! If you haven't done it before, blocklaying is slow. On your own you may lay one course of blocks in a day, or even many less, bringing a wall just above ankle height. What an achievement the first day! But the next day it still hasn't reached your knees. When several people work together, however, the wall fairly flies up. One lays mortar, one places blocks, one plumbs the wall and sets out cavity ties. Someone else delivers blocks, another cuts them; two mix and deliver

Who built this wall?

mortar. Seven people with a sense of achievement – much better than seven disconsolate who won't volunteer their labour again. Of these seven only a few jobs require strength and only one requires skill: the mortar layer.

Similarly in work allocation there is always something for anyone to do. Consensus design needs all-round balance – so non-specialists are at least as important as specialists. Otherwise things lean too much toward the arty, the practical or the challenging. For a balance of thinking, feeling and doing, we need feelers and doers as well as thinkers – and best of all people who just live – doing all these in daily life.

This approach uses co-operation, not as expedient, but as a decision- and task-organizing principle. It enjoys multi-viewpoint holism, but multiple viewpoints can bring chaos! The structure of four-layered observations and questions, however, lead us from the obviously commonly shared to that which we find we now share. Individual and especially individualistic energies are strong and potentially centrifugal, but structures such as I use lead them to converge. This is leadership 'by the people, for the people'. In fact it has to be, for this is the only way it really works.

Knowledge: power or fertilizing enabler

Whenever I'm invited to work on a project, I always make the assumption that I know nothing – or anyway, nothing like as much as the people there know. But I also know I know – in my own specialist area – much more than they know. Even if I hadn't thought so at the outset, I soon discover that I do. Does this mean that I have to either take charge, abandoning my social ideals, or abdicate the responsibilities that come with knowledge?

I know things in two ways, both of which can be shared. I know *about* things: facts. And, through experience and sensitivity refined over years of practice, I am

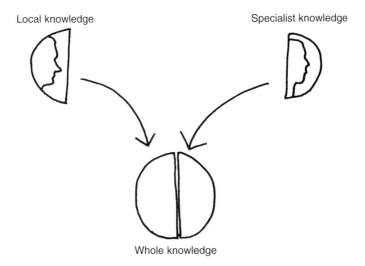

Locals don't know everything; nor do professionals. Two halves make one whole.

aware of how things work, how qualities of place affect us, how situations will change, that sort of thing. These two sorts of knowledge are the reason we engage – and need – experts. And because this is *specialist* knowledge and experience, it is, by definition, narrow. That's why we need teams to round out viewpoints – best of all, teams well-grounded in everyday life: 'ordinary' people.

Facts are easy to pass on. It's not for me to decide whether a floor should be chipboard or wood. But I certainly have a duty to describe what chipboard is and does: its glue content, the formaldehyde or phenol it emits,[1] and their health consequences. Naturally, most people choose wood once they know these facts. It's not a case of imposing my preference on unwilling others; they choose as I would have.

Sensitivity is also possible to share, but in a different way. I can ask, for instance, what should a doorway do to us? Should passing into the room in question be an awakening experience? Or a calming, or reverence-inducing one? Perhaps it should be respectful, even humbling, as in older buildings where you had to stoop, both bowing in deference and – sometimes more important – unable to raise your sword arm.

When I ask this question, then use my experience to gesture the shapes that answer each preference, we – not I – agree how things should be shaped. And not just shaped, for this applies to tactile texture, acoustic and light quality, focal or diffuse heat, indeed to everything where sensory experience works on human mood.

This isn't just a way to use experts, yet reach decisions socially. It also raises consciousness. This makes it a growth process for all concerned. For me because I can expand my own privately developed sensitivities into the social realm; for others, what they intuitively felt, knew, becomes clarified and conscious. They become aware that what they were already seeing and feeling is shared and valued by others.

This is only one way in which the consensus design process is also a personal growth process for each participant. Whenever somebody makes a suggestion or criticism, I try to refrain from instantly drawing it.[2] Instead, I put a pencil in their hand and say, 'show me'. Note that this is a pencil, not a felt-tipped pen. Most people feel a little inhibited, but can at least hover with a pencil and sketch faint marks. It's enough! The decision, the shape, may change – just as anything I have drawn will – but their suggestion has become substance. No longer is it a case of them telling me their verbal-only wishes and me choosing a form for them. The process is no longer expert dominated, but expert facilitated.

I do the same with clay at the modelling stage. This is generally harder, partly because it's hard for enough people to get close enough to take part. Also, some find it too messy for their smart clothes. To overcome inhibitions, I try to get several people massing out general shapes or modelling existing buildings and features. Once they've had their hands on clay it's much easier to get them to mould it into new shapes as required.

Once, but only once, I worked with a group who, for the design of one single building each made their own model of how they'd like it to be. Every half-hour, they moved on to their neighbour's model, to improve that – and so on round the circle. Eventually, all models had been worked on by all hands – but this didn't mean they were the same. My task was to find the common themes and develop a synthesis of all those ideas. Challenging for me – but an excellent way of uncovering what everyone wanted and what felt right for all. This approach is based on *drawing out* the latent in someone else's work, not squashing it to impose your own wishes. Many groups aren't ready – at the outset – for such selfless social listening, which is why I normally use other techniques.

In some participatory design techniques, participants move around blocks of wood representing buildings. I prefer clay. Blocks of wood assume rectangularity. All you can do is decide where to place them. Clay can be squidged back and forth – you can make practically any shape you want (with card for roof overhangs and balconies and twigs or matchsticks for posts and beams, you can cover the whole range). Another problem with wood is it's so solid, confident and apparently fixed in size and shape. Anything that starts by suggesting form risks focusing more on buildings than the places between them. This happens enough in architecture anyway – especially style- and icon-led architecture. Clay modelling doesn't require drawing skills. It may be more inhibiting to start, but is more liberating once you get going.

All these techniques both involve people in the physical design itself and also empower them to shape it in ways that resonate with them. This is critically different from just delegating it to the professionals. More than all this, it's an inner awakening process – a growth process for all involved, empowering, self-esteem-raising and fulfilling.

Notes

1   Even today, with low formaldehyde adhesives.

2   I do sometimes, but I try not to and, except when time pressure is intense, mostly I succeed in this!

CHAPTER FOURTEEN

Social technique

Social technique with unequal groups

> Modern society has entrusted too much responsibility to architects and engineers. Once
> an architect initially controls the agenda, the layman is reluctant to offer any meaningful
> input. The attitude of the layman is this: 'Architects and engineers are professionals that
> do this stuff everyday for a living. What could I, as a layman, possibly offer that they
> don't already know'.
>
> Once the presence, vocabulary and status of the architect and engineer are in the same
> brain-storming room with the layman users, the entire process takes on a more
> restricted path.
>
> *Richard Erganian, Developer*

With architects and engineers uncommitted – even hostile – to consensus process,
this is a major risk. Firm process technique can overcome this, but only if the whole
group works, not as specialist and review panel, but as one.

I've also had the experience that influential members – the architect is usually the
most influential – can agree to, even say, all the right things, but *do* something different. I could (unwittingly) easily do this too. This is why, when designing, it's
important that as many people as possible – ideally everyone – put their hands to the
clay model and pencils to the drawings. Agreeing words, then deferring to someone
else to give them form is *never* enough.

Group process

A group may share a vision – or a question, a worry, an opposition – but every group
is composed of individuals. Each individual has a particular way of looking at things,
has an agenda, a list of problems and, more significantly, a list of solutions. This isn't
the only problem of groups. There are also personality aspects: power seekers, self-
effacers and clashes of interest, viewpoint and dominance. We may all be concerned
with a single issue – or a single *family* of many sub-issues – but each from our own
angle. How can we transcend rather than deny our differences? How can we act as
one trans-individual being?

I'll describe how I do it. Firstly, our *physical*, spatial relationship affects how we
interact. Chairs lined up to face a table can never make a relationship of equals.

Chairs in a circle go a long way towards reducing inequalities. A central table focuses on the project in hand. For a very small group – two to five persons – the table, and what's on it, also absorbs some of the intensity so that vulnerable personalities feel psychologically safer. The table is best round, or if that's not possible, the seats are *around* it, or at least side by side, not *across* it. This also goes some way to countering the dominance implied by drawings one way up. While some architects can draw upside-down, most people can't, nor can they understand upside-down drawings, so it helps to rotate papers frequently.

Tables are fine for small groups, but larger numbers can't all get round a table. We therefore sit in a large circle. If we're too many for the room, it's better to be squashed side-by-side than have two rows. Those in the rear never feel equal to those in front. Even though I'm the invited dignitary, we are now spatially equal. The process we will now go through will reinforce this equality. This isn't just ethical principle; it's also the best way to get everyone, especially the timorous, to contribute. We'd miss out on much if they didn't.

Usually I, at least, am a stranger. So before addressing *why* we are here, comes the question: who are we? We go round the circle, briefly introducing ourselves: who we are at several levels: name, what we do, our contact with the project. This sets the scene – and incidentally tells me a lot about the skills and will-energy that the project can muster, also the values and expectations bound up with it. I'm not a good rememberer of names so I usually make notes and hope people don't change their positions before I've anchored name to face!

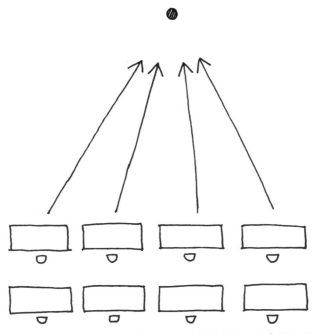

All attention focused on one person, giving this one multiplied (here eight times) power.

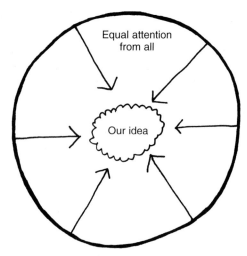

All attention focused on thing discussed, making everyone equal.

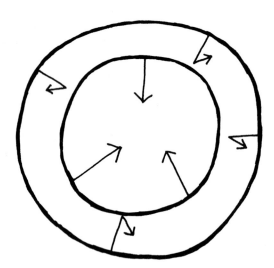

Second row blocked, so harder to get a word in. (OK for powerful personalities – but these tend to sit in front!)

As early as possible, I like to lay out the ground rules. In fact there is only one: *all ideas are group property*. Once something is voiced, it's no longer *my* suggestion, thought, observation, but *ours*. Nor is it yours, or hers or his. Only *ours*. This rule is key to the consensus design process.

Because suggestions are group property I have a different relationship to them than if they were *yours* – yours in distinction to, in competition with, *mine*. To act as a group we need to rise above personalized competitiveness, antagonisms, petty irritations, alliances and subserviences. So if somebody makes a suggestion I don't like, before I speak I need to be clear what I don't like about it. I can then *evaluate* instead of criticizing or rejecting. This is more objective, less putting-down, less dominating, and leaves everyone free. Even better, if I can phrase it as a question, like: 'Is this turn of direction too abrupt for this circumstance? or do we need this jolt, awakening here?', 'is this proportion too cramping or is it necessary to enhance the spatial expansion that follows?', 'what does it feel like to go directly into this activity from this one?', 'although it's only one minute's walk, will people go to the shop if it's this far away?'. Before we reject things, there's also a 'how?' option: 'how can we make this path the obvious way to go?', 'how can we give such urban vitality to the experience that you don't notice the minute's distance?'.

The same applies to *my* suggestions. Rather than 'I suggest ...', it is better to use 'what if we move this here, emphasize the upward gesture, compress the space, concentrate the activity ...'. 'What if ...' leaves other people freer as to how they respond. It also protects me from being exposed as a fool if my suggestion was ridiculous.

Ridiculous suggestions are important. Not so many that we descend into trivia, but enough to give levity to an intense, serious and long process. But ridiculous suggestions do more than this. They can jolt us into a new way of looking at things. They open chances for unexpected insights that we would never have found by proceeding along the linear track down which our concentrated focus leads us. Some people make serious suggestions that others think stupid. I've learnt never to dismiss these. Dismissal isn't only insulting; our superior sophistication easily blinds us to the insights that naivety, impracticality and over-simplification occasionally bring.

As this stage of the process is *always* preceded by the place-study stage, all the suggestions we make have a shared aim. Their *only* purpose is to support the spirit of the project, already agreed by the group. This isn't, therefore, about putting forward individualistic ideas. These may make individuals feel important, but won't add to our shared aim. We therefore aim to avoid individualistic ideas at all stages of the process.

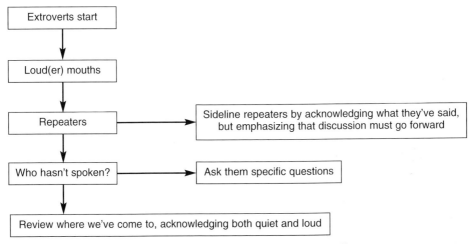

Ensuring loud-mouths don't dominate, but everyone contributes equally.

We may have equal rights, but groups are never equal. Every group has assertive members and reticent, under-confident and shy ones. In the early stages – place-study – this is no problem because everybody has their say in turn. This greatly helps quieter members gain confidence to speak. Then comes the stage when we all work together, formulating precise answers to questions like, 'what should a place say?'

Usually, the stronger personalities assert themselves now. Still no problem; it gets things going. Once the ice is broken, the quieter voices start to be heard. Part of my job, of course, is to ensure that everyone who desires to do so makes a contribution. This is when those with low confidence, who felt they didn't have anything of value to offer, realize that their observations *are* valuable.

So far, so good, but at the end of the day, when we're all tired, invariably fresh questions and sometimes even fresh agendas come up. Tiredness, too much to do, time pressures – all these weaken inner discipline and shorten tempers. At this stage, the strong personalities tend to reassert themselves, sometimes irritably, usually bringing up the fixed ideas they had before the process even started. Fortunately, this doesn't happen very often, but it does happen.

Clearly, I shouldn't shut people up, even when they bring us back to our starting point, potentially unravelling the whole day's achievements. It wouldn't just be rude, it would inevitably cause resentments and lead to cliques manoeuvring against cliques. I have, however, one golden card: our time is limited. To finish by 6 p.m., 10.30 or whenever people have to go home, there will be other issues that we must resolve. So let's put contentious matters temporarily to the side, complete the process and finalize the non-contentious. In this way we can end up resolving the difficult issues, simply by approaching them non-frontally. This may not *guarantee* success – though it has always worked so far. If nothing else, it prevents us getting bogged down. We will, at the very least, get a lot more done.

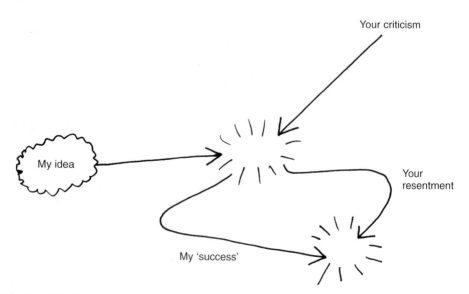

Idea-based design.

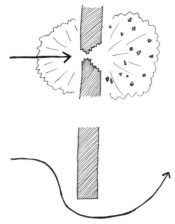

Two ways of dealing with problems: head on, or approaching from a different viewpoint. I'm lazy; I prefer the second way.

Confirming decisions

Sitting in a group – or standing around a table – is only one aspect of group work. Different sorts of work go in different directions: place-study involves walking around the site; design work leads to paper and clay; project planning to discussions and eventually to written documents – conventionally 'minutes'.

I have little love for minutes. I've been to too many meetings where half the time (or more) is taken by reading the minutes of the last meeting. I prefer shorter and more focused records. Whenever decisions are agreed their precise wording is proposed, discussed, agreed then written down and read back for confirmation, *at that time*. If – and this is rare – there are dissenting voices, these, with their reasons, are also recorded. We can then pass to the next point.

Such records brief the next meeting as to what has been decided, how and when it will be done and by whom, also what needs further review, what has been deferred and why. This gives a framework for meeting to build on meeting to really get things done.

There is always the problem that not everybody can get to every meeting. Indeed the likelihood of finding a meeting date to suit all decreases by the square of the number of people involved. Here I'm afraid I tend to prefer the path that gets things done over the democratic. This doesn't mean by-passing people. If each meeting's agenda is circulated in advance, those who can't come can at least have their views represented by others, or by letter.

This is much the same as the 'mandate system'. No committee, group or meeting can decide every detail. There is always too much to do. Eventually someone has to be given the freedom to get on with the job. In the same way, larger groups can mandate to smaller ones which are easier to convene, more task focused and quicker to make and implement decisions. Mandating means deciding the parameters within which the mandated group – or individual – is free to act. Freedom to act means freedom to do things other than the way I would like. But – as no freedom means no initiative, and possibly no action – this is something I have to accept. That is a small price for getting things to move forward. The alternative is overload, invariably followed by burn-out. Bad for individuals, bad for organizations, bad for momentum.

Recapitulation: anchoring where we've got to

Reports from mandated groups bring us up to date. Minutes refresh our memory. Both appraise us of the current situation. We strengthen our focus on this each time we recapitulate. So, at the end of meetings I like to recapitulate decisions. And at the commencement of each subsequent day, or session, we recapitulate (briefly) the process that has brought us to the present. In this way we both connect with the stream of form-condensing that is taking place and refine the *essence* of the situation.

Recapitulation is especially important when we've slept a night. Sleep frees us from the detail, the emotive distortions and the primacy of the most recent. It allows us to gain more of a picture of the essence of things. But it also starts the process of forgetting – hence the importance of recapitulation.

What is this approach all about? Fundamentally it is a *listening* approach. This accords full value to every individual, even the reticent, self-effacing, (apparently) un-skilled ones. And people really blossom when so treated. In fact it is just from those who thought they had nothing worthwhile to contribute that many important contributions come.

Listening, on an equal and group-sharing basis, means that we can hear that which comes from the group *as a whole*. When a group works as one trans-individual being, what it produces is always greater than the sum of its parts. There is more to this than numbers. When ten people form a group to pursue gain (namely self-interest), they become ten times as powerful. When ten gather for the greater good, their transcendence of egotism allows the group to listen selflessly to the energy behind things. They become a hundred times as strong! Strength and power aren't the same thing. Power can crash through things – but it gets expended. Strength may not be forceful, but it can be sustained. Hence: 'in true strength there is gentleness; in true gentleness, strength'.

A group working with a listening attitude isn't just listening to its members, nor even to the whole group, but also to the spirit of the group, of the initiative. When we also try to listen to the spirit of a place and to unify all these through a listening *process* of design, we are carried, aided, deepened and enriched by energies beyond our own.

CHAPTER FIFTEEN

Technique and non-technique

Dead technique, live technique

I have a personal confession: I'm put off by 'techniques'. I've been to too many workshops (about two) which are run by formula techniques – and I don't like it. Why then do I use a technique?

The method I describe has enabled me to work with groups of many complexions and to penetrate rapidly to insights and insightful solutions. So successful have I found it, that I feel the need to share it. It's not the *technique*, however, that's important, but the reasons that underlie it, and which have given it form. As with most things, once we understand underlying reasons, we can adapt, or create, methods appropriate to whatever circumstance we find ourselves in. If we don't understand

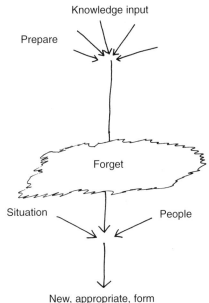

Dead technique has rigid forms. With live technique, situation shapes underlying knowledge into spontaneous form.

the underlying, then we just have empty formulaic technique – enough to put any-one off!

Preparing lectures, or lessons – the better prepared, the better the lesson; but the more rigidly stuck to is the preparation, the worse the lesson – not a living dialogue, just a rigid dead outer form with no inner life. Dialogue takes into account the indi-vidual listeners and what they are ready to hear. Once we understand something, we can allow technique to form as we go.

The demands of circumstance

Different scales of project ask for different processes. The number of people involved, the size of the site and the complexity of the project all influence what we need to do.

A single house rarely involves more than the family who'll live in it. Moreover, they know – or think they know – what they want. Such a small group is usually too small for individuals to balance each other, or to build 'group consciousness'. This isn't about broad or narrow minds, just numbers. Rigid ideas tend to dominate, but I will probably meet resistance if I try to free them by stepping back to an idea-free process. Better to use the prematurely formed suggestions I'm given – which are anyway (hopefully) shared by all family members – as a *starting* point.

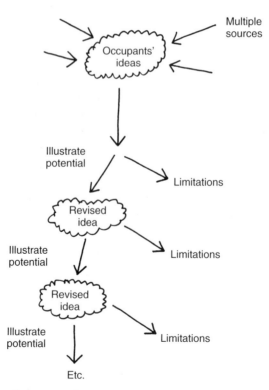

Consensus design at family house scale.

For most families their home is the focus of their attentions. Other things, however, can easily be forgotten. Commonly, the focus is so much on the house itself that its relationship with its surroundings, how you arrive there, how the building greets you, and how you journey through it have hardly been considered. Likewise, though moods of rooms and spirit of the home are implied in the ideas and examples they've given me, they're rarely made explicit.

Four-layer place-study, even if brief, is never time wasted as it always casts fresh light on things. For a house, the approach, entry and internal journeys have a significant bearing on how we feel about it. In this context, the moods, and subsequently the forms, of the interior and exterior spaces can grow *from* the images and ideas I've been given, into what the family couldn't articulate, but in fact *really* want.

The social dynamics of families can be demanding. They're frequently patterned by habit, making it hard for me to distinguish between domination and free agreement. I've twice (only twice, thank goodness!) co-designed with couples, but later received a letter from the wife claiming that I was doing the opposite of what 'they' wanted. Yet she had agreed with everything, even when questions were directed at her! I had obviously failed to notice domination by the (in these cases) husbands. (Wives do it too – also grown-up children to their elderly parents, and the reverse.)

I'm more alert now to when one person is dominating another, but it's still easy to miss. One technique is to ask the (possibly) subservient person to summarize our decisions and how what we've (jointly) drawn meets 'their' needs.

Most families have never worked with an architect before, so they don't always understand, or aren't fully understanding when they think they are. All this, therefore, requires very careful listening to *how* people say things, how they agree – or acquiesce – and what they don't say.

A building, or group of buildings, used by a group of people obviously fits easily into the processes I describe. The different viewpoints, perspectives, knowledge and experiences balance and complement each other. Also relationship intensity is looser, so it's easier to build 'group consciousness'. But what happens when the project is of a size, use or placing that impacts its neighbours?

Here, there are two distinct interest groups: those that want something, and those that are concerned about, indeed often fear, it. To make matters worse, only one of these groups has asked me to become involved, and has agreed to give time to the process. And, because they pay me, my allegiances are suspected by the other group. Perhaps rightly so, as it's hard not to want to push a project that you're enthusiastic about.

Places can be bounded by more than one owner, use or building. Ideally all neighbours should take part in the design process. After all they will be affected. But this isn't straightforward. There can be problems finding them and getting them to come. Neighbours' agendas are inevitably different to project agendas. Their concerns are spatially different. The issue for them is *interface relationships*, whereas the project group is more concerned with the *heart* of the project.

This suggests two different area focuses for place-study: periphery and centre. As both affect each other, it is only appropriate that neighbours take part in the design. If they're open and self-disciplined, they can bring unique knowledge and experience, make valuable contributions and become full members of the process. But, of course, they haven't chosen the project, appointed me or committed themselves to its desirability. Why should they? If they're determined to feel negative, I can't do much about that. More commonly they feel excluded, threatened and defensive. This changes when they feel included and listened to. There are, however, parameters to their involvement. Their remit is the *interface zone*, spatially and also in terms of spillover impacts like noise and traffic. I try to make it clear that however strongly they feel about things, we can only go forward if we dispassionately *assess* them – even mood, feeling and emotion things. Even irrational strong feelings need to be taken seriously, but as only some people hold them they're no easy basis for whole group discussion. Were they to seek to block us by complaining to the planning authority, they would be subject to much the same terms and remit. In that case, they would only be able to block some (rarely all) of what we want to do, but have to put up with the rest. If however, they work *with* us, they can take part in the form-giving process so that the design that emerges has positive *benefits* for them. This isn't about mere damage-limitation, but about creating something that is better for everybody than if it hadn't happened. Win-win instead of damage-control.

A very important part of the process from the neighbours' point of view is the stage where we consider hypothetical interventions. We can usually identify the most probable scenarios. If, instead of a multi-cultural centre with park (see Chapter 21), the land remained derelict, became a shopping centre, or – as already classified – light industry, would neighbours be safer, suffer less traffic, gain in property value, have somewhere for children and young people? Looked at emotively, racist issues start to creep in. Looked at objectively, all these highly probable alternatives have significant disadvantages.

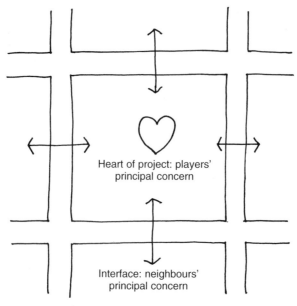

Heart of project: players'
principal concern

Interface: neighbours'
principal concern

The interface between project and surroundings will affect neighbours. Can they be involved in this interface design?

What about large groups: hundreds, even thousands of people – too many to work together as a single group? One way round this is to create layers of mandated representatives. Decisions – and places – always fall into strata of scale: overview, coordination, areas of interest, fine details. National transport plans aren't about pedestrian crossings. Village plans are. The first step, therefore, is to clarify the strategic issues and the levels of detail at each layer of decision-making. Depending on scale, this can be a public meeting or representatives around a table. Next is for 'lower' groups, like street community or tenants association, to choose representatives to the layer above. These are mandated to speak and decide for the group they represent.

This can even be done at urban planning scale. In New Delhi a squatter community of 500 families elected representatives to design their area within the framework of a government-funded infrastructure. A more familiar, if tarnished, example is the system of soviets introduced in post-revolutionary Russia. A collective farm or factory would vote a member to the area 'soviet', this in turn would vote one to the regional soviet and so on. Ideal in theory, but disastrous in practice. This system had one fundamental flaw that led to its corruption: 'upper' echelons had power over 'lower' ones. If delegated power is to respond to community needs rather than just build its own power structure, it's essential that the upper layers make as *few* decisions as possible. Only those that *cannot* be decided at a lower level. Everything that can be passed *down* for more local decision-making must be.

With this sort of structure, participatory planning is possible even at a town scale, if not larger, with the nut-and-bolt decisions made by street, block, and apartment floor sub-groups. Regardless of scale, the same four layers of being apply to every issue, every place, every community. The spirit at the heart of things, the emotional consequences, the time-continuum context and the physical results. The motivation, mood, flow and substance.

How this is done, however, very much depends on the number of people involved. For small groups, anything that smacks of 'technique' can feel heavy-handed, authoritarian and too rigid to be receptive to the individuals involved. Large groups, on the other hand, need firmer technique or the process will be dispersed and dominated by the 'strong idea-ers'. For these, the stronger the technique, the freer is everyone.

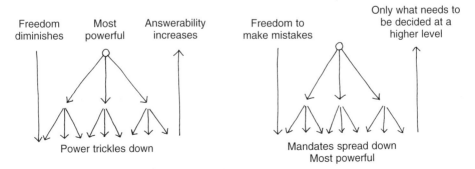

Top-down versus bottom-up decision making.

Thinking the process versus doing the process

Understanding the principles and mentally imagining the process (which I will describe more fully in case studies) may be a useful foundation for understanding places and designing them. But to gain real value from it, you must *do* it. Until acted out in the physical world, it is abstract and personal – limited by, and bound to, a single viewpoint. You need to actually do it for the *social activity* to clarify focus, the *diversity of viewpoint* to sharpen impartial listening and the *time taken* to bring balanced perspective.

Similarly, if we don't include others – especially those who'll be impacted by the project – vital knowledge can be missed or resentment bred. Shyness, inertia or impatience makes such omissions easy, as I know to my cost!

Taking time

Time is central to the *process* of design. The methods I describe *take time*. It is a lot to ask two days, or even one, of a busy person – and there are many who won't give it. So why do I ask for so much time? And why is that time begrudged?

Everybody has time, but also lots of things to fill it with. If I don't have time for something, I actually mean that this is too low on my list of priorities. As a culture, we don't very much value time, nor place. We give monetary values to both, but what we are actually valuing is what we can *fit into* time, not the benefits of *taking time*. Likewise, what we can fit into space, rather than the space quality. Awareness of the value of place-quality is growing, however. Few restauranteurs these days would expect food quality alone to make a restaurant a success; they also need 'mood'. Even with the best gastronomy, it would be hard to build up customers in a canteen atmosphere. Taking time, however, doesn't get much value. Nor does continuum. It has become normal to gut and refurbish offices every 12 years, houses every 40, and in the USA, to build commercial buildings that last no longer than their ten-year leases.

If we don't value time, we won't give it, but the four-layer design process *needs time*. Its steps *must* follow each other in prescribed sequence. This is the only way that the essence, the spirit of a project, can condense into form, into changes to place. Skip a stage and we no longer listen fully, but start to impose our own, always prematurely formed, ideas. The full process takes time, but this is always time well spent. But it isn't only design time we need. We aren't ready to undertake this till we know the place our design will happen in, what the new will be growing out of, and the continuum which gives context to our acts. All this takes at least a whole day; for a project of any size or social impact, at least two. Not just for me, but for everyone centrally involved. A lot of time for a businessman, doctor, teacher, charity-manager, parent, or indeed anyone.

There is naturally the temptation to rush through the steps or to blur them together. Sometimes time constraints make this unavoidable. So much happens, however, when the whole consensus design process is followed through, step by step that *I strongly recommend taking the time for it*. Although this has often been contested at the outset, never yet have I known anyone to begrudge this time when we've finished.

For one thing, when we slow down, our output speeds up! Whenever I've tried to short-cut the process by a few hours, it has cost us days in wasted time – as described in Chapter 23. Time commitment invested now prevents delays and the expense of remedial work. Patient observation coupled with extrapolations of chains of consequences enables us to foresee and remedy many problems – from foot traffic eroding a hillside to the changing scale of theatre productions invalidating a business plan – well in advance.

This isn't just about 'more haste, less speed'. The less time given to the process, the earlier must ideas become formed. Once formed, they're very hard to see around. Alternatives are screened out by what we've become focused on. Speeding things up risks forcing things into form before they are ready to find *their own* forms. Rushed forms will never be as appropriate as these – and we will pay for this forever on. That is why taking enough time at the pre-form stage is time well spent.

Finally, because this process (for new development of any larger scale) spans at least two days, we have the opportunity to 'sleep on things'. The old adage, to 'sleep on it', is full of wisdom, for we easily carry our thoughts into sleep as an overwhelming confusion, an over-simplification, or an emotional turbulence, outrage or conviction. We're unable to 'see the wood for the trees'. But through sleep we are rejuvenated. We *re*visit things after a digestion period and we are freed, if we sleep soundly, from all the near-sighted turmoil. For this reason, in the morning we see a clearer picture. Both for creative and scientific processes, there is nothing as effective as sleep in bringing fresh and balanced perspective.

Taking time saves time, of course. We don't have to have endless meetings to deal with complaints, rectify mistakes, refute criticisms and generally soothe the aggrieved. We don't have to have design professionals and users, indeed sometimes everybody, arguing with, resenting and out-manoeuvring each other. This brings benefits in morale, in all pulling together in the same direction, in the suitability of the end result. Deferring decisions until our 'listening' has made them obvious may sound like going slowly. Indeed the start always does seem slow, but then suddenly everything comes together. In fact, it has been my experience that this 'slow' way usually goes *much* faster than the conventional way.

Understanding behind doing

I describe techniques – and give examples of programmes, agenda and so on, and these I believe would be useful to follow the first two or three times you work with consensus design. Even at the outset, it's best if these techniques are leavened by understanding. Before long, however, the understanding should be shaping the form: the programme, the timetable, the group dynamics. This doesn't mean an individual way of doing it for each person, but one for each *situation*. The furtherance of a leader's individualism and prestige signature isn't going to help group consciousness. But every process born anew for every individual group, project and place situation gives it a life, relevance, respect and focus that no repeated formula can.

That is why I have urged you to read, and work with, the principles behind the practice.

CHAPTER SIXTEEN

What can go wrong? What can go right?

Do the processes I describe always go smoothly? In my experience so far, they have every time. That is, they've *ended* smoothly – and mostly, but not always, been smooth the whole way through. Always, when I start, I feel as well equipped as a beginner swimmer standing on the high diving board. For, despite process method and social technique, anything could happen. Indeed it's most important that I'm as open as possible to anything happening – otherwise the consensus design process would just be a sham.

My consensus method is built on a 20-year background of scores of projects, designed jointly with clients and users but in a less structured way. So far I have co-designed nearly 50[1] projects in the way this book describes. This includes seven exercise workshops – harder because there's no 'real' end product to motivate consensus. (Three of these were with architects, the hardest group to deal with!) Many of these projects have taken the consensus process beyond the clay-model stage, to a larger scaled card model.

Generally, these have worked well but, inevitably, some things *have* gone wrong. Objective listening to forces beneath the surface isn't as easy as it might sound. On one occasion, we didn't listen acutely enough to what the place was telling us. The historical movement of glacial deposits *should* have awakened us to potentially mobile sub-soil. It didn't. And our building – which felt so right *on the surface* – needed expensive foundations below.

Ironically, most problems result from the success of the consensus process. This process liberates so much energy; energy normally suppressed by inhibitions or just marginalized by the 'proper' professional way.

One consequence is that individuals feel freed to do their 'own thing'. Now that the architect is no longer boss, they don't need me, they don't need the group. This isn't consensus design any more. Once this starts it's not too easy to control, for, once broken down, consensual decision-making is both hard and – because I have to invoke hierarchical authority – *unfortunate* to re-establish. Here I depend on the group being sufficiently mature to remain trans-individual. In such situations, the process structure needs to be firm.

Another problem is that the enthusiasm of the user group with whom I design can out-run their decision-making remit. I've had the experience of developing a design well into card-model stage only to discover that there was another group – a committee – that should have authorized the work. And naturally they were not a little peeved.

Because I work largely on my own, together with the client/user group, and many projects are overseas, we usually need executive architects to carry the job to completion. I'm anxious that executive architects don't perceive the design as 'my' design, but as 'our' design, so I'm keen that they're part of the consensus process through which the form incarnates. Herein lies the first problem: who pays for their time? Clients rarely want to pay for two architects where one would do and the executive architect often doesn't want to spend time without being paid for it. One way round this is for the client to pay a standard fee and the two of us apportion this on a time-record basis.

The alarm bells start however, when (usually at the last minute) the executive architect can't come. After that the project has – in their eyes – two stages: mine and theirs. One once said to me *'you* inspire them [the client group] then *we* do the work'. 'Doing the work', for designers, normally means putting their own design signature on something. In other words, the early design emerges by consensus – then an outsider architect redesigns it. Yes, this has happened. It's galling but it's life! Here it's useful for me to have been clearly and conventionally appointed so that I have the authority to redirect the design back onto its group-agreed track. But it's very unfortunate to have to resort to the hierarchical way. In these times we should have grown beyond it.

Then there is the problem of finding where other design-critical specialists, from ecologists to acousticians, come into the process. If engineers are to be more than just calculators of beam sizes they need to be involved with the ongoing design. Likewise environmental consultants concerned with energy conservation and natural ventilation need to feed into the design early on. But when in the process? Who pays for their time in the place-study phase? Can you meaningfully be part of the design stage without involvement in the place-study? By the end of the clay-model stage the design is substantially formed. True, the clay can be remolded – and will inevitably need to be, but the major form issues have been more or less decided. The initial, rough, clay model gives form to the synthesized needs of project, place and people. As we develop it we increasingly concern ourselves with environmental performance and quality, also buildabilty. These issues will develop further on paper and with the card model. Consultants may be outsiders to the process, but the point at which the model has been first formed seems the best point at which to first involve such people.

Specialists can bring valuable contributions – but what happens when these haven't been invited? Not everybody believes in feng shui, earth energies or sacred geometry. Regardless of their relevance, if one person senses these but others don't, the group can only either accept or reject their recommendations. We can't *share* the experience. By appointing specialists, the group has agreed to value what they bring – but with self-appointed specialists it hasn't. This can cause feelings of unfreedom and rejection, both divisive. Fortunately it doesn't have to. Just as spirit-of-place is manifest in physical matter, so do even the subtlest of energies have material manifestations. These physical signs (and movement and mood influences) we can all experience. If we can't, there's something not quite whole about the specialist knowledge. If we can, it doesn't matter whether this has a special name (which implies some people know more about it than others). It's enough to know it's true.

Just as gesturing movement and meetings of forms and spaces helps us experience the flow of 'chi', so do leaning trees and animal paths evidence geodetic energies.[2] Both we feel.

This is why the four-layer consensus process, dowsing and feng shui always (in my experience) reach the same conclusions.

There's also the practical problem of finding enough time to design together. Inevitably, however much we group-design, there comes a time when I have to work things up on my own. As rough drawings get more precise, they invariably need some modification. This especially happens each time we enlarge the scale at which we're working. As this involves a myriad of small decisions and it often isn't easy to contact everybody rapidly, I usually just keep going, noting down the changes for my client's approval. Normally this is given, but I have had one client who felt that I was unilaterally changing what had previously been agreed – albeit in rough at a smaller scale. This is the unfortunate price of distance. Whenever we can sit down together, things go smoothly. In this case, the executive architect – sensitive to the design process – could sit with them, explain the reasoning behind these (very minimal) revisions and sort everything out.

Surprisingly, not everyone wants to be part of the design process. They might want to, but have such low confidence that they won't believe they can do it, so refuse to become empowered. I've had one community project cancelled for this reason. Once the group got a grant, they hired another architect to do the whole job for them 'properly'.[3] This is extreme, and rare, but the low confidence and low self-esteem it stems from are all too common. Once we get going, however, confidence and self-esteem always grow.

Though avoidable with hindsight, these difficulties aren't random, but linked to the process. Genuine disadvantages though they are, they're not so serious as the disadvantages bound to the conventional design process. Not infrequently, that process goes like this: clients have unworkable ideas. Architects have personal, usually stylistic, aspirations. Unworkable ideas and stylistic aspirations don't match one another – so a process of proposal, rebuff, criticism and new proposal ensues. Clients and architects can become polarized into camps, neither of which respect the other – the 'difficult client, difficult architect' mentality. Users don't get a look in.

Architects seek to get round clients or win them round, and then engineers, with their over-cautious, over-dimensioned structures, compromise this further. In due course the building contractors compromise the whole lot. And when the buildings are occupied, people don't use them in the right way – they further compromise the design by the alterations they make. And they even complain that the architect never thought about the way they need to do things! How unappreciative! It may not always happen like this, but I hear enough dissatisfaction stories from clients, building users and even from architects, to infer that non-communication, non-listening, non-respect and frustration are by no means uncommon.

The whole conventional process is one of sequential *order*. Nothing wrong with that, but the means by which order is established hardens relationships into money-exchanges. It atomizes – even polarizes – the different parties and desiccates the soul out of what gets designed, what gets built. This doesn't mean nourishing places can't be achieved by this method, but that they don't *result from* the process. They *rise above* its limitations.

By contrast, consensus design does not demand exceptional skills, sensitivities and experience. Soul-nourishing and physically practical places are the natural outcome of the process. A much easier starting point from which to raise places to the spirit-transforming level of art.

Notes

1 Forty-seven at the last count.
2 After Guy Underwood (1974). *The Pattern of the Past*, Sphere Books.

3 Later, even this fell through. But so battered was their confidence, they could no longer think of doing the project themselves.

PART SIX

Projects

First it should be said that those of us who were involved in that process with you remember it as one of the, if not the, most inspirational of times. [I] don't remember the steps (wish I did) you took us through, but do recall the gradual unfolding of what the land spoke, meeting what were perceived to be our needs. As a result the latter seemed to find its rightful place on the land. And it was very good. The process opened us to such a degree that ideas flooded in. Many never thought of before. And yet over it all there was sense, not a fantasizing.

Belinda Feillion – Teacher, USA (East Bay Waldorf School project)

The extraordinary cross-section of people from various cultures, religions and age that are actively involved in the creation of the ASHA Centre were able to input their creative ideas and community & cultural needs into the overall vision and design of the Centre. The atmosphere in which everyone worked was relaxed, while at the same time being dynamic. The overall result were buildings and gardens that were both beautiful and an inspiration to the 'collective community' that is the new millennium.

Zerbanoo Gifford. Director – ASHA Foundation UK

I've described the theory. But theories are only theories. How does consensus design work in practice?

Firstly, it's exiting, liberating, fun – and hectic! Too hectic for me to take photographs or record the process at the time. (I do, of course, record the decisions.) Only a few have I been able to write-up afterwards. This has influenced the selection here.[1]

Secondly, nothing works quite the way it's meant to! Things never do![2] By reading several project descriptions, however, you'll see how the core principles remain, but their application adapts to each circumstance. In particular, Chapter 20, shows how the process can adapt when there are no users; Chapter 21, what can happen when there are potentially hundreds of participants; and Chapter 22 describes the use of the process with a very small group. Most of the projects described here are about healing damaged places, using new buildings – and designing these buildings in detail. Chapters 17 and 18, however, show how the process can work to remediate existing buildings as well as the places they are part of.

These projects also illustrate how different groups relate to each stage: how, in particular, approach to mood and spirit ranges from touchy-feely-ism to firmly grounded business mission-statement; from anthropomorphizing parts of a place to describing the elemental identity. Likewise, place-biography ranges from the predominantly site-focused to the predominantly surrounding-area-focused. Only physical description is the same in all projects. As it should be, for physical facts are the same for all, regardless of how we relate to them. My only requirement at this level was that, buildings or none, indoor or outdoor, our study is about *place*, not building form.

Notes

1 While I've tried to be scrupulously accurate, including what went wrong as well as right, slight inaccuracies are always possible, particular where I've had to draw from memory.

2 Hence Murphy's law.

CHAPTER SEVENTEEN

Reversing moods: lunatic asylum to Steiner school, Brighton

In 1997, Brighton Steiner School had just moved into a new building. This had started its days gracefully, as a convalescent home, but then became a 'lunatic asylum', then mental hospital – with electro-therapy, only slightly more humane. All in all, it had quite the wrong aura for a Steiner school. Nor was it very suitable in practical terms. The building was too cramped, classes – and teachers – too dispersed and separated by zig-zag corridors. There was no integration of building with garden, nor with the locality – both creating an atmosphere of imbalance. The fundamental question, however, was, could a former lunatic asylum ever become a satisfactory Steiner school?

The teachers asked me to help transform the place. The negative, oppressive message needed urgent redemption. There were material issues as well. In three years the school had grown from seven to ten classes so desperately needed more space, not to mention workshops and a hall. Even more urgently it had just received a £5000 grant for interior renovation and another £5000 for the garden. Money needed – and needing to be spent – *now*.

Teachers are only free at weekends – and most have families – so weekend time constraints prevailed. We couldn't meet before 9.30, and were scheduled to finish at 5 p.m. Could we do it in one short day? Obviously yes, because we had to … but not as thoroughly as we might like. We would need to keep to a tight timetable – always hard with a large group. We were 13 in number. I hoped this wasn't a bad omen.

One-day process

Place-study

9.30: We gathered in a circle and briefly introduced ourselves. Equally briefly I outlined the day ahead.

9.45: We walked the approach journey, from around the street corner to the school gate, then in to the building, up stairs, along corridors to the endmost top floor classroom – the nicest, indeed the only pleasant one, as it happened. The teachers, of course, knew this journey well, or anyway what can be seen of the first part by car, for those that drove to work. This was an introduction for me but a 'new eyes' refresher for them. There was much contemplative looking – more conscious than a 'normal' first-impression. This first-impressions walk actually only needed five minutes, but in the event, took 40. As we walked in silence, it was hard for me to hurry everyone without breaking the silence. (I now stress – and repeat – the necessity of keeping to time allocation!)

Back in the classroom we built up a 'first impression' picture – what a newly enrolled child sees and experiences. There was a clear distinction between the Edwardian-designed front and the utilitarian pragmatism of the rear. The many dis-coordinated additions and alterations over the years added up to an impression of chaos. Moreover, the very first impression of the school was of all the cars wedged into every available bit of the tarmac that fronted it: a car park, not a place for children.

From now on, we limited our journey to the bits we could do something about: effectively just the property and its boundary fence. We started by identifying the parts it could be divided into and agreeing who would study which of these: gate to front door; front door to stairs; staircase; corridor to classroom. Two or three people in each group.

10.20: We now observed what was physically there, agreeing to meet and share our observations in 20 minutes. (It took 25.) Despite the short time, the observations were thorough and acute. Each group spoke in turn, so building up a 'sequence picture'. This took 40 minutes, longer than I had allowed, but 40 minutes well spent.

In summary: our arrival journey started with a long narrow pavement edged by a chain-link fence, changing to iron railings, then wooden boarding funnelled towards two iron gates. We then walked across the car-stuffed tarmac, in deep shade from the three-storey building with its peeling paint and cobweb of drainpipes. Then entered the building by an apparently rear entrance. Once inside there was a metal inner porch. Beyond this, we came face to face with a wall. Corridors led to left and right, one zig-zagging deep into the interior, the other turning 90° to the staircase. Upstairs was another zig-zagging corridor, diminishing in width and acutely constricted at some corners, especially by lift-shaft, bathrooms, fire-reels and other nailed-on after-thoughts. It was solely fluorescent lit and had doors all over the place.

11.25: We now moved to the time and life stage, repeating our journey, but this time focusing on sequence and flow. For this we again allowed 20 minutes. The narrow strip of pavement, fenced one side, open-view to the other, swung into the downsloping entrance funnel, broader but with opaque sides. Once through the gate, a lawn opened to the right. The tarmac path now widened out into carpark. Then downhill across this open space towards the storage buildings, a series of sharp corners. Swinging right to an entrance porch we met a sudden check at the inner screen, and a stop at the blank wall ahead. Now came an abrupt turn into a corridor, its ceiling stepped down and its width narrowing at every zig and zag, then a short passage with doors randomly to the side. Next, a light-flooded staircase drawing us upwards, then again zig-zag narrowing corridors till at last through a narrow opening, the space expanded into the classroom. This in turn, opened onto a rooftop terrace.

We built up this journey with verbal descriptions, sketches, bodily gestures and movements to 'caricature' the space experience sequence. Three teachers in particular acted this out with penetrating insight and humour, one demonstrating how the children ricocheted off every protruding corner as they rushed and collided down the corridor. This took 20 minutes to half-an-hour.

12.15: We now observed the moods along this route, and the feelings they induced in us. For this, as time was running short, we allowed only ten minutes. The 'rebuilding' through description took 20. Once through the gate, and therefore within our power to alter, the moods started with meeting a welcoming tree, and glimpsing the lawn to the side, but then became increasingly unwelcoming as we picked our way through parked cars. We felt confined and confused once within the building, more mood-elevated at the generously daylit stairs, then again oppressed in the upper corridor. Near the narrowest point, where a recently built bathroom jutted in, was a section some described as haunted. Children would rush uncomfortably, even fearfully past this point. One teacher told us that this was where electric shock treatment was administered to patients. The aura of the mind-destruction and physical agony this entailed was still palpable. Again, the classroom was a relief – it had had a history more of convalescence than 'treatment', with all the brutalities that entailed.

1.10: We now asked what the place said it was. Several phrases came up: 'I was once grand, but have now declined', 'I am an adult, but with adolescent problems', 'I am trying to be, have questions, want help, have potential', 'I have a charming face (the front facade, which we never actually met on our entrance journey, and the children only meet when it's dry enough to play on the front lawn) but hide degraded interiors,' 'I dwell on former glory and resist change.' More condensed: 'I have a beautiful face, but am rigid inside'. Then: 'I am bitty, confused, not together – I have an identity crisis'. 'An identity crisis because I have no physical *heart*.' This brought all strands together: '*I have no heart*'. And we could hear the building cry: 'I am open – wanting to be loved, but I am rigid'.

1.30: This brought us, somewhat late, to lunch. About three hours and 25 minutes of focused place-study plus introductions and 'first impressions' – all-in-all about four hours. This left only a short afternoon to condense proposals for improvement, rehabilitation, rescue – for healing the building.

Design

2.00: Lunch over, we re-commenced by briefly recapitulating the morning. This took five minutes – worth it to clarify and anchor what we had gone through. We then asked what the school *should* say? This was easier – after all, teachers knew what ideals they were committed to – so it only took five to ten minutes. 'I have freely chosen to be a place of *life, warmth and love.*' 'A place of stability, strong, enduring and at home with itself.' 'An oasis, welcoming, inspiring, secure – but looking out into the world.'

2.10: What did this mean for our mood journey? All of us together re-walked the route, suggesting and discussing the moods that each part *should* – and could, without much difficulty – convey.

As we walked past the side, the first views of the building from outside the fence – hence our introduction to it would need to say: 'calm, elegant, inspiring', 'somewhere worthy of respect', 'interesting, coordinated', 'a sense of the whole', 'fun, alive, organic', 'wow! I'd like to be there', 'versatile, different things going on', 'I wish I'd been a child there'.

At the gates and through the approach yard: 'welcome, joy'.

In the corridors: 'joy, happiness, love – and I love to be here'. These spaces needed the clarity, interest and stimulation of revealing the activities in every room – in distinction to the present anonymous doors and 'hidden' rooms, hard even to discover how to get into.

Again, we walked the route; this time considering what flow of experience would achieve or reinforce these moods. We spoke, sketched and gestured, by pointing, posture exaggeration and eurythmy movement. As this was late November and daylight fading fast, we included suggestions for physical improvements in this stage. Also, because of impending dusk, we took 25 or so minutes to look at the workshops and storage sheds round the back of the building with a view to converting these to classrooms. The agenda expanded as the day shortened!

Starting at the gateway, we sought to address the building and its front door from this point on, instead of an entrance which pointed at outbuildings, then swerved to the side – as an afterthought, as it were. This led us to move the gateway to the left and angle it, then swing the path so as to face our destination.

Both pedestrians and vehicles enter here – a potential conflict, if not risk – suggesting a two-gate entrance. Teachers, however, arrive before children,[1] so this conflict could be resolved in *time*, rather than *space*. Children arrive by school mini-bus. This vehicle we could accommodate with a pull-in lay-by adjacent to the entrance. The chain-link fence needed a hedge grown over it to obstruct view, as some teachers had noticed 'creepy-looking' men staring at little girls playing.

We agreed that part of the sense of arrival depends on crossing a *threshold*. But what sort of threshold could mark entry here? Someone suggested this be an archway. Fresh from California I asked if we should make this a rose-covered frame. Once through this, did we need something else to differentiate this land as a *children's* – not car – realm? There was no room to separate 'drive' from 'path' – and anyway these uses occurred at different times. We decided, therefore to give this drive/path a footpath *mood*. This suggested that it point to the main pedestrian, not vehicle destination, have a foot-responsive texture and be human-scaled to walk on, hand-scaled to look at. This led us to choose a brick-paved *path* (but still usable as a *drive*) swinging towards the main door.

The building had once stood in stately grounds but contracting boundaries and broadening roads now left only an amorphous strip, part tarmac, part grass, around it. We realized we could use the path as an edge marker to form 'places', distinct in character. What else could form, or imply, place-edges? Someone suggested a pool – water always being popular with children (even if not always so popular with parents!).

We wondered where we'd get the water. Buy it? Rainwater would be cheaper *and* more environmentally responsible. One teacher suggested we develop this into a lesson in nature's cycles and human-directed recycling. The sort of lesson children would imbibe every day, without ever needing to be 'taught'. As rainwater is constantly added to, it can't just sit in a pond, but has to flow. This implied a stream. Wind-pumped to a header tank in the roof, this rainwater could feed toilet cisterns, then overflow via a sand filter for slow release to the stream. This could lead, by a series of cascades, from a header pool to a second one to 'finish' its journey. Aquatic plants cleaning the water would add to its educational purpose.

The school's space requirements had never been explicit. Every so often someone thought of another room nobody had yet mentioned. One such was a parents' room and kitchen. A hut, perhaps also including a cafe, shop and display area, could be interface between school and public. Pivoting the path around this would reinforce the gateway portal experience.

We now moved to the building entrance. This too had problems. It had a 'back door' atmosphere – not surprisingly, as that was indeed how it had started life. The original 'front door', on the (sunny) 'front' of the building had since become its inaccessible back, and the original (shady) back, now front.

Here, after the threshold, we needed to out-breathe, have space, levity and light to carry the joy of arriving, of being here. After demolishing the inner draught-screen, we would need a small exterior porch, fully glazed. This would open the interior hall to be a 'place' – further reinforced by new (and necessary) fire-doors to enclose it.

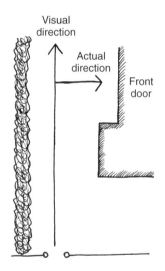
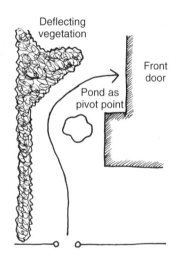

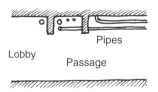
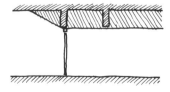

Small changes; large effect.

For the corridors to right and left, shaping the ceilings so that a sloping plane interceded between wall and ceiling wouldn't only make them gentler, but also hide the utilitarian mess of pipes. Likewise, both the ceiling steps and corridor zig-zags could be softened with angled planes – cupboards or ceiling plaster-board – so that spaces that belonged together could flow into one-another. The narrower parts of the upstairs corridor could be widened by removing the redundant bathroom, and could be shaped – as downstairs – with 45° cupboards so that space – and children – flowed rather than ricocheted. Individual shaping and recessing of classroom doors, together with small windows in them could make more legible what went on where. More cohesion, more clarity and fewer ghosts.

This all took about two-and-three-quarter hours, bringing us to our agreed stopping time when about half the teachers had to go home. The other half remained to open up the new agenda: which classrooms should be where? Where could a hall go? Another classroom, the kindergarten, an apartment for a teacher or caretaker?

Now in the current of how the place wanted to be shaped, for the next two or three hours we discussed how the school could expand. Then came the issue of who would get which room. Naturally every teacher wanted a sunny, spacious one. More to the point, however, was which classrooms *suited* which classes? We evaluated the *physical*, spatial, needs of the different class sizes, the character and *moods* appropriate to different ages or specialist activities. Also the *journey* through the building (hence the relationship between classroom and entry, playground and anchoring terra firma) appropriate to each age. Classes would cost next to nothing to move around. But there weren't *enough* classrooms. This was where finance-group members made

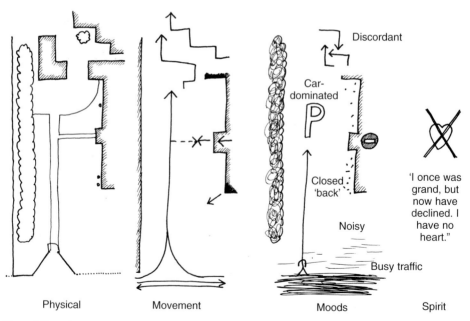

Physical   Movement   Moods   Spirit

The existing place.

important contributions. At bearable expense, we could move the current caretaker's flat down to the classroom that had formerly been a kitchen, creating both a more satisfactory classroom and a more independent flat. Moving the kindergarten off-campus into a converted house would free up two more rooms for classrooms. Economically, this was viable. Mortgage repayments would be covered by kinder-garten revenue. If this didn't work out, the house could be resold; the only loss being the cost of additional toilets. This would leave the school just one classroom short of those needed for an upper school. Reviewing what was physically there, we could find a place for this if we built it on the roof terrace and used the disused goods-lift shaft for the necessary fire-escape stairs. This would also enable the upstairs corri-dors to be shortened, so enlarging two classrooms. These new escape stairs would also help simplify the complicated passages.

The zig-zag blocks at the rear could, with only minor demolitions of redundant stores, tanks, walls and paving, become a sort of pedestrian 'street'. But now came the issue of the hall – where should it go? Could it be fitted-in? Built out from the main building, it could also face the entrance, so welcoming anyone outside the school community who might use it. (It would hope to partly finance itself by being rented out from time to time.) Its rear face would now enclose a currently nondescript, unformed, back-area; a forgotten litter-dump. In this new courtyard so formed, there was already a tree. With a pool and flowform as well, this would become an outdoor room, attractive enough to let for wedding receptions and the like.

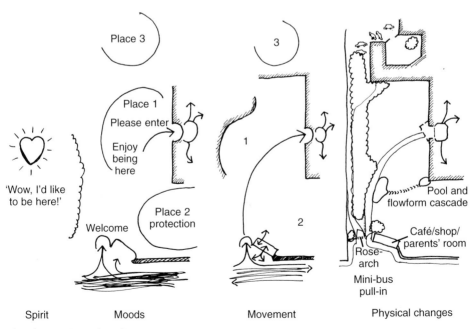

The place as it needs to be.

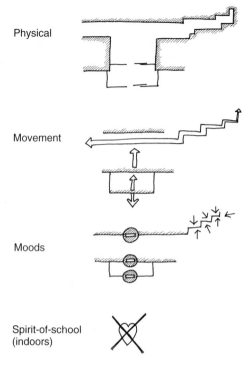

Physical

Movement

Moods

Spirit-of-school
(indoors)

Present entry journey.

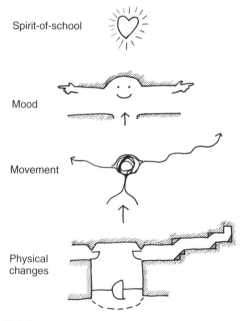

Spirit-of-school

Mood

Movement

Physical
changes

Entry journey as it needs to be.

Reflections

This brought us to the end of what felt like a week, but was only a short day's work. A day of listening and avoiding 'having ideas'. How much, I wonder, might I have been able to accomplish on my own, 'unencumbered' by a community of users? I certainly couldn't have done so much in one day – nor avoided endless revisions to accommodate criticisms, suggestions and counter-suggestions. Qualitatively, as well, we achieved more than I alone could have. For instance, I'm sure I would have tried to make the entrance more welcoming, but the key to this was establishing a child-welcoming mood from the gateway on. Without recognizing that teachers' car arrival was separated in time from children's arrival, this mood couldn't have been achieved.

Then there was the haunted corridor, the children's movement induced by the space, the absence of a physical 'heart' and many other crucial things that left no visual trace. Without the teachers, I might have designed something that looked nice, but didn't help the school's mood, moving-around or physical functioning. Most particularly, I, on my own, couldn't have changed the 'message' the school emanated in any meaningful way. Indeed how appropriate, meshed into place and authentic in spirit would my suggestions have been had I worked in the more conventional way? How much of all this could have been achieved, found this form, and also enjoyed consensual support amongst users, if we had worked by the conventional 'architect-led', idea-suggestion, method?

Note

1   To meet together and start the day with
    a meditation.

CHAPTER EIGHTEEN

Redeeming buildings: East Bay Waldorf School, California

Short-, medium- and long-term development

In 1995 the East Bay Waldorf School in California was preparing to move from rented premises to a new site: a derelict, but intact, school on around ten acres of land. They asked me if I had any ideas to redeem the appallingly ugly buildings, also for the development of the school and its grounds. I said that I tried not to have ideas these days, but would work *with* them.

The building, dating from the 1940s, was indeed ugly. Wartime brought rapid expansion to Californian armaments industries. The school had been rushed up to serve the accompanying population surge. Industries had since declined, the school district became bankrupt and the school was sold.

With its aggressively jutting flat-roof overhangs in plywood imitating concrete, and steel-mesh-reinforced fibreglass windows, it was indeed the ugliest building I've ever seen (even after Russia with its crumbling grey tower blocks, mastic dribbling from their broad cracks!). To make things worse, it had uniform grey paint over everything, including – to prevent vandalism – over every window. The land it sat on had been brutally ripped into mechanically stepped terraces. In fact, everything spoke of a military engineering approach.

So much for the first impression: ugly, regimented, forlorn.

The school had a packed agenda for me: rescuing the existing building, developing a plan for a high school and, as well as this, a public lecture, all in two days. Too short, in my opinion, but that was how it was. And the group: varying numbers, up to 24 teachers, development group members, parents who would be doing the building, two executive architects,[1] – one of whom had nobly recommended me to the school (instead of keeping all the job!) – and myself.

Rescuing the existing building

Place-study

After introductions, the first day was given over to the existing building. We walked around gathering first impressions. At the rear, the ground was just asphalt playground; the building, predominately machine-stamped strips of aluminium sun-shades along its face, grey as everything else. Other impressions I've described.

We chose to walk the journey from vehicle drop-off point to school entry, then down gloomy corridors to a classroom – also gloomy behind its grey painted windows.

We then broke into groups, one to each part of the journey. We concentrated first on only what was *physically* there, meeting after 20 minutes to build the whole from our separate observations. I visited each group in case anyone needed help, also so that I could ask relevant questions when we met.

What was there? Approach started with the steep, cracked, patched and uneven paved road. To its side was a drop-off loop around a scrubby grass and weed island. Then came a 30° slope of dry grass, scrub and poison ivy, with a galvanized-pipe-framed chain-link fence and gate along its top. The school was atop this terrace. Three flights of concrete steps with steel pipe handrails went straight up the slope, concrete-filled steel-tube bollards obstructing each landing. Our route now angled across asphalt to the grey, single-storey building, its flat roof eaves jutting some eight feet. Around two corners was the entry door. This opened to a central corridor, long and dimly lit by far-apart roof lights. This ended in a right-angled 'T' to another long, equally dark corridor.

Our destination classroom had fibreglass windows along one wall, shaded by an aluminium sun-screen. Above the opposite wall was a strip of roof light, also sun-screened. Its ceiling was dominated by red-painted steel trusses and fluorescent lights.

Next, we looked at how the journey *flowed*. From parking lot to fence it went frontally up the slope, at right angles to the road below and fence above. It then turned diagonally across tarmac to the building corner, so accenting the sharply jut-ting corner eaves. Around two abrupt corners came the entrance. Once inside, another right-angled turn brought us into the long, straight corridor arrowing to col-lide at the T-junction, with another, equally long. The classroom door, flush along the wall and identical to every other, required a sudden side-step. The classroom itself, with transverse trusses and ceiling sloping up from the windows, was visually busy.

Then the journey *moods*: the steps were regimented, unfree and unappealing; the school, dull in its greyness, aggressive with its jutting angles. The corridors were forcefully straight and drearily dark. The classroom, though cacophonic with its busy ceiling of steel lattice and fluorescent tubes, was a dead box.

And what the place *said*? We didn't have much difficulty agreeing that it had no love for children – treated them as nuisances to discipline and process. Not much about individuality, freedom. Not at all what we would have liked a school to say – any school, especially a Waldorf school.

Design

What *should the place say*? Certainly there should be something about how children are valued, about care, nurture and growing into freedom.

With this in mind, we repeated the journey, this time all of us together, asking what *moods* would support this? The starting point clearly needed to be more wel-coming, even celebratory. We agreed the ascent should rise with a mood of expectant arrival – not obligatory delivery. The entrance should be inviting and spirit-raising;

an entry to welcome you. The corridor – though unavoidably still a corridor – should be more joyous, and the classroom calmer, spirit-uplifting. And everything needed to be infused with the message: 'You are welcome. I value and appreciate you. Be light in spirit, happy here'.

Again we re-walked the journey, now asking what *flow* of movement, space and gesture would support these moods? A more defined vehicle entry, constricted then expanding, would enhance our sense of arriving somewhere special, then feeling at ease once there. Instead of the abrupt barrier of un-enterable facade ordering us to go around two corners to the building's back, a fluid, sweeping ascent would bring us to *meet* the entrance. The entrance needed an embracing gesture to invite. The eurythmist[2] gestured this. Once through the portal, spatial expansion, light flooded, would let us 'breathe out' freely, relax and pause. Off this lingering space, the corridor route should *flow*. If only by moderating its arrow-like energy and abrupt turns, harmonious changes of direction, a soft sectional shape and varying punctuation by doorways would soften its unaccommodating institutional severity.

Once more, we walked the route – now sweeping to the side up the new entryway. This time I asked the group what *physical* alterations this implied. A rose-clad archway and sign with wooden boom-type gates would emphasize *arrival* – and improve security. (A concern made all the more pertinent when a teacher noticed two strange youths poking around the back of the building.) Then up a sweeping brick path with a streamlet cascading alongside it. (Dry and hot as this region is in summer, winter brings some 50 inches [1250 mm] of rain. Multiplied by the large areas of asphalt and roofs, there could be plenty of water if only we could store it.)

Cutting the acute angle off the roof overhang would swing its gesture along the entry approach, instead of stabbing across it. Glazing inserted into the structural framework of the walls would open up and light-flood the entrance. (Orientation and roof overhang would shade this sufficiently). Replacing the industrial aluminium shade screens with a vine-shaded arcade would soften, cool and seasonally enliven both the facade and the light through it. By incorporating porchways to each classroom and rising to a 'welcome porch' at the main entrance, this would break its domineering straight line into bays, presenting an inviting facade, in place of the present repelling one.

Inside the main entrance, the secretary suggested the reception office should be the first thing you see, but it should greet you, not confront. The library, a room to pause in, could be to the side.

To reduce their longitudinal force, the corridors asked to be de-symmetrized and differentiated in light and mood from each other. Doors likewise needed individualizing with colour and architraves; some could be inset.

The dead boxiness of the classrooms would be relieved by gentler and differentiated light. Sunlight through foliage would do this by day; by night fluorescent tubes could be replaced by compact bulbs in lampshades and blackboard-focused lights. Plywood triangles across window corners would both brace for earthquakes[3] and soften window shapes. Painting trusses to match the ceiling would reduce their dominating visual impact, so focusing attention more at the human level.

Thanks to a contractor parent, we could utilize seismic bracing to de-institutionalize a corridor.

Reflections

This day had been dedicated to transforming the spirit of the place. From forgotten, disciplinarianist and materially functionalist institution into welcoming, joy-filled, child-valuing Waldorf school. From somewhere oppressive to a place nurturing development and inner freedom.

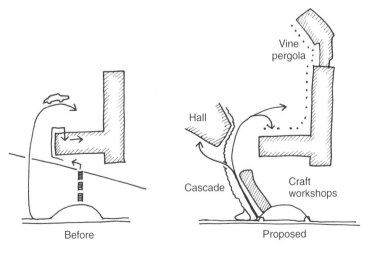

Arrival journey.

Before

After

Before

After

The approach: before and after.

Before and after: improvements partly completed – photos courtesy of East Bay Waldorf School.

Notes

1 Greg van Mechelen and Bob Davidson.
2 Eurythmy is an art of movement which both works with energy flows and gives visible form to soul-state.

3 Recent regulations (following recent earthquakes) required additional seismic bracing.

CHAPTER NINETEEN

Future growth: East Bay Waldorf School, California

After the day focused on how to redeem the existing building (see Chapter 18), we moved on to thinking about the school's future growth. We began by considering the development of the site as a whole. How could a high school, eurythmy room, hall and kindergarten fit onto this site? Ideally there would be workshops for craftspeople and living spaces, at least for a caretaker, perhaps teachers as well? Only after a day of this broader strategic planning could we design the high school building. For this we had four days.

> *Timetable:*
>
> Day 2:   Site development strategy
> Days 3–6:   High-school building development.

Site development strategy

Place-study

Where previously our concern was one *route* (see Chapter 18), now we had to deal with the land as a whole. We started, therefore, by walking around the *whole* site. This was somewhat obstructed by fences, also corrugated iron stables and paddocks in the middle of the upper level. Recent rains made part of our 'walk' into a muddy slide down the steep artificial slope. After sharing *first impressions*, we divided into groups, one for each sub-place:

Sub-places

- downhill (and to the shady north) of the existing school
- the asphalt level to its south
- the slope up to the next level, wooded to the east, grassed to the west
- the middle level (where the stables were)
- the topmost level and tree boundary
- the rear boundary, a tree strip, but with gaps.

As usual we started with physical observations. Overall, the land was cut into three levels with 45° steps, about 30 feet high. One fell away from the northern boundary fence into a steep long natural slope; one cut through the centre of the property; and one was just within the south boundary. Monterey pine, leaning and wind-bent, grew on these steps. The lower level was all tarmac and buildings, generously littered; the middle and upper ones, mostly thick, head-high shrubs except for the stables and paddock in the centre of the middle level. To the East, some ten to 30 feet below the property level, a rough roadway climbed steeply to state park-land. Westwards, the land fell away, sometimes naturally, sometimes artificially steeply. In one place, erosion gullies backed right up to the property fence; elsewhere the slope was more stable. A band of eucalyptus trees, some 70 feet tall, grew along this boundary.

We then looked at the place's biography. The stables, dereliction and shrubs were relatively new, the school having only closed some seven years previously. Though dividing the land in half, these were a 'temporary state'. The landform, though barely 50 years old, was now, however, a 'permanent state'. Clearly a ridge had run down from the hilltops to the south. This had been bulldozed into massive steps; almost certainly half cut, half fill. Only on cross- and boundary-slopes were there trees, all about 50 years old. The leaning pines showed how the ground was sliding downhill. Many trees were dying, some already dead. It was amongst these that, without warning, a pine limb crashed amongst us on a later visit. Even before this 50-year-old re-shaped landscape, the California landscape itself is 'new'. The town below, though growing fast, is recent. Indeed most 'development' in California is less than 50 years old. Less than 0.1% pre-dates the gold-rush 150 years ago. Even the topography is geologically new. In fact, as frequent earthquakes remind us, it's still moving.

What of the future? The pines were approaching the end of their life, but were already seeding new trees – which would widen the original strip into a copse. The

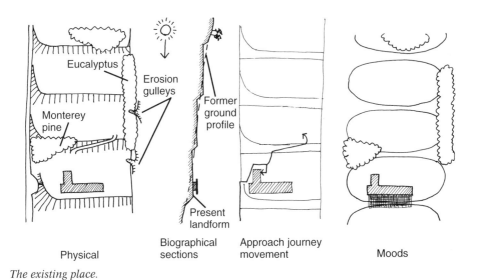

The existing place.

shrub plateau was ready to develop into a tangle of low trees. The slopes were slow-ly settling to smoother contours – though this would take a long time. The erosion on the west boundary would soon be stabilized as growing woodland intercepted rainwater runoff from the tarmac area. The valley to the East had a planning application for housing development (which we hoped road and sewer costs would prevent). The virgin grass, shrub and hill land to the south was state park-land (hopefully) guaranteeing immunity from development.

We next looked at the moods of the place, starting at the school level: the gloomy, over-shaded north strip, with land falling steeply from its fence and cracking paving, felt insecure. The asphalt 'playground', edged on the north by the grey, industrial-shuttered school, felt desolate; though more refreshing to the west, where eucalyp-tus rustled in the ever-present breeze. To the south it was enclosed by a high bank, grassed at one end, wind-soughing pines at the other, so felt more alive at its edge. By contrast, the upper level was sun-drenched and wind-sheltered by shrubs. With pine trees below it, eucalyptus to the west and a mound of pines framing a rising view of cascading grassy landscape and hilltops to the south, it overlooked the state park fire-road and valley to the east. The middle level felt abandoned in its centre, but the further we went towards the southern boundary, the more pleasant did it become. Unlike the school level, this was somewhere to be in.

Outline design

The whole place spoke of a once heavenly countryside, raped then abandoned: beau-ty abused. But what *should* it say? We easily agreed it should be beautiful, spirit-uplifting – a joyous, inspiring place. Others added that it should welcome children, tell them how much they are valued. The school, therefore, should 'offer a jewel of beauty'. To this pivotal phrase we added: 'kept healthy by natural forces' and 'some-where the spirit could feel free'.

It was now time to consider what *activities* would need to be accommodated. A high school means classrooms, art, science and workshop rooms, also library, stu-dents' social room and staff-room along with other bits and pieces. Both high- and lower-school needed a hall – a large building occasionally issuing large groups of peo-ple. A kindergarten, to foster that special magical mood that infants live in, would need its own entrance and garden. While nobody liked the asphalt playground, sev-eral teachers pointed out the necessity for a hard-surface play area. There would also need to be a sports field, children's garden plots and so on. And, of course, parking – much more than was currently there.

What moods would these facilities, and the activities within and around them, need and generate? With these moods in mind, where should each activity go?

Should we build on the already-destroyed lower level? This would redeem, rescue it. But would this make the school too socially compact? Would it confuse the iden-tity of each stage of school and the experience of growing up through it?

This was going too fast in the direction of positing ideas, then testing them – Newtonian rather than Goethean scientific method (see Chapter 7) Such solution-based questions were premature; we needed solutions to condense, not be thrown against each other. We therefore asked instead: what moods of place *already there* would suit – or be reinforced or redeemed by – the moods that would come with particular activities? How could we bring these existing moods-of-place and future moods-of-activities into matching and mutually beneficial relationships?

The lower level, all asphalt and buildings, was so ugly it was a relief to leave it. The uppermost level, breeze-washed and with views drawing the eye up the unspoilt hills, appealed to all of us – so much so that we all agreed it shouldn't be spoilt by buildings. This left the middle level: the obvious place for new buildings. Obvious? What impact would they have? Would they, by filling up the centre, divide the site? Or, by spreading-out the school, suburbanize it? Should the heart of the land be buildings, playground, swimming-pool, sports-field, children's garden plots, or what?

We returned to issues of mood. What mood – hence, what activity – should be at the centre of the school grounds; at the physical centre of the spirit-of-school? We easily agreed it shouldn't be buildings. But what about athletics and sports-ground, playground, gardens or decorative landscape? Each had its advocates, but each represented a different aspect of the school and of child development. I therefore asked what core aspect was common to all these. The answer that emerged was growth, vigour, freedom of movement, doing things together. At this point, the athletics teacher suggested a 'sports garden'. Spacious, sun-drenched and airy, this level was well suited to expansive sport: running, organized games, outdoor gymnastics, swimming. More wind-protected, but still sunny, the western part would be good for garden plots.

But what about the high-school? Where should it go? Could we define the mood it needed and find a location for this mood?

Central to this mood would be the *social* mood – all the stronger for adolescents as their world is predominately a peer-group society. A teacher described their developmental journey: their increasing independence and interest in the wider world – the world beyond school and home, beyond the safe and allowed. This suggested to

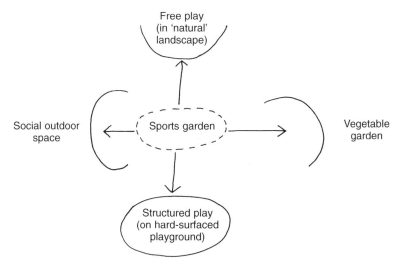

Activity-moods and their hint at gestures.

us that the high-school needed to 'rise' up here – independent and 'growing' uphill. It also needed a wider view of the world, unlike the more self-contained lower school and protected 'own world' of the kindergarten. We entertained several placings, but though each had a rational case, none had a wholehearted advocate, nor felt as right as when, as an undulating ribbon, it crested the eastern escarpment.

But should this be one building or a group of buildings? A single building would have space-economy, practical and cost advantages – but what would it say to the pupils? The teachers felt its scale would be too imposing, and its monolithic nature too institutional. They felt that more individualized classrooms and specialized activity-rooms better reflected the pupils' developmental needs. Moreover a single building would largely retain its social focus *indoors* – anti-social for the school as a whole.

A finance-group member pointed out that 'affordable', not 'cheapest' was the issue. Progressive small increments would be much easier to finance than one large building. Indeed they could be largely self-financing.

The teachers anticipated two-room growth increments: one a classroom, the other a (temporary) specialist room. This began to suggest a growth pattern: double-room units with service rooms, such as toilets and storerooms, as linking elements.

We next turned our attention to the hall. What was it for? To the teachers – somewhere to unify the whole 'being' of the school, as well as its use for drama, music and eurythmy; to the development group – a facility for the wider community, not just to earn income, but, more importantly, to increase public exposure. We realized that, different though these perceptions were, the hall being *used* differently by public and school community, in both cases it should *speak* of the spirit at the heart of the school. Someone observed that it would have a multiple bridging role: between high and lower school, hence upper and lower levels. When rented out it would also bridge between the school, socially enclosed, and the wider public, for whom it should be open, accessible and inviting. With these bridging aspects in mind, none of us could imagine it anywhere other than *between* upper and lower levels, private and public spaces. This more or less fixed its position astride the step between levels.

The library still needed a home. One teacher pointed out that, as a facility for the whole school, it also belonged in this bridging zone. But where? Its mood – and use – would be more towards the high school. Moodwise, it felt right cutting through the belt of trees between levels (in an already existing gap), its gesture a snaking link between hall and high-school.

One element remained unlocated: the kindergarten. Kindergarten teachers were emphatic: small children need a different mood – dreamy, magical and secure – from the rest of the school. This meant a distinct and dedicated separate realm. Ideally, it would have a totally separate identity and separate building. But everyone was just as emphatic: there was no money for this now. It would have to find a short-term home in the existing building (see Chapter 18). But where? Where could we find hints of an appropriate mood? At first sight, nowhere – there was nothing dreamy, magical or child-scaled about the grey, harsh and hideous school. Its only security was by prison-like fence – nothing of a secure *mood*.

When we reviewed the physical characteristics of each place, however, a different picture began to emerge. The strip behind the school, though shady, was quiet, tree-edged and totally withdrawn from any playground frenzy. Though not this day, most of the year shade would be an advantage. If divided with fences – low, but above child-level – it would no longer feel a corridor-like strip. And once full of life, it would cease to be forgotten back-land. With these few, inexpensive, alterations, it could provide a protected outdoor child-realm. It was teachers' eyes, not mine, that first saw these possibilities.

But how would this, currently 'back' place, offer a 'front' to greet the children? Could the approach journey emphasize its special identity? A new path slanting up the sunny hillside[1] would give it its own individual approach, safe from hurtling bigger children. Tunnels of laced branches, especially of scented, flowering shrubs and trees could offer precursors of the magic of the kindergarten day. These outdoor considerations fixed the kindergarten's interior location.

The development group had suggested craft-workshops – partly for the children to experience, partly as a link with the wider community and also to ensure a living presence during holidays. Both these and the caretaker's flat would be semi-independent of the school. Fulfilling a gateway role, these felt right along the entry slope.

Finally the issue of parking came up. As something nobody likes (but everybody wants) it's easy to forget about it until too late. Currently, it covered the playground. Additionally, as teachers told me, many students drive to school – something I, coming from Europe, had never imagined. We agreed parking shouldn't intrude its mood into the 'jewelled haven' of the school, but grow off already 'car-y' areas. Amongst other possibilities, could we park along the road? No; too narrow. Then someone suggested cutting into the base of the slope and using rainwater cisterns as retaining walls to widen it.

Like hall capacity, peak parking demand is only occasional. Asking *when* that occurred, I was told special and evening events, like open-days and concerts. This opened-up time-share possibilities. Concert-goers could use the hard-surfaced playground; play by day, parking in the evening. For occasional special events, over-spill parking could even be on the playing field.

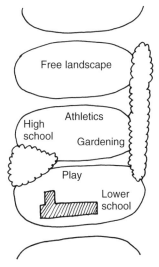

Location of activities matched to mood.

We now considered what *gestures* would be appropriate for each activity. The high school, though its *outline* outer-face crested the ridge, had its *social* front facing the playing field. Like the adolescent scene – outward aspiring but peer-group society – this implied two faces. Classroom windows face towards the outer world, doors towards sports, play and school society.

As *social focus* was an important reason for its group-of-buildings choice, what did this imply mood- and gesture-wise? The linked buildings and social outdoor area began to develop a 'village' relationship: individual 'houses' with socially unifying common-ground. But what social *gesture* should our village have: 'street', 'square' or 'green'?

The 'cliff-edge' row of buildings answered view-to-outer-world needs and left the rest of the land free for other uses. But nobody felt it had enough social identity. Ribbon plans are socially dispersing; this asked to be more socially condensing – a shape to enclose a social realm. We realized we needed a more circular gesture. Not a closed circle, but one which, though socially focusing, left people free. Instead of closure, it needed to interact with the whole school social area of games, pool and garden. This brought us to two enclosure-implying arcs interpenetrating each other

So far so good – but what *actual* gesture would this mean *on the ground*? This we tried to pace out amongst the head-high bushes. We stood, pointed and walked, as best we could; pegging and stringing was impossible with so many obstructions. I drew an approximate plan of this, corrected by others' observations and paced measurements. In the circumstances, this couldn't be accurate, but did record key limits, angles, relationships to existing features and the *quality* of gesture we refined between us. This more or less fixed the layout's *social* face. We then did the same for its *outlook* face.

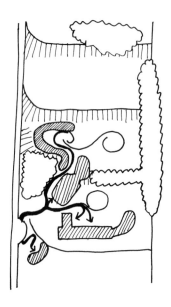

Space movement gestures.

We next turned our attention to the hall. Central between high and lower school, public and 'private', it could act as a pivot point. But how would public and children meet it? Precise location and gesture – especially facade and flank angles and approach paths – would be critical. Obliquely placed, it could greet different groups by day and night. By turning the entry path it could focus it, by day, upon the school entrance. A branch path, at night emphasized by lighting, would lead to the hall foyer. The rear of the building would enclose the playground, strengthening its mood focus and increasing security – and, additionally, make a good ball-bouncing wall. The library and common facilities could now cascade down the slope from upper-level high-school to lower-level lower school, so tying-in the large bulk of the hall.

The land was now becoming differentiated into more human – and child-sized – bits, each different in mood. The asphalt playground, however, remained a desolate rectangle. But even this was slightly softened by an invasion of weeds in one corner – a process to continue. The gardening teacher observed how, by varying the grass-to-tarmac edge and planting shrubs and trees, we could form bays. The land, though one school, was currently cut apart into disconnected levels. Breaking the straight-line of the tree edge would help integrate these. It would be easy enough to plant new trees on the grass slope; even easier, as the gardener pointed out, to encourage wind-sown saplings.

But how could we link the two school levels? There was a slanting track slashed between them. We decided to retain it, but we also needed a more direct route through the pine trees. There was already an informal track here, direct but so steep we could only slide down it. We all agreed steps here, alongside the future hall, seemed the obvious connection between levels, and between schools. What about a wheelchair path? If cut into the eastern scarp and extended with curves, it could slope gently enough. We had already discussed edging the entry route and hall access with running water: rills, flowforms or cascades as appropriate. Why not extend these cascades back along the staircase edge? This 'stream' could now rise in a pool to centre the upper court, the whole lot powered by a wind-pump.

We now knew where everything wanted to be, and – within a yard or so – the critical edge of each building or outdoor 'place'. At this stage, rearward faces were generally elastic enough to address later. These social-front gestures we could now mark on the ground and record on a tracing over the site plan. This gave us the shape of outdoor 'places' and any building faces that enclosed, defined or generated them. Not too little for one day's work.

High-school building

Nine months later, the old buildings renovated, repainted, and to some extent re-shaped, were now in use. Some improvements had been completed, some deferred, some half-done – most notably, the rooflight sunshades had been removed, but the canopy and pergola to replace them not yet built. This we acutely felt when indoor temperatures allegedly reached 120°F.

I was back to start the high-school design process. The first half-day was spent in discussion, preparing for two days of design workshop – what should be in a high school and how should these bits relate to one another?

Recapitulation and reconfirmation

The next day, the group having new members, we introduced ourselves around the circle, then recapitulated what we had done nine months previously, and why we had come to the decisions we did. Changing circumstance, experience of the new location, geo-structural investigations and a long period of 'sleeping on it', however, cast some decisions in a different light.

The hall, in particular, which asked to be all things to all people (sports, music, drama, festivals) and hold the largest audience possible, but still be affordable, could have taken a whole day's discussion. Each activity was considered essential on educational *and* financial grounds by its proponents. (I pointed out that something large enough for sports and with the environmental quality necessary for music would not be cheap. A pole barn for sports and a separate smaller hall for the more environmentally demanding uses would be more economical.) As there was no money for it at this stage I had a good excuse to return to the task in hand. Most of the earlier decisions still stood, but we only had two days to shape the high-school, and provisionally design the hall and library.

Shaping the building

Focusing now on the high-school site, we briefly repeated the four-layer observation and incarnation (outline design) processes. This fixed the extent of the undulating crest line and the gesture of the socially enclosing arc. On engineer's advice, we had to move everything back from the edge for soil stability reasons. We were, however, still able to retain the outlook over the lower school and valley – the pupils' past and future.

We again paced both building faces as best we could among the bushes, located them in relationship to features identifiable on the site plan, then drew this at 1/16":1'0" (approximately 1:200) scale.

Next we laid out paper pieces representing classroom, hall and specialist rooms onto this plan-gesture drawing. Being rectangular, they naturally overlapped or left gaps – but then the rooms probably wouldn't be rectangular either, so no problem. For upper storey rooms, we laid paper above paper.

A tracing of this with ambiguously loose lines gave us a rough plan at 1/16" scale. This showed room relationships and approximate areas, but no form. There was some discussion, some refining, but in principle, this would remain the high-school plan. Next we made clay rectanguloids of the approximate proportions of the principal rooms (not toilets, stores and suchlike smaller rooms). Like the paper rectangles, these didn't fit so had to be moulded together. The small-component volumes helped join, or extend, the larger ones to serve the gestures we sought.

This basic building *form* modified the *plan*. So did a review of room sizes, orientations, entries, and storage needs. By the end of the day, we had the basic high school plan.

Design development

A month later I was back to further develop this design. To refresh memories, visualize and re-appraise the design, we walked around the high-school site. There had been many 'slept-on' afterthoughts in the meantime, so much discussion and many changes, but only minor ones. The clay model had dried so the revised forms had to be rebuilt. This was the heat-wave of the decade and as the temperature climbed, moist clay dried and we wilted. Shading – particularly topical! – was given serious attention, further modifying both model and drawings.

The design now had enough substance for us to draw meaningful sections: what levels were needed for view across the valley, concealing the car park? Would the stream flow downhill (as streams should)? With the sections, we could refine wind-shedding, cross-ventilation, indoor air movement, and – again – shading. We also optimized winter sun penetration for heating – though, sweat-soaked as we were, it was hard to feel enthusiasm for this. The design, though not complete, was now well rounded – insofar as it ever can be at such a small scale. That evening, therefore, we enlarged the drawings to 1/8″ (approximately 1:100) on a photocopier.

At this enlarged scale we could instantly see which elements we had oversized and which undersized. Doors and toilets, for instance, hadn't looked wide enough at 1/16″ scale so were drawn too large, while lots of little things, from stair-landings to cupboards, too small to bother with at that scale, we now needed to find space for. It may not sound much, but we – about 15 people – were a full (and hot!) day refining the plans and sections at this scale.

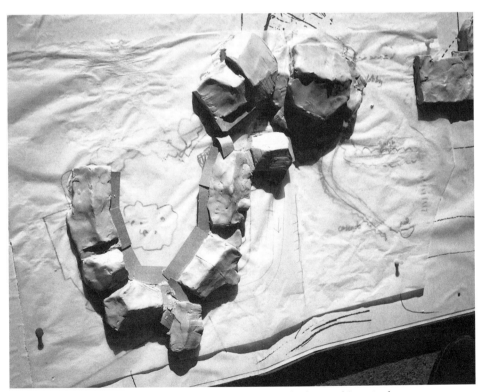

High School model – the product of a 24-member group – shade-tested in actual sun.

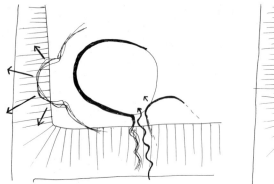

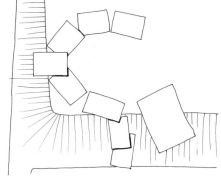

Mood: enclosed, sheltered, socially focusing, but outward looking.

Rough plans (paper rectangles).

Gesture to support this mood.

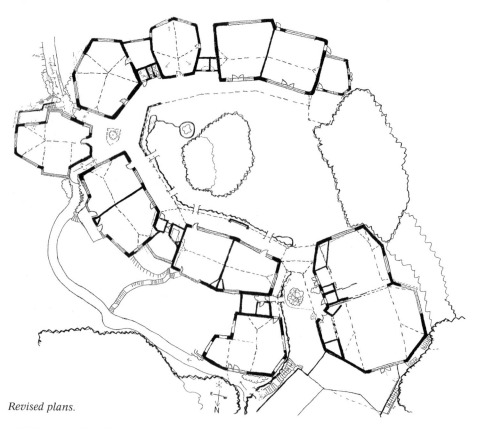

Revised plans.

These roughly drawn, but substantially accurate, drawings I then took back to my office in Wales to refine, work out more sections and elevations and re-draw in a legible form.

The first of the new (straw-bale) buildings. Design: East Bay Waldorf School, Greg van Mechleren, Bob Davidson, Christopher Day and Vital Systems (the part professional, part volunteer, building group).

Reflections

Of the five-and-a-half days groupwork, rescuing the existing building took one, site development one, and the high-school design, three-and-a-half days. How easy was it to achieve five-and-a-half days of consensus? Well, it didn't happen automatically, nor all the time, but it did *most* of the time.

Mostly, the process of gradually condensing design went smoothly. Occasionally, however, some members rushed too fast toward form. For larger things I felt it important to hold this back, but for smaller matters, when everyone seemed in agreement, it felt better to just keep momentum. Things tended to go less easily toward the end of each day, when we were all tired. This would be when idea suggestions increasingly appeared – and were argued about. Also some forceful personalities would resurrect their favourite pre-process ideas. At times like this, I had to assert my steering role and asked what decisions had we reached at the *previous* level. What, then, did *that* decision imply? This steered us back onto a consequential-decision path so that individually held ideas fell to the sides. Despite such – albeit rare – lapses into idea-pushing, the process as a whole was consensual. Certainly *every* decision was by consensus and so, therefore, was the design.

Notes

1 Sunny in the mornings. In Waldorf schools, the kindergarten 'day' is mornings only – it's enough for small children. Because of parents' needs, however, many schools make provision for children to stay on to rest and play in the afternoons.

CHAPTER TWENTY

Working with a developer: mixed-use urban development, California

A different climate, culture, project

In 1993, after two intense weeks of lectures and meetings in California, I finally had two days to relax with friends. When an unexpected phone-call invited me to 'hop on a plane to look at a little project'. I was so tired I almost said no! I didn't, and my host turned out to be a developer. His 'little project' was to be ten acres of mixed development in the centre (but not downtown) of a Californian city. Having showed me round – and driven me to breakfast for the culture-shock! – he asked me if I could design a sustainable development 'with heart' for him. I said this was a totally new world to me. It would be much more productive to design it *with* him.

Though he was already committed to ecological and social responsibility, 'sustainability', at that time, meant 'economic' to him, 'ecological' to me. The longer I worked on the project, however, the more I realized that economic, ecological and social sustainability depended on each other. We could only achieve one by achieving all.

Naively optimistic, I quickly realized I knew nothing of the economic side of development, nothing of en-socialing design in an automotive society, nothing about hot-dry climate design, nothing about public spaces that were not friendly but dangerous. Everything was, in fact, the absolute opposite of what I was used to. If it hadn't been for the co-design input of others, I'd still know nothing – and the developer would be bankrupt.

I worked on this project in six-week blocks; two a year, for about five years. Every block started with my client taking me on a several-day tour to see developments that worked and ones that didn't. A good education in what goes wrong in development.

But avoiding pitfalls is a bit like avoiding sick building syndrome. It may prevent failure in the first two years, but isn't enough to guarantee sustainable success. Furthermore, our site and situation had particular demands:

- no sense of place
- no geographically located community
- no vernacular or settlement-pattern continuum.

Building codes and retailers required three to four times as much parking as floor area – making it hard to create a 'place of heart'. Summers at 117°F (48°C) meant air-conditioners everywhere – not very sustainable. Local regulations were more anti-sustainable than I could ever have imagined. As for local building materials, we could buy almost any sort – as long as it wasn't natural or local!

I quickly realized climate would be a major form-driver. Public places delightful to linger in would be essential to any development with heart. Naturally cooled buildings were essential to sustainability. The myriad of other factors, even water-management and crime prevention, would make less demands on layout and building form. (Water was mostly about ground-levels to retain all rainwater on site; security about view lines from residential and 24-hour activities.)

It took longer to understand how the demands of ecological, social and economic sustainability reflect each other. At the outset, it seemed each compromised the others. After a while, however, I came to realize how inseparably they are interwoven. So much so that I can't now look at things in any other way. Most difficult of all, however, was adapting consensus principles to a small team with no users represented, and who – anyway at the outset – expected a designer-led approach.

Place-study

On my first trip, I was joined by an environmental engineer. My intention was to start the design with place-study then condense the design, refining it for climatic concerns. There were, however, so many pressures on my client's time that we could never find a two-day slot to all work together. We therefore had to use the four-layer process in a less structured way. This had no impact on consensus technique, but it made it harder to allow decisions to condense on their own.

The consultant and I looked at what was there, on-site and around it. The site was in the corner of the busiest intersection in the city (six lanes of traffic, swelling to nine). There were two square retail buildings, one Las Vegas chain restaurant, a farmers' market, the developer's house (re-located from another site) and large areas of parking. For fire control regulations, most of the rest of the land was bare: dry dust. In the centre was a farmers' market (a rose-shrouded arbour by Christopher Alexander); at the back, the developer's house and garden.

We next looked at the place's historical journey: desert, then irrigation and vineyards; engulfment by the growing city some 30 years previously; dirt roads asphalted, then broadening from two to nine lanes. We looked at how and when buildings came. Also the evolving context: the city growing at around one foot a minute, its wealth migrating northwards, inner-city blight spreading ripple-like behind it. This blight ripple would engulf our site unless we could create a counter-ripple, fed by a mood of delight. This certainly wasn't there yet.

Moodwise, the roads dominated two sides of the rectangle. The farmers' market was a real soul-heart, but only for two mornings a week; the developer's domestic garden an oasis of refreshing nature and bird-song. The rest: abandoned land or desolate parking-lot.

The place cried out for life – but not life as all around. Not the rootless, visually cacophonic and meaninglessly styled strip-malls, with sweltering asphalt and petrol-fumed 300 feet (100 m) parking-lot strips fronted by 40 feet (12 m) pylon signs.

Design

The developer had already told me what the development *should* say: 'I am a place of heart'. Economic viability would depend upon this 'heart' spirit. Without it, no inner-city location could compete with urban-fringe discount warehouses, their retail prices lower than wholesale prices for smaller retailers.

This spirit, in turn, would depend on appealing, delight-filled moods-of-place. Twice a week, the farmers' market provided such a heart mood. But we'd need much more. More places, more of the time. For these, attractive design would not be enough. They would also need human vitality – urban buzz. Hence project growth must be shaped by, and continually feed, activity. For this project, a *meaningful pattern of growth* would, therefore, be crucial to viability.

Several key factors would shape this project growth:

- socially: making *places*
- environmentally: *micro-climatic* improvement (especially noise-reduction, shade cooling, and air-quality)
- economically: building by *small increments*. This would be the only independently affordable way. It would allow development to be self-financing; also to incorporate feedback, correct mistakes and continuously adapt to changing circumstance.

Growing a site model: what one building would bring the existing buildings into relationship? What second building would start to make a place? *What subsequent buildings would substantiate place, grow new places ... and so on, until the whole site was 'developed'? The end result isn't a* master plan, *but from the process of growth, we can condense a* development strategy.

We therefore modified the process sequence to focus on growth. For this, we modelled the whole site at 1":40' (approximately 1:500). This was easy – the land was almost flat and all buildings rectangular. We now, the three of us, asked a series of questions:

- What single action would strengthen the incipient heart?
- What single building would bring disparate buildings into relationship?
- What additional building would start to make 'place'?
- What further buildings would strengthen this place (spatially, socially and micro-climatically)?
- How could this single place start to grow others?

Although *growth* questions, these were about establishing moods-of-place and transforming the spirit of the place. This led us to:

- *A cafe* (with toilets): This would service the farmers' market arbour, so allowing its use seven days a week, (and eventually, 19 hours a day). Spatially, it would unify the farmers' market with the two retail buildings.
- Then an inexpensive *pole framework* for market stalls awnings: this would further enclose space and also establish activity (which could later condense into lock-ups, then shops). This combination of enclosure and human activity would create the first *place*.[1]
- Then a second retail building: this would further enclose space and focus human activity. As importantly, it would also shield noise, allowing the mood to be coloured more by people and life than by traffic.

These we modelled with clay (and matchsticks for the pole structure). After this first 'place', we now had to address future growth. How could we grow a (pedestrian-dominated) street, then a second courtyard. Then a third, a fourth, and so on, eventually developing the whole site. Our clay model grew, simulating progressive development. Certain for the first building (but modified by a metre or two when we marked it out on site with straw-bales), probable for the next ones, possible for the later ones.

All this had all hands involved – though unfortunately not all the time. The developer could only spare two hours engagement in the mornings, and two hours appraisal in the evenings. Mostly, we reviewed issues at breakfast.

While model development was shaped by incremental place *growth*, the character of its places sought to match *moods* to their varied constituent *activities*. Crucial to mood would be micro-climate. This shaped *physical* form.

Working in the open air, we could assess shade as the sun passed overhead. Also, by tilting the model table, see how it would be in other seasons.

Participation without users

This development being speculative, there were never any real users. On three or four occasions, I had discussions with prospective tenants, but none of these eventually leased buildings. The core team settled down to be the developer (half-time), myself, one or two helpers (mostly disillusioned architects), the executive architect

Growth from (certain) past to (possible) future.

Marking out a (straw-bale) building with straw bales. Such full-size modelling enables better space fine-tuning than does any drawing. It's also easier for non-professionals to understand and simulate using. And lots of hands can build – and adjust – it!

(10% or less of time) and, belatedly, the design engineer. Additionally, the developer arranged a constant stream of people to view work in progress and advise. These ranged from city officials and fire officers to farmers and customers from the market, 'friends of the city', the local green movement and shopkeepers. There were also specialist consultants selling their wares, from feng shui to building-biology experts. (I found that these latter asked so much advice from me, I wondered whether I should set up shop in fashionable southern California!)

Amongst those I found most valuable were:

- Building contractors. These had a 'can do' attitude – a breath of fresh air after the 'can't be built' attitude so common in Britain. (Particularly irritating as invariably this is about something even I – not a qualified tradesman – *have* built.) I later discovered, however, that 'can do' means 'leave me alone, and I'll do it my way, ignoring anything we've agreed!'.
- Shoppers. Their general response was enthusiastic. Some described the project as 'just like Disneyland'. This was said as a compliment, though not heard by me as one! It actually meant: somewhere enjoyable to be in, not boring and bland. But it also indicated that, to many people, integrity behind the form-giving process meant nothing. The most common comment was 'how nice to be able to shop, eat, relax in a car-free area'. But this would be followed a few minutes later with 'But I like to park at the store (shop) door'! This made me realize what an uphill

struggle it would be to create human-flavoured places. Windscreen views don't make for social contact – and cars don't have hearts.

- Other developers. With their hard-nosed appraisals, much came together. I had to concede that customer acceptance depended on easy car access, but they in turn agreed that environmental quality was essential for delight – vital to economic viability.

These meetings weren't part of a structured process, but they forced me to listen closely to the unpalatable (like automotive convenience) as well as the palatable. This meant I could sympathize, and agree, with nearly everything in principle and most things in practice. Whether true or not, some (fortunately rare) comments, like those linking race and youth with crime I found repugnant. Yet even from these I learnt something: how vital it is to reverse culture-cide and re-build cultural self-esteem. For us, this meant maximizing minority-culture valuing opportunities like ethnic food, craft, music, children's activities and cultural events.

Normally, when I introduced the project, I would describe our aims and values (the spirit of the project), then the atmosphere (moods) we sought in each place. I'd then trace the relevant journeys – for instance, from parking to store (shop) – and then, with sketches to back up the model, show the physical form and appearance. I don't remember any dispute about spirit-of-project or moods-of-place. Most people liked both journey and physical form, but these sometimes brought fresh observations, reservations, (occasionally criticisms) and contributions. With widely varied viewpoints, values, priorities and expectations, we couldn't accommodate every suggestion, though most we could. We weren't always able to reach consensus, but about 90% of the time, we did.

One chain-store executive had, for instance, no problem with the idea of sustainability. In fact, he liked it. He liked also the moods-of-place: pedestrian-dominated, the delights of leaf-shade, water-feature cooling and the sensory appeal of natural materials. He was keen on all this – so long, however, as our store dimensions matched their standard plan to within half an inch (1 cm). It also needed all its parking (five times floor area) immediately in front of its door. For instant recognition from the freeway, it must incorporate a functionless tower and look exactly like all their other stores. And, of course, cost the same, be built and cooled (air-conditioned) the same. Apart from this, we could do whatever we liked – indeed the more sustainable, the more heart, the better! Had I missed something by thinking spirit, mood, journey and physical substance belonged together?

However sweet the cash injection, to accept such a disconnected approach would compromise the project irrevocably. Nonetheless these comments were useful; they helped us enter into that kind of thinking. While never our approach, it would be important to *also* evaluate our ongoing design through like eyes. As even unacceptable contributions taught me something, every one was valuable to hear.

It was unfortunate that these were added 'from outside' and hadn't emerged from the process. Had they done so, they would have both been more relevant and easier to assimilate. Without users as part of the process, however, this was inevitable.

With the developer and the design team, it was different. We continually reviewed all levels, often simultaneously. I also routinely questioned requirements and assumptions – even those I knew would touch emotional triggers. I felt bound to.

Viability couldn't be risked just for an easy life! We never argued about proposals, but evaluated them rigorously. If I – or anyone else – would notice a potential disadvantage – even one acceptable to us, but possibly not to others' criteria – we'd ask how much this mattered, and modify the design as required. Nothing went forward unless we *all* agreed. This was consensus not by process, but by attitude.

Card models as design tools. Preceding drawings, their purpose is to show internal space, construction and structure. If rough enough, we have no inhibitions about cutting bits off or sticking bits on. More effectively than drawings, they show us how buildings will look. Later, they can be improved to (rough) presentation standard. Working on site allowed us to alternate designing by model with walking and viewing the actual location.

Reflections

While, mostly, design and working relationships and progress went smoothly, here were three problematical areas. These being (normally) invisible, we were slow to recognize their significance:

- everything below ground
- cash-flow
- local politics.

Underground would be all the things we didn't want to see. This was about *physical wholeness* – or our avoiding dealing with this. Fuller attention to the users' whole-*journey* experience and its physical implications would have brought up this issue earlier – when easier to deal with. Cash-flow is about the economic propellants of *growth*. Although money is (theoretically) the epitome of *material* possession,[2] its *flow* is about *life-vigour*. Politics is about ethical context, namely underlying *values*.

To obtain a pedestrian atmosphere above ground, unavoidably meant lots of parking below. The developer suggested building on pile foundations; subsequent excavation between these would provide underground parking. The local structural engineer, however, designed 5 foot (1.5 m) diameter piles at 10 feet (3 m) centres. No room to park a car, twice the cost of the building above and, by the time we gave up on local engineers and started to work with one I know from Britain, four times the architectural fees! After this new appointment, things went smoothly. We were able to set-out, and adjust, the first two buildings with straw-bales prior to finalizing their design.

There were two aspects to politics: municipal corruption, which for us meant the necessity of local front men. The other was my first exposure to 'office politics'. Our consensus-based work, in which we worked as equals, encouraged the environmental engineer to try to take over the job. When other work took me to Siberia, rendering me incommunicado, he slandered me to the developer and offered to take over the job. This was all resolved on my return – when the client sacked him – but the episode left a bitter aftertaste. The lesson here was that consensus equality doesn't mean the right to be 'more equal than equal'.[3]

Cash-flow had seemed simple when we looked at incremental growth. But underground parking would require heavy up-front investment and only deliver returns when a third of the project was built. By eliminating all return on investment, self-financed growth would be impossible. External investors were out of the question. In that area, short-term criteria are the norm: five years to cover costs, five for profit, then abandon and move on. No sustainability there! This prohibitive up-front expense, though essential for long-term viability, set the project back seven years. Could it have been avoided?

Had we but looked at the physical pre-conditions – namely a business plan – early on, this issue should have become clear. The mission-statement (spirit of the project), though never formally written, was clear enough. The steps to achieve this (creating activity-*mood* places) we understood on the surface, though not below ground. Our comprehension, therefore, was unbalanced and incomplete. Consequently, the cash-*flow* to achieve these steps wasn't matched to the whole picture. For this, there wasn't sufficient cash or flow! Had we attended to these layers of business planning, we would – early on – have had to consider practical means to raise cash: to make the project *physical*. Practical means that wouldn't compromise flow, mood or spirit, like trusts, non-voting shareholders, lenders and ethical finance sources were not without ownership issue ramifications. These, however, could have been sorted out well before we got involved in design.

How would I do things differently next time?

- Booking *'process time'* well ahead would (hopefully) have guaranteed we could start out on a sound place-study and design-incarnation basis.
- Identifying key – and fringe – *players* early on would have enabled us to bring many viewpoints together and build a balanced outlook from the beginning.
- Identifying key *issues* early would have enabled timely prioritization of effort and a well-targeted sequence of strategic decisions. This is never easy as many issues only emerge as you get to understand things. Nevertheless, once numbers were given to cash-flow, the obstacles – and hints as to ways round them – became clear. While some of these numbers depended on design, the principle ones – especially those about underground parking – didn't.
- Now recognizing that, for many, there is a disconnection between spirit and mood, and journey and physical form, I would have tried all means to draw the second two stages slowly and seamlessly out of the first two. Questions as to appropriate moods, how to achieve them and whether we were going in the right direction would have helped substantiate their connection.
- Recapitulating, review-evaluations and extracting the *principles* that gave form to the design were always scheduled, but always overridden by the pressure of events on our (or on the developer's) time. Regardless of whether or not he thought this was what he was paying for, I should have been inflexible on this.

All in all however, both the developer and I learnt a great deal – especially about the inseparability of environmental, social and economic sustainability. We enjoyed ourselves and built a deep friendship. While we brought different viewpoints, experience – and blinkers – we didn't argue, but questioned each other and the many others – and were questioned by them. The development strategy, detail designs and tenants' architects' criteria, through sweated over, condensed consensually.

This was consensus born of a listening respect.

Notes

1   For more about how 'boundaries' and energy 'fields' make places, see Day C. (2002). *Spirit & Place*. Architectural Press.

2   In fact, most money these days has *no physical substance*. It is just electronic signals.

3   To paraphrase George Orwell's *Animal Farm*.

CHAPTER TWENTY-ONE

Multiple viewpoints: multi-cultural, multi-faith centre, London

At the turn of the millennium, I was invited to lead a consensus design process for the ASHA[1] Centre in London – a multi-cultural, multi-faith centre celebrating cultural diversity and the one-ness of divine spirit. This one-ness, however, manifested in a multiplicity of religions, turned a simple concept into a major challenge.

Multi-ethnic and multi-faith inevitably means multi-viewpoint. Many people assumed this would mean multi-dispute and multi-compromise, so take forever to reach even rudimentary agreement. But it didn't. The primary design emerged during a five-day intense process: one day of general meeting, four of structured process. Consolidating this design took another three.

As preparation, I worked out who needed to be involved, how long to allow for what, and, from this, a timetable. I had hoped to start with both neighbours and ASHA 'players': religious and special-activity representatives. We would study place and incarnate design from two directions: neighbours from periphery, players from centre. But things didn't work out like this!

Timetable

Day 1:   Project launch
Days 2–4:   Site development strategy
Days 5–9:   Developing the buildings

Project launch

On the first day, I had anticipated meeting people who would be involved throughout the design process, familiarizing ourselves with the site and extracting the essence of what each faith hoped for from the centre. In the event, it was more of a general meeting to present the project and gather support.

I found myself, not sitting in a circle with everyone else, but on a panel facing a room packed with over 100 people – some dauntingly famous. There were representatives of all major religions. Also of some less conventional ones, including King

Arthur (his sword, cloak and trainers raised some establishment eyebrows, but his words gained instant respect). Only Rastafarianism was missing, though Caribbean culture was represented. No neighbours came. We paid for this later when their justifiable (but unfounded) worries about traffic, parking and noise were exploited by local racists.

The meeting opened with silence, a Hindu prayer and then short contributions from the panel, mostly about ASHA's aims, support, funding and how the project would progress.

I explained the principles of listening design and of holding-back ideas: that while I would listen attentively to all contributions, I did *not* intend to incorporate ideas, but rather attempt to identify the essence, the spirit-core, of each one. From these spirit impulses, the design would emerge. As religious practice is manifest in activities, I needed to know what would go on there. Also what these activities would need in terms of space, physical amenities and soul qualities.

Next came the plenum phase. Amongst the hopes expressed, a policeman described the nihilism of so many young people. How even vague interest from someone over 30 brought automatic rejection. The need to remotivate them was desperate. Most contributions, however, were neither concerns nor visions. Nor were there many ideas, even about activities to be housed. Almost all were expressions of support – many from distinguished or influential people. Inspiring and wonderful to receive, but not yet a starting point for design.

In the afternoon, we divided into groups, each focused on particular activities. I asked these groups first to try to define spatial needs and then to describe their activity in nouns (*what* it needs), verbs (what will *go on* there), adverbs (what *qualities* these *activities* need) and lastly adjectives (what *physical qualities* its building, room or place needs).

To avoid spokespersons ignoring issues raised in discussion and merely presenting the views they started with, we asked each group to schedule the last ten minutes to summarize their findings *and agree* what their spokesperson would present. Only one group addressed the verbs, adverbs, adjectives and nouns. Most mixed loose activity definition with formed ideas, like 'the buildings should be round'.

This led to a general discussion, initially related to these activity-place themes but rapidly broadening. Quite a lot was about what people would like to see. For the children's centre, for instance, an ideal school as described by children would have a heart-shaped front door, with a heart-shaped cat door in it.

There were also some fully formed solutions, like a ferro-concrete dome sprayed onto a polythene balloon, to house 2500 people, and cost only £100,000 ($150,000). Two domes stuck together to make an 'egg' could be floated on a lake – beautiful and striking! The designers told us they were advised by a sea-captain. (This really sparked my imagination – what was his role?) Unsure if the silent audience was spellbound, I felt it would be petty to bring up questions like daylight, breathability and insulation.

Plenum summary

The project should:

- be uplifting: beautiful, healthy and environmentally friendly
- have periphery activities to invite and involve people; around a sacred core

- be inspiring and empowering for the young and disprivileged
- celebrate diversity as an enrichment of the new Britain
- have an integrating effect on society through the single *spiritual* source of this materially manifest diversity
- offer an inspired and hope-filled future, fed by what we bring from the past: traditions and cultures
- be of millennial spiritual significance; a beacon to the world.

Some valuable organizing themes emerged from this discussion, which became central to the design. Most notable were themes about the relationship between sacred space and secular activities: a Sikh suggested the activity-realms be like the layers of an onion, secular and socially permeable without, progressively more sacred within; a Zoroastrian, that the journey to the sacred space be a *will journey*. The need for circular gestures and soft, fluid movements was repeatedly emphasized. Many asked for nature – gardens and water, also enhanced awareness of the elements, cycles and processes of nature, to be everywhere in the project, indoors and out. Especially, there must be a meditation garden. Someone pointed out that 'paradise' in Persian means 'garden'.

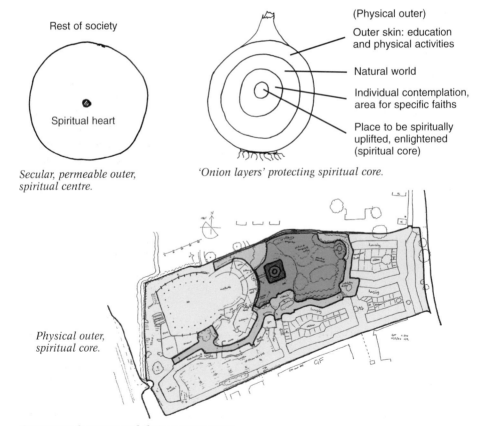

Rest of society

Spiritual heart

Secular, permeable outer, spiritual centre.

(Physical outer)

Outer skin: education and physical activities

Natural world

Individual contemplation, area for specific faiths

Place to be spiritually uplifted, enlightened (spiritual core)

'Onion layers' protecting spiritual core.

Physical outer, spiritual core.

Organizing diagrams and their consequences.

To conclude the meeting, I summarized the principal organizing themes and described how we would proceed in the next days. Faced with 150 prospective participants, I stressed that only those who planned to see the project, and the five-day design process, through should take part. I hoped this would reduce 150 to about 30, but it didn't work like this, for few participants had been forewarned. (Actually they had been, but hadn't read that section.) Some were outraged that, not being free in the next few days, they would be excluded. One said that I talked of democratic design but practised authoritarianism. We therefore modified this to allow any to drop in when they could, with the provision that they respected the process. Other voices, including spiritual leaders, said 'we trust you, we are happy to leave the design in your hands'. An honour to hear, but not what I had hoped for.

In the event only a small core, about a dozen, saw the process through, and even of those, only three students and myself were present *all* the time. Even though we worked late into the evenings, less than ten (and none of the outraged group) dropped in and out. This wasn't the involvement I'd hoped for, but nonetheless, we represented eight religions and nine cultures.[2]

Short as was the first day, it was intense. All-in-all it was an exhilarating day of diverse and strong support.

Site development strategy

Place-study

As always, we started the process with a silent first-impressions walk. Our ten-acre site was a former military headquarters, now used for government offices. Security fences meant we couldn't see a lot of the site. What we could see were two long strips of buildings (mostly asbestos), the street between them and some, not all, of the back lands behind them. All the buildings, however, were scheduled for demolition in two weeks' time. Everything we saw as disconnected bits would become one large muddy field.

Sharing impressions, we identified sub-places to study: the roadside entry, spine road, two back strips and a meadow beyond the buildings. Not much would outlast demolition, but at least the sub-place auras would remain.

When looking at what was physically there, we were acutely aware that it soon *wouldn't* be there. We therefore extended our interests to the context beyond the site boundaries. This still would be. So would a few things within our boundaries: a spring, a conduited stream, a two-metre slope across what looked flat, and the enclosing railway and road embankments.

Then to biography. Tree-lines, soil and vegetation, corroborated by street names, showed the former route of the stream and its marshy source, prior to re-routing and canalization. Old maps told us of the gas works, demolished, but still polluting downstream water and soil. Before this there had been a farm and smithy, with pond. The mature oaks showed field patterns before the railway embankment sliced them. In the 1920s came suburban houses and the slow engulfment into London, with the road steadily growing till the present dual carriageway. This unfolding tableau *around* the site became clearer and clearer, the more we looked. On the site itself, the transformation from field to wartime buildings was sudden. Since then, despite civilian use superseding military, time seemed to have stood still. The place looked like a film set for a 1940s air-defence HQ – as it had been!

But how would the future develop? In three weeks there would be just a pile of rubble and deep tractor ruts. Many of the trees were elms, which at around 15 years develop Dutch elm disease, so in a few years would all be dead and felled. Major transformations. More significant, however, was how the *surrounding area* would change. Rising property values suggested warehouses to the south would soon be replaced by a business park. In 50 years the railway might well become a multi-layer transport corridor, topped by a motorway. Though our site had barely altered in the past 60 years, in the next 60 we could expect major changes all around it. This flow of time *around* our boundaries had clearer continuity than the more random steps of change within them.

Now to moods: the rear meadow was peaceful; the southern back strip, sleeping; the empty, lifeless heart still echoed with its long-past hive of activity, heroism and desperation. Only one part was obviously loved, three winter flowering cherry trees incongruously protected by a motorway crash rail.

What then did the place say? Not quite 'abandoned, derelict', but more 'I am waiting' – or, more poignantly: 'I am *still* waiting'.

Moods

Northwest (corner): human scale.
North: people/busy (currently with demolition work).
Northeast (corner): electrical transformer makes this uncomfortable.
West: peaceful, soft.
Southwest (corner): darker, cold, dank.
Southwest (gate): activity.
South (back-land): haven.
Centre: cloistered but disconnected; abandoned, nostalgic.
Three trees: soul heart.

What the place says

I am an eccentric old man/old woman.
I am a sleeping beauty – my time has come.
I am waiting.
I am *still* waiting.

Outline design

We opened the third day by recapitulating the themes from the general meeting, the findings of the previous day, and how we had reached them. I then asked what ASHA should say. 'I am a celebration of shared heritage and creation', 'I am timeless', 'I am yours' were the phrases that emerged.

We then listed activities, gathering these into mood-families. Where would be the most mood-appropriate location for each one? We soon realized that the two large-area uses (the 1500-seat auditorium with linked 1000-seat amphitheatre and the three acres of social housing) were so large that their placing would fix all the other elements (multi-faith sacred space, museum of migration, holistic health centre, children's realm, park, meditation garden and car parking). Housing seemed to want to go in the sleeping, domestic mood area. The auditorium foyer asked to face the cherry trees. Obviously loved for many years, these had become the 'heart' of the place, though, at 60 years old, the trees themselves were near the end of their lives. We drew these rough areas on the site plan, then looked at massing by placing rough, unformed, Plasticine volumes on the model base.

These locations resulted from matching future activity-mood to current mood-of-place. While there were some *present* influences on moods, like shade, noise, damp ground and, of course, buildings, the strongest influences resulted from *past biography*. The 'ensouled heart' was solely due to care in times past. But what about *future biography*? We could expect increasing traffic and noise from the west. This meant buildings here would have a noise-shielding role. When rail-links (already planned) were complete, more people would arrive by train than road. This meant two 'main' entrances: one for now, one for a decade hence. We also needed to keep an access option to additional land under negotiation – its future ownership unclear. Such considerations significantly modified building layout and form.

On the fourth day, we succinctly recapitulated the whole process to date, each stage by a different person. This briefed incomers about the decisions we had reached, reminded us of the reasons behind them, and kept process continuity in view. The onion layers, will-journey and cherry tree heart were beginning to organize the routes from the two site-entrances (road and rail) and hence the layout.

Unlike clay, cold Plasticine is barely malleable, so slow to form. For speed, therefore, we resorted to drawing. Unfortunate, because modelling before drawing is more creativity-freeing. Nonetheless, we formed enough of a model to be able to condense a rough plan by the end of the day.

The buildings

Design development

After the daily recapitulation, we concentrated on key elements, particularly the auditorium and multi-faith tower. Parking demand for Asian weddings emerged as a major issue, requiring a three-floored parking structure. This necessitated re-shaping the social housing.

Though the core group worked every day, others came in and out. Those less involved in the process brought ideas with them. But, like all ideas, however good, their *source* lay outside the project. With Islamic, classicist and organic proponents, there were many sacred cows, even deeply held design-philosophies. These bent the design in new, sometimes contradictory, directions: organic flow alternating with classical composition, Islamic geometry with the randomness of life-vigour, marketable prestige with informal, human scale. I found this hard to know how to deal with. While the project was about *unity of spirit* within diversity of manifestation, here the *diverse* was constantly pulling in one direction or the other. Indeed the design seemed to oscillate between flavours every few hours.

Initially, I approached this as a challenge to diplomacy and assimilation skills. *Diplomacy* was the easy bit. Turning statements into questions and asking what these *implied*, made it easier to choose the consensually agreed *appropriate* over the personally favoured *attractive*. But these still diverged in stylistic approach. To *assimilate* them, I tried, therefore, to understand what lay at the heart of each. Once *approaches* were translated into *essences*, we could talk dispassionately about the contribution of each. Which mood and aspect of life did each bring; and where (and for what reasons) would this be appropriate?

What, for instance, would a classically organized arrival journey – with axial symmetry, controlled movement tempo, visual composition and carefully chosen proportions say? Might it be too rigidly organized, unfree, for a welcoming experience? What, on the other hand, would a life-shaped organic journey say? Would its potentially chaotic life-vigour be too un-directed, un-quiet, even too multi-ethnic product-focused and secular?

In line with the onion-layer principle, a theme began to emerge: a sensory-rich soul-journey from life-vigour-formed periphery to still, sacred, heart. This resolved the classical-organic polarity: principal buildings and sacred elements organized by sacred geometric proportion along an axis, but the *journey* to and past them, organic, responding to pressures and energies along its route. This informality would help the project feel open and accessible. Vital, as such a project could all too easily be perceived as closed and clique-dominated. By working with their *essence*, we managed to bring such disparate approaches into synthesis.

At the close of this final day of whole-group process, we had reached the basic plan of the centre. We now worked through the general design of each building in the same ways. Whenever the general layout condensed to the point when a particular

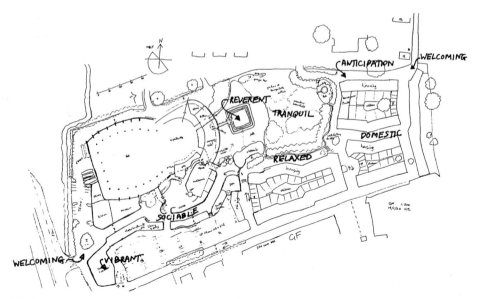

Mood zones to support the appropriate spirit and 'onion layers'.

building needed more precise form, I would divert the group to this. We would discuss what the building was for (its primary activity). How would we describe its essence? What message should it therefore convey? What would be its constituent parts – and what size should they be? Then, what mood would be appropriate to each part and how should we best journey through these to reinforce the spirit-of-the-building, the essence of its (spiritual) function.

Some buildings, of course, had several functions, entries, destinations and journeys to or through them. We worked with all these, first at the stage of condensing form. Then, as the design hardened up, we would review these mood-journeys daily. Did they still reinforce what the building should say?

While people dropping in and out of the process made for discontinuity, there were compensating advantages. Some, particularly the developer, sea-captain, film-maker and project-initiator, brought new – and sharp – eyes to each review. Doubly advantageous, because in a small group it's easy to convince ourselves that we're doing everything right.

We spent the next three days developing and consolidating this design. The larger group having left, four students and myself (five nationalities), were left, with occasional others from the main process dropping in, bringing invaluable observations and contributions. These ranged from viability (from a developer's perspective) and relative costs of surface, under-building and upper-level parking, to the requirements for Jewish Orthodox kitchens,[3] Islamic weddings and the museum of migration.

We started each day by reviewing key experience sequences, both approaching and within buildings: would we meet the right things in the right order? This was about

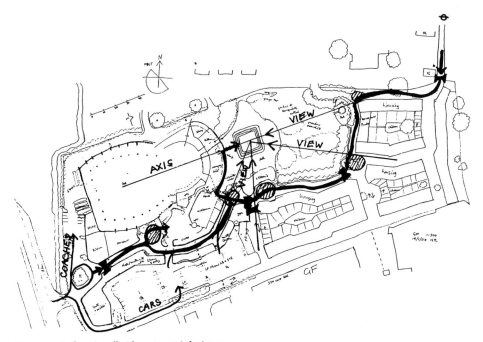

Movement: dancing fluid route; axial views.

the 'redeeming buildings' experience: what approach journeys say. We also checked room areas, adjusting them accordingly. A reality check – vital for cost control. We then firmed-up and refined the drawings and Plasticine model and sketched their implications.

The project as a whole had posed the problem of unifying many approaches, interests and mood-rich activities – all laden with conflict potential. The four-layer condensation process had steered us through this minefield. But what about the sacred building? Much bigger mines lurked here – or would have, had we started with competing faiths. Fortunately, everyone was committed to the 'unity at the heart of diversity' ideal. The problem was to give this form.

As every religion (that I know of) has forms associated with it, it proved hard to find any building form that didn't lean towards one or the other.

We discussed forms and spatial organizations, like domes, axes to altars or shrines, and cruciform plans; also patterns, images and symbols. We also considered a single large space with separate faith areas or niches. All these approaches felt too specific and bound to lead to unbalanced – and competing – results. Not to mention problems like Christian icons or Hindu fertility-figures, compromising Jewish and Islamic icon-prohibitions.

We realized that here, more than anywhere, we needed forms, not to be chosen, but to condense from the spirit at the heart of the project. Diversity was easy, but how could unity find form? We asked what principles were common to all major religions. From the experience of the eight we represented, we listed:

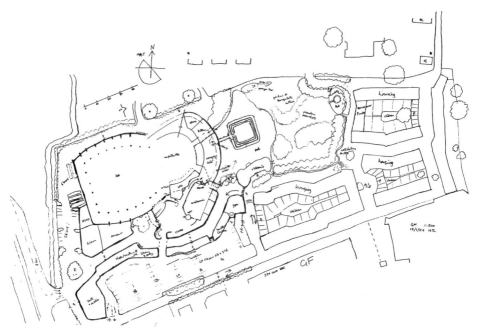

Resultant plan.

- inner peace – a sacred centre to a hectic, material, world
- inner development – progressive enspiriting of an outwardly material body
- divine light – the illumination of otherwise dead, dark matter
- reverence for the divine – focused in place or in rituals, usually both.

What qualities, journeys, spaces, forms and matter encapsulated these? Inner peace brought up the Sikh's onion contours again. Inner development is a journey, often given form in architecture as well as ritual. In many rituals, it's manifest as a progression through elemental levels from matter to fire; in nature, from winter-earth to warmth-ripened seed. Divine light furthers this principle of elevating the material elements. Reverence suggests a ritual journey.

Further materialized, this led us to a journey through the elements, rising from earth to fire. A journey inwards to the divine, spirit-core, but upwards to the light. Inner-spirit-feeding (hence will-strengthening) on the ascent; outer material-world-fertilizing (through our strengthened, spirit-fed will) on the descent. This led us to a bridge portal, then a cube – in occult tradition, the form of matter, earth – progressing upwards through a coloured-light-flooded octagon to a glass cone. We realized these forms – cubes, cylinders, pyramids, stupas, spires and minaret-crowns – are found in so many religious buildings that they touch deep archetypes. Through this condensation process, however, we didn't need to select forms or lists of symbols from a multi-faith 'menu'. They just appeared.

At the end of eight days – of which one was all talk (for me: listening), one of site study, and one mostly printing and paper-sorting, we had three stories of plans and five sections for seven acres of development, a three-level sacred tower in some detail, a 2400 × 1200 cm (8 × 4 feet) model and a number of interior and exterior sketches of how bits and pieces would look.

A lot of work still to do, but a lot achieved in six and a half days of place-study and design.

Reflections

What would I have done differently if I did it again? Life would have been easier if we'd known what should go into the project and what size things should be. These required much discussion. Even more fundamental, however, would be to find the key people – from hall and museum managers and religious representatives to next-door neighbours – and book their time for the design process. (Never arrange anything to start immediately after New Year! Key people can't be contacted. Nor supplies easily bought. Especially, never, never, do this after a millennium holiday!)

Although trivial by comparison, better supplies would have helped greatly. Using tracing paper rather than semi-opaque newsprint, and clay rather than Plastacine would probably have got us two days further ahead. Nonetheless, we did achieve a lot in a short time. Utilizing the four-layer process and adapting its principles – most particularly, stepping back to the previous level – wherever potential impasses appeared ensured we wasted neither time nor morale energy in criticism and defensiveness, but all pulled together.

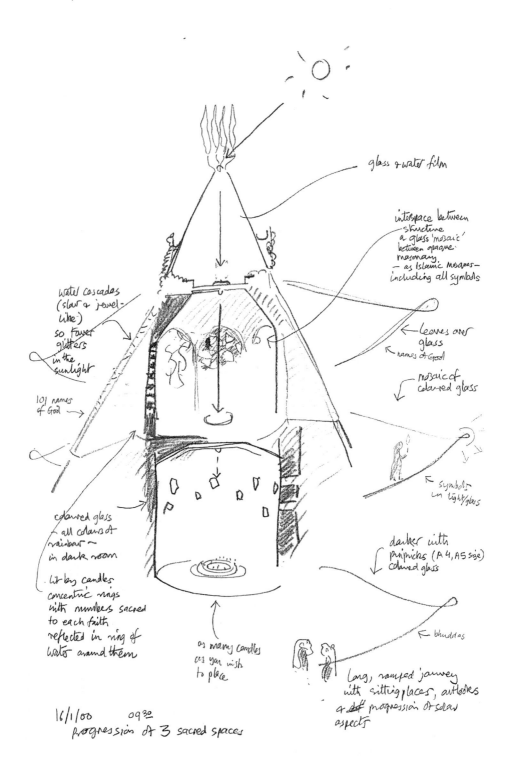

glass & water film

interspace between
structure
a glass 'mosaic'
between opaque
masonry
— as Islamic Mosques —
including all symbols

water cascades
(star & jewel-
like)
so tower
glitters
in the
sunlight

← Leaves over
glass
← names of God

mosaic of
coloured glass

101 names
of God →

← symbols
in light/glass

coloured glass
— all colours of
rainbow —
in dark room

darker with
pinpricks (A4, A5 size)
coloured glass

Lit by candles
concentric rings
with numbers sacred
to each faith
reflected in ring of
water around them

as many candles
as you wish
to place

← bhuddas

Long, ramped journey
with sitting places, outlooks
& progression of solar
aspects

16/1/00   09³⁰
progression of 3 sacred spaces

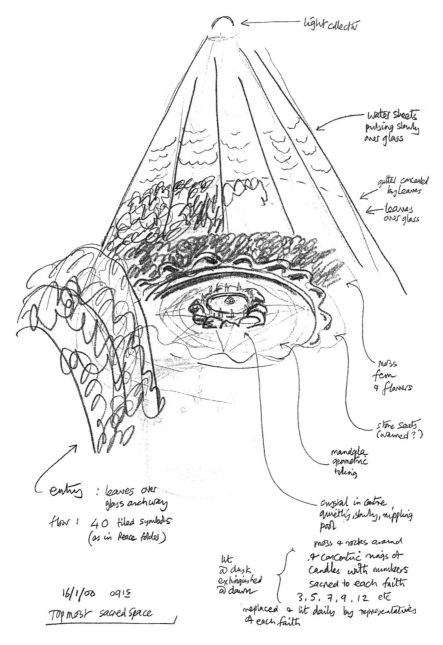

light collector

water sheets
pulsing slowly
over glass

gutter concealed
by leaves

leaves
over glass

moss
fern
& flowers

stone seats
(warmed?)

mandala
geometric
tiling

crystal in centre,
quietly, slowly, rippling
pool

moss & rocks around
.& concentric rings of
candles with numbers
sacred to each faith
3, 5, 7, 9, 12 etc
replaced & lit daily by representatives
& each faith

lit
@ dusk
extinguished
@ dawn

entry : leaves over
glass archway

floor : 40 tiled symbols
(as in Peace folder)

16/1/00   0915
Topmost sacred space

Public meeting requests (sacred centre, four-elemental qualities, landmark to London, indoor med-itation garden) given form. The sacred tower had three levels: the first earth and matter bound – internally a cube, dark with tiny rainbow windows and a candle bed in the centre. The second, an octagon of stained glass with symbols and motifs from all religions. The third, a faceted glass cone, water sheets pulsing over it. Inside, a pool at the centre with a crystal lit by a sunlight-catcher from the apex. And outside, at the very tip, a permanent – 'eternal' – flame, reinforcing its London land-mark role. The pilgrimage up would be disorientating, so will-demanding. The journey down, reori-entating, connecting the enspirited will with the wider world.

More significantly, except for those outside the group process, we worked consensually throughout. This project, above all others I've been involved in, required a coming together of world-outlooks, at one level totally opposite. Religions easily give people strong convictions, occasionally even dogmatic 'knowledge'. How could I ever reconcile such (apparently) inimical outlooks, aspirations and requirements without resorting to lowest-common-denominator compromises? Indeed, did I?

The answer is that *I* didn't. *We* did. We did it by stepping back to the level before religious differentiation, the level at which we share a single spirituality. Easily said – and relatively easily done. More difficult, however, is to *remain in* that shared, archetypal, 'spirit' level and yet *go forward* into a more and more concrete design. This is where the process I describe was invaluable.

Far from the untold difficulties, political wrangling and compromise others foresaw, both process and outcome went smoothly, building consensus decisions upon consensus decisions.

Did I just have blind confidence to help me past problems? No. From the outset I knew I was totally out of my depth. But I also knew the *only* way to achieve consensus was to work from the shared pre-form values and help condense these in their own unique way.

Notes

1   ASHA means 'hope' in Sanskrit, 'divine justice' in Parsee.
2   Buddhism, Christianity, Humanism, Hinduism, Islam, Judaism, Zoroastranism and Chinese religion. Our group came from Australia, China, Egypt, England, India, Iran, Pakistan, South Africa, Wales.
3   Two separate kitchens and complete sets of equipment if meat dishes are prepared, to ensure milk and meat are kept separate in every way.

CHAPTER TWENTY-TWO

Desert ranch: single-family house, Arizona

In 2000, I was invited to design a house on an Arizona ostrich ranch. Being in the desert there would be no utilities (services); it would need to be autonomous, and make hospitable a climate inhospitable in the extreme. The consensus design process may work well with communities, but for this project, we were just four people: two clients, the executive architect and myself. As half the group would be paying for the house and living in it, fulfilling their wishes was more important than any issue of equality or group consciousness. Despite this, we *worked* as a round-table consensus group. This chapter shows both how we could utilize the process structure, and how we had to modify it for these circumstances.

Timetable	
Day 1:	Place-study & outline design
Days 2–4:	Design development

Place-study

Except for livestock shelters, trailers and a mobile home, there were no buildings nor – at first sight – any landscape features to relate to. Only desert ringed by mountains and – a mere four miles away – a nuclear power plant. Transfixing beauty and blasphemy side by side.

We started, therefore, by walking a loop through the whole site. Some places were obviously unsuitable for buildings: the gulch, which flooded to a brief torrent every few years, and the centennial flood plain edging it; also the land nearest the nuclear plant, within earshot even at this range.[1]

While we were all drawn to one particular low mesa above the dry river-bed gulch, we nonetheless checked out all other possibilities before making any decision.

We returned to the first mesa, noting it was above the 100-year flood level, open to cooling breezes and – perhaps once a year – might hear running water. It was also close to the gulch-side trees, a welcome rest to the eyes and an effective screen for the power plant's night-time floodlights and morning steam plumes. A window through these trees focused on a twin-peak mountain to the west, and the ring of mountains from east to southwest was in full view.

It also had practical advantages. The land was so bare we would be destroying less of the fragile desert vegetation by building there. Also, from the dirt road there was a level(ish!) route unobstructed by washes or gulches. This location-choosing took the whole morning.

But where would the house actually be? And how would we arrive at it? To establish the exact route from ranch dirt-track to mesa, we let landform and gaps between vegetation (creosote bush, cactus and chaparral) lead us. We could now focus on the last stage of this journey: the building approach.

We looked first at what was physically there: the vegetation, contours, surrounding mountains. In so doing, we found an old native American trail. This reinforced our sense of the route's 'rightness'. Next we looked at the flow of the journey: how our route turned off the road, picked up the track, skirted miniature dry creeks, wound between clumps of creosote bush and sought out the bare, stony clearing. Then we noted the place's elemental qualities: dry, airy, hot (even on a winter afternoon). And finally asked what the place said, what it was asking for. It asked for elemental balance, in particular for water, shade and a sense of coolness. As an anchor point in the landscape, it was the only place a home could feel 'at home' in.

Outline design

We then asked what a homestead here should say: something of an oasis quality. Then which activities – rooms and outdoor spaces – should go where? This we could walk out on the ground, checking the view and solar orientation. Then, from this, what moods and elemental qualities should be where? Where succulent, where dry? Where sheltered, where open? This brought us to ask how we should *meet* the building. Then the question: what building and wall gestures should *greet* us? What, therefore, should be the *entry* gesture? In such an empty landscape, the building, shaded under a long sheltering roof, needed to hug the ground. We focused, therefore, on the plan gesture: an open-sided courtyard, half its perimeter being building, half dwarf anti-snake wall atop the mesa edge.

This was all very rushed as winter sunset came early – and in sub-tropical latitudes, swiftly. We roughly sketched our plan and track decisions, all too aware of fingers of mountain shadows rapidly engulfing the land. We had only just enough time to get home before darkness and night chill closed down the day.

Design development

We began the following day by making a list of rooms and their sizes. Then cut out (and labelled) 1/8":1'0" (approximately 1:100) scale paper rectangles for each one. These we laid out to make a diagrammatic plan in the gesture agreed on the ground. Which room should go where? We agreed that the kitchen as 'heart' of this house would be the place to locate first. The whole plan grew from this point. Returning to site, we checked orientation to views, sun, shade and breeze.

In such a harsh climate, cooling was a major shaping force. This meant reducing exposure to low westerly sun, deep roof overhangs to the south, good vertical and cross ventilation and earth-berming wherever possible. At the same time we wanted to maximize views of the mountains, an arc from east through south to west. The best views faced west – overheating problem direction!

We then reviewed movement from room to room, modifying the plan accordingly.

This started to firm-up our plan, but measuring its area for cost check, led us to shrink some rooms. We now had a *plan*, but not yet a building *form*. For this we built a clay model on a tracing of the plan. This resolved much that was unclear about the roof shape, clerestories, solar chimneys and cooling towers. Next we drew rough cross-sections to check that windows would admit winter sun, but be shaded in summer, also to show cross and vertical ventilation. At the end of this day we had a clay model together with a rough plan and sections.

The next day we enlarged the drawings on a photocopier to 1/4":1'0" scale (approximately 1:50). With these, we could tighten up dimensions, both for plans and sections. As usual at 1/8" scale, a few things – like cupboards – had been left out or drawn too small while others, like bathrooms and passages were too large. This allowed us to contract the plan. We could now go through it room by room, looking at furnishings, use and space – and adding in things the husband missed out on when away driving to the photocopier (a three-hour trip in all).

At this scale, it became obvious the building was too high, too prominent in the landscape. This meant changes to roof form and building width. Lowering the eaves helped visually and improved shading, though not the air-space necessary for cool heads. After many revisions, mostly to the sections and model, the form began to work out well, both for cooling and fitting into the landscape. But the plan had expanded again! For a cost check, we calculated the floor area – and again had to contract the plan. With this revised plan, we revisited the site to confirm orientations and fine-tune placing. This led us to move the building about eight feet (2.5 m).

This was a short day. Electric generator problems and frozen water meant we couldn't get started before dawn, which was late. Farm work took up half my clients' time. Decisions taken by any three of us, invariably were reversed by the fourth. (Unfortunately, consensus doesn't work when someone is left out! This means

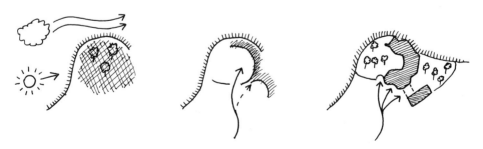

Spirit-of place wanted: oasis. Mood to support this: shady, airy, protected but good view. Gestures and movement-flow to support mood. Physical form to embody this.

absence slows things up a lot.) Hence it was very late before we could mark out the building on site. Under the pressure of imminent dusk, this was somewhat rushed. After dark we firmed up the 1/4″ scale plan. Having lost another half a day we were now behind schedule.

On the final day we began by reviewing and improving the plan. On site, we rechecked orientation for views, sun and courtyard gestures. This led us to open up the 'wings' some 10–15° and relocate the sleeping porch. Again, electrical and water problems had delayed our start and half the day was spent with the dowser (and probable building contractor). By now, our timetable had slipped one day.

In the evening, we looked at how the house would be *used* and asked whether we still had the right mood in each room. Then considered how the cooling would work, each season having different demands: winter, spring and early summer are dry, but late summer unpleasantly humid. This last, with temperatures around 110°F, was the most difficult to design for. Moreover, high humidity and dry heat place opposite demands on a building. Winter, though brief, could be covered by solar heating.

Again, plan revisions. We could now crudely peg out the building outline. Farm work, animal injuries, generator breakdown, water and car problems took up yet more of my clients' time so the programme slipped further into contingency time.

To better understand the building and its construction, we drew more sections. From these we could draw elevations. This led to revising the roof, in turn affecting the floor plan – and sections and elevations. We now had a plan we could mark out precisely on site, and did this using a coloured spray.

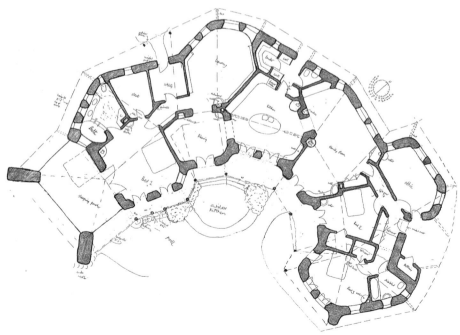

Resultant plan.

Elevation.

After dark, we 'walked-through' the plan, room by room, imagining every passage, door, even tables and furniture. This should of course have been done much earlier, but it was hard to get both clients together to do this.

So at the end of four days (only two-and-a-half of joint work) we had plans, sections, elevations and a clay model of a house. Not just a house, but a large, rather complex one with exacting environmental performance demands. Very exacting, as the desert climate is quite unforgiving.

To check indoor spaces, constructibility and sun and shade, we now needed to build a card model. From this, I would develop drawings. The lost day and a bit meant I would have to do this on my own in Wales. The substance of the design, however, we had grown together over two-and-a-half days of intense work. This was slower progress than I am used to. The price of rarely having everyone together, meant lots of reversing and re-deciding. Whenever we were all together, things went faster.

Reflections

Single families aren't like communities. There aren't enough people to balance personalities, so different methods are necessary. Whereas large groups are freed by the trans-individual nature of the consensus design process, attempts to stick rigidly to it could easily seem tyrannical and unresponsive to each individual in small groups. This requires the process to be more like a flexible agenda. We can still use a sequence structure to condense design, but must always be open to re-examining earlier decisions. Large groups that constantly re-open old issues end up going round in circles; they become so frustratingly ineffective, people drop out. Tiny groups that don't feel tyrannized.

A major problem in this project was competing demands on our time. Everyone, of course, has life and work outside project design, but our time on site was finite. We had to keep momentum but how could we decide what others wanted in their absence? To some extent, we could switch to developing non-controversial aspects, but at the price of the most efficient work sequence. Consensus is anyway hard when only one of the two essential people is present. Hence reversing each other's decisions wasted a lot of time. We did always reach consensus, but this was often only by refining what was common to all parties.

What was required – in practical terms, like what rooms and what sizes, which entrance was the most important and what rooms each should lead to – wasn't clear to anybody. There's nothing wrong, nor exceptional, in this; most people have never had houses built for them. Had we realized that the requirements we were given were still in flux, I would have focused on these at the beginning of the design stage. What should the home say? What moods did this imply? What relationships between them? And – critically – what rooms, of what size for what activities? Was this total area compatible with budget?

For my part, I should have brought a compass as the survey map (at two miles to the inch) was useless. We overcame this by marking out a solar-clock on site, firstly by estimating solar noon (correcting clock noon by longitude; this *was* on the map!). This gave us south. We confirmed this by marking sunrise and sunset angles and dividing these.

While such problems compromised efficiency, they didn't compromise consensus. The design, while it advanced, retreated and moved sideways by fits and starts, nonetheless emerged, and became consolidated, through a slow and progressive condensation process. Despite inefficiencies and small-group, non-quorum problems, this was still design by consensus and through four-layer process.

Note

1   From the point of view of exposure to radioactivity should there be an accident, four-and-a-half miles is no better than three-and-a-half miles. There isn't even a lot of difference between four and 40 miles.

CHAPTER TWENTY-THREE

Science Centre revisited: Goethean Science Centre, Scotland

In November 2001 I re-visited the Goethean Science Centre (Chapter 11), to co-design its (probably) final two buildings: residential building and social centre. Being my eighth working trip, I thought this would be easy. It wasn't.

> *Timetable*
>
> Day 1 & 2:   Residential building
> Day 3:   Social centre

Residential building

Place-study

After explaining the process, we started with a silent walk from carpark to (future) residential building. Having 'found' and re-found this and the social centre at least three times already on previous trips, we took their location as fixed. Ten years on from our original study, the place had changed. While physical changes were mostly small, the transformation in mood was striking.

With too much to do in too little time – and even less daylight – we tried to short-cut the process. For this we suffered. As three of the six of us (biologist, builder, potter, student and two architects), had been involved in earlier place studies, we decided to compress physical observation and spatial movement into a single half-hour session. We then discussed the place's present mood, then what it 'said' ('melancholy, lacking warmth').

Outline design

Next we asked what our building, and the place it would form, should say, and what mood would support this. Under pressure of cold and approaching dusk, message,

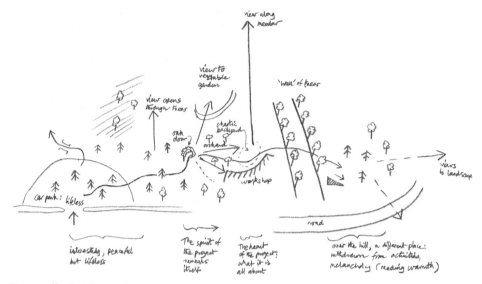

Entry walk: first impressions map.

mood and even physical implications became blurred so words and phrases like 'welcome!', 'I am a home to withdraw to', were mixed up with 'domestic mood', 'humanly warm', 'respectful of the tall trees', even 'I am a marker that people live here' and 'I stand tall when seen from the road, but am a protective "retreat" when approached from the workshop'. These premature form implications should have alerted me that with the process too rushed, things were going wrong.

We next staked out the limits of the 'domestic-compatible' mood. In so doing, we recognized two trees were dying. Had the physical and time-process stages been distinct, thus more focused, we would have noticed this earlier. After imagining these trees away, we could extend the northern place-boundary about three metres. How high could the building be without blocking views through the bare pine-trunks? How high *should* it be? Should it be in scale with the tall pines or low to respect their verticality? We also wondered whether a building as large as we needed could even fit here. At this point, fixed ideas – some bound to ten-year old sketches – started to come in.

Once contributions shifted into 'I think it should be ...' mode, we rapidly became stuck. Exacerbated by rough ground, which broke the group into twos and threes, consensus broke down. We were paying full price for short-cutting the process.

We could only get back on track by stepping right back to the key, pre-design question. What should the building – and, even more important, the place it would create – *say*? Should it make an assertive statement: 'people live here!' or be more respectful, even retiring? Even about this, we couldn't agree. With dusk approaching, bitter cold and two people having to leave, we decided to measure-up the mood-zone we'd pegged out and continue the design indoors the following day.

Reconvening, we re-addressed the fundamental question of what the place should say. There was no simple, single answer. The building needed to *both* assert human (domestic) life *and* be humble to its surroundings. Discussing these apparent irreconcilables, a consensus emerged that the building should assert human presence where we would *meet* it – the entrance court. Elsewhere, it needed to be humble to its surroundings. Again, haste had encouraged us to think of polarities as alternatives rather than compatible facets. Had we but taken time earlier, we'd have got here much faster.

The dual-facet spirit we had agreed began to suggest building gestures – low and horizontal, though rising confidently above the road. Also, to not obstruct views from the previously fixed 'spine-path', height had to be limited for at least half its length.

We now considered the 'mood-zone'. How much could be building? How much could be garden or – though otherwise untouched nature – influenced by the building? These building boundaries we established and pegged-out on site the next day.

Of what materials should our building be? Cob could be dug within yards – and had been for the nearby workshop building. But this was a woodland site. As someone with arboricultural experience pointed out, this meant plenty of tree roots, most within foundation depth and all needing aerated soil. 'Wild' trees typically have few main roots which, interwoven with those of other trees, run long distances. We therefore decided a lightweight structure on point foundations would do the least damage. This implied a wooden building – but should it be on stilts or ground-connected? This brought up issues of view: should we see over or under it? Some wanted strong architectural statements: one person wanted a tower, an architect suggested stilts. Others preferred something lower. I therefore asked what the different scales and rootedness or airiness would say. Deference to surroundings and view from the spine path decided us in favour of a low building. *Mostly* low, for, to assert human presence, we agreed it should rise where it enwrapped the entry court. This also ensured continuity of form-language with other buildings – not to mention easing disabled access.

The form that emerged was, not surprisingly, different from that speed-designed (outside appearance only) ten years previously. Nonetheless, its mood-quality was much the same and the space-gestures and building materials were almost identical.

The social centre

Having learnt our 'more haste, less speed' lesson, we took more time in the early stages when focusing on the social centre. We started with a brief recapitulation of all previous design sessions, then, in more detail, our recent first-impressions walk.

Place-study

We next stood in an outward-facing circle at the centre of where the social building would be. What could we see? Each of us in turn described, as objectively and unemotively as possible, everything directly in front of us. Between us, this built a 360° picture of the physical surroundings.

Physically in front of me:

A rectangular(ish) space, approximately 90 metres wide, 250 long. The first 30 metres slopes down 10%, then rises 5–7 metres on the left, 10–12 on the right. Ground-cover: predominantly grass, bracken and hemlock stems. To the left: a 'wall' of 5–7-metre willows and birches. At the end: 10–12-metre birches, larches just visible beyond them. To the right … (my neighbour continues) …

Next, still in a circle, we imagined what had been there before: land-forming pressures, glaciation, forest, Neolithic tomb, agriculture, then (mostly from those of us who'd known the place over a ten-year span) more recent changes. Then we moved from present into future, each describing how the view before each of us would change: deep winter with bare trees and snow; full-leafed, tall-brackened summer; next year, the half-built workshop completed and in use; in five years, the orchard tree canopy meeting overhead and the residential building built and occupied – so more people, more things going on; in ten years, younger trees mature, closing long views – and so on into the future.

Next we observed the circle of activity-places around us. We described their moods, then considered their influence on the activities and moods of the places between them and us. What mood did this give to the place in which we stood? As somewhere that gathered all the in-streaming influences from the activity-moods around us, it felt welcoming. What then did it say it was? Just as a physical heart receives message-bearing in-streaming blood and re-invigorates it, this spot absorbed and integrated in-streaming influences and radiated balance, warmth and social re-vitalization in return. It felt like the 'heart' of the project.

Outline design

We now asked what the social centre building *should* say. 'I am the heart of the project' came easily to all of us, re-affirming the rightness of this location. What moods, then, should each interface space have? The courtyard between centre and workshop needed to be active, interesting and welcoming. The approach path between this and the orchard, inviting. Between building and vegetable garden, round to the valley meadow, needed to be relaxing, moving from comfortably restful to calming. To the east, the 'wall' of trees formed a boundary.

What should be the extent of these *places*? How far should our *building* come? The front wall, facing the workshop, was easy to define. Too far to the south and the courtyard would be too narrow, linear and confined. Too far north and it would be too open, too loosely bounded. About the two front corners, one a pivot point, the other a gateway edge, there was a 500 mm (18 inch) difference of opinion. This took only ten minutes' discussion to resolve. Next: where should the invitation condense into an entrance? The activity-energy from the workshop door, the visibility sequence from the approach path and the focusing gesture of the workshop building quickly fixed this. This concave facade line we now pegged out.

The east wall was more or less fixed by the trees' drip-line. If it didn't come this far, the 'gateway' – and hence the courtyard – would be weakened. Further would threaten tree health. As the kitchen would need its own entrance, this asked for a receiving concavity in this, otherwise straight, line.

At first sight, the rear and west walls could be anywhere. But the spaces between social centre, vegetable garden and meadow would become *places*, threatened if the building extended too far. This quickly fixed the southwest corner. We soon found we only had around one metre (three feet) elasticity in locating the remaining walls.

Standing at the focus of four activity-influences, the building could easily obstruct their relationship, unless partly transparent. Not necessarily to be seen through directly (bad *feng shui* as someone pointed out), but where view would lead to view as you entered and walked through the building.

We now had all building *limits* and – where binding – facade lines pegged-out. Back indoors, we laid paper 'rooms' on a plan of these pegs. Since we had these room dimensions in mind throughout the marking-out process, we found that they fitted. Major room relationships, layout and orientation seemed obvious, though there was still some flexibility in what went where.

Design development

Once we started clay-modelling the social centre, two basic arrangements emerged. For rapid comparison, we modelled both at 1:200 (approximately 1/16":1'0") scale. Each had its advocates. In one, the social room was at one end of the building, in the other it rose out of surrounding support rooms. As far as I was concerned, both were 'nice', but which was most *appropriate*?

It was time to ask what each one 'said'. One social room gave the impression of a 'mother' heart, her skirts around her. The other seemed the culmination of the whole building – a 'crown' radiating out to all the activity-places around. Attractive and cosy as was the former, it was this unifying and 'raising' quality that encapsulated everything the centre was about. It also allowed a less high room, not as daunting and 'holy' as the other would have to be. Moreover, it could have eye-level windows on three sides instead of only a clerestory lantern. Just as the most ethical course invariably turns out to be the most practical (whereas the apparently most practical is always too blinkered to be either practical or ethical), the most appropriate-in-spirit seems to work out the most practically functional.

We fine-tuned the plan of this second model and I drew rough sections and elevations to check scale and sunlight. Out of curiosity, we then looked at the sketches drawn by a different group (only two of us had been in both) in our first (whole-site) study ten years previously. The similarity was striking!

This brought up the observation that for nine summers a marquee (used as the temporary social room) had stood on the exact place we had pegged out for that room. Also where we'd marked out kitchen and dining had for nine years been a fire pit and circle of log seats. Coincidence, intuitive sensitivity to place-moods, or residual aura of (now invisible) use? Whatever the reason, we felt reassured that this was the right place for this building.

Social centre and workshop, 1991 version.

We had now, over a decade and with seven different groups, designed seven build-ings in some detail. Their functions differed widely: residential, social/educational, byre, craft-workshop, pottery and one that contained a bit of everything. So did the locations and their micro-climates: woodland, hilltop, road-edge and meadow. Moreover, they had to demonstrate a variety of constructional materials: cob, adobe, *liechtlehm,*[1] stone, local-timber, and round-wood, cruck and gridshell construction. While, not surprisingly, their forms differed, they nonetheless had a metamorphic unity. No surprise here, for the four-layer consensus process accesses soul arche-types through the underlying levels of place and project. Sub-places, micro-climates, project-activities are diverse, yet unified by single underlying principles.

In a metamorphic development, there isn't a single fluid continuum, but progres-sive *steps*. Each vertebra of the spine, for instance, is different, but each is a recog-

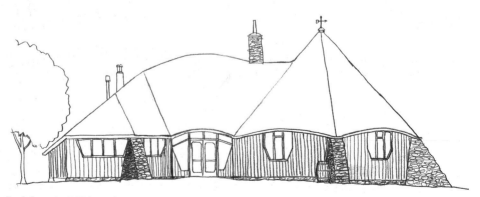

Social centre 2001 version.

nizable development of its neighbour. What unites these separate steps is a single form-generating principle. Though central to every metamorphic progression, this principle *never physically exists*. Only its manifestations do.

Just as in every metamorphosis, these buildings share form-generating principles but are individually formed in response to each individual circumstance. It wasn't necessary to impose any form language. Their coherence is a direct result of the consensus design process

Metamorphosis of buildings.

Residential/farm building.

Workshop.

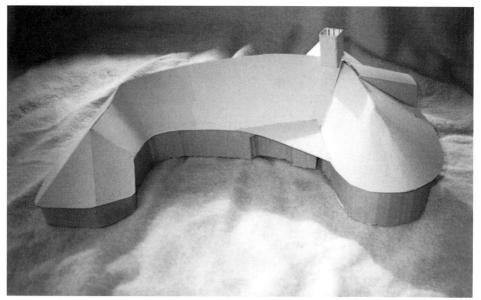

Residential.

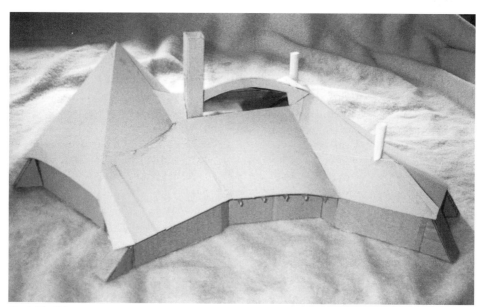

Social building.

Different buildings for different activities in different locations and micro-climates, and designed by different groups. The activities they house, however, are all parts of one project, the locations of one larger place, and the buildings formed by the same spirit-of-place- and spirit-of-activity-responsive process. Their metamorphic unity is, therefore, neither accidental nor contrived. It results from the listening-to-the-underlying consensus design process.

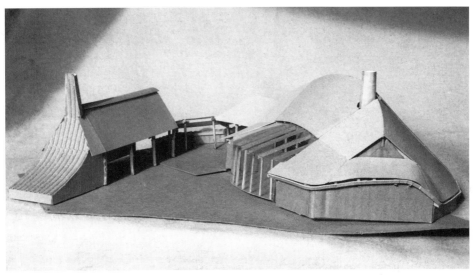

Laboratory (right) and solar herb-drier.

Reflections

What would I have done differently next time? Retrospectively, it was clear I should have insisted that the early stages enjoy the full time allocated to them. I also should have been more assertive in ensuring personal opinions were re-phrased (and hence re-thought) as de-personalized objective questions. I ought to have recognized short-cut-ism in time to re-assert the appropriate process layers before we reached an impasse. With any (apparently premature) contribution, merely asking how what we had just agreed *directly led to it* would have achieved this.

While this design workshop proved unexpectedly difficult at times, whenever we recognized that conventional ideas-generation was subverting the progression of design-condensation, we could re-assert process. Immediately blocks fell away and the forms that condensed felt 'right' to everybody.

Note

1 Low-density clay-straw (mostly straw).

PART SEVEN

Broader implications

CHAPTER TWENTY-FOUR

Social process as artistic method

I was recently asked what is my greatest passion. Not an everyday question. One that took a little thought to answer. I suppose it must be the creation of beautiful, spirit-healing places. Yet I increasingly work, nowadays almost completely, through consensus. Are these two compatible? Isn't the artistic the polar opposite of the social common denominator?

There is a common view that to suit everybody you have to dumb things down, that only the lowest common denominator will appeal to all. Hollywood takes this view. Not that films from there can't be well-made and worth watching. But they confirm a world-view we already hold. Only the 'independents' dare jolt this view, stretch our consciousness.

There is also a view that to suit all, you suit nobody. This is the 'camel is a horse designed by a committee' attitude. But there's another way of looking at this. Don't places that resonate with everyone have more to do with archetype than dumbness?[1]

To resonate, places must nourish the soul. Most soul nourishing places haven't been architect-designed nor professionally built, but were self-built, designed by amateurs as they went along. What makes them special isn't construction proficiency or sophisticated aesthetic sensitivity, but the fact that they have been, and continue to be, *loved* by their occupants.

Whatever intellectual guff arty-farties might say, artistic value only *means* something if it *resonates in the soul*. Our soul response is the direct result of the soul involvement of the people who built, lived in and loved the place. So soul involvement is crucial to whether a place is nourishing or not. The best way to generate this from the people who live there is not designing something beautiful *for* them, but designing it *with* them.

Can people untrained in the arts design beautiful things on their own? Potentially yes – folk-museums are full of beautiful things. Nowadays, however, we're subjected to commercially driven images. Advertising and the media are full of them. These are disconnected from the time-flow continuum. Though datable – and in a few years dated – they don't flow out of the everyday life around us. They may be fashion-leaders, but they're unrelated to life.

It's harder to make beautiful things these days; we can no longer do it unthinkingly – in fact thought usually gets in the way of feeling. Also the growth of design professions has so mystified design that few of us now have confidence in our own abilities. Fortunate for me, as it means I still have a job, but unfortunate for the world at large.

People who have made things look after them. Places designed by the people who live there suit their needs better than had they been designed by others more remote. Two reasons why such places and buildings last longer. They can more easily be adapted to match evolving lifestyles. Somewhere you resent may be adaptable, but minor mismatch with current needs gives an appealing excuse to destroy it and start again.[2] Hence user involvement encourages building longevity.

Because places formed by users endure and encourage adaptation, they are 'future-suited'. Contrast this with places whose *forms* were shaped by future imagery. How long did the futuristic social utopias of the 1960s (and their less idealistic derivatives in the 1970s) last?[3]

This brings up questions of appropriateness. Appropriateness to now, and to a future as we imagine it. Something appropriate to *me* should reflect *my* needs. But to what extent will my desires, self-image and aspirations guarantee suitability to place and situation (from which other people can't be omitted)? Things will only feel right – and last – if they harmonize with this three-fold web: people, place and situation. The more something rigid – like a building – is tied to my individualized personality, the more is it tied to how I am *now*. Once personalization moves into self-image projection, just like fashion, it rapidly looks dated.

By contrast, the more it answers the needs of the place that is its context, the more timeless will it feel. The situation, though bound to present time and personalities, is also inseparable from its place and time contexts. It moderates between fixed place and flowing time. Design that condenses out of situational issues finds forms within the current of evolution.

While architectural history is largely the history of architects, it was never as ego-led as today. Medieval towns mostly just happened. Gothic cathedrals were designed by individuals: master-masons with years of occult study behind them. But the cathedrals themselves are largely ego-free.

Architect design, as we know it, started with renaissance classical buildings. Their architects, however, worked within a strict rule-book framework, so largely subjugated their individuality to an archetypal, cosmically proportioned, system.

Nowadays, however, individualistic art favours the individualistic and novel over the established and archetypal. This dominance of individual wishes makes it effectively a-social, occasionally even anti-social.

Gothic and Classical architecture was socially excluding – commissioned by the rich and built by the poor. Building style, scale, materials and workmanship were inaccessibly different from anything the poor could afford. Nonetheless, through archetypal form and space language, they were connected to the people who used them. Today, we're searching for new languages to suit our poly-cultural society, changing ways of life and new technologies. The slowly multi-generationally evolving forms of past generations don't necessarily suit modern life. We don't even necessarily share cultural archetype. Things acceptable in the past aren't today. Social inclusion (or, more commonly, exclusion) is a central issue for our time. This – and the divergence of 'design' from 'life' – make it more important than ever that people who live and work in places take part in their place-formative processes.

This is also an issue of health. It's not just that those who live in buildings have a greater interest in non-toxicity than those who finance, but don't live in them. Health isn't just non-illness. The World Health Organization defines it as 'a state of complete physical, mental, and social well-being and not merely the absence of disease or infirmity'. This definition links the social to the personal. Any situation that excludes, disempowers and de-values anyone's input undermines self-esteem. Both low self-esteem and social exclusion have documented links with ill health.[4]

Health is a state of maintenance. Healing is an activity, a transformation. To heal, environment must resonate with our inner needs. This being my specialist area, I used to think I had a reasonable idea of what was right for other people. But nobody can ever know as well as those people themselves. For healing, soul-comfort isn't enough; we need to experience transformative beauty. Can I achieve this? Can others? Perhaps, but most probably not. Yet, when – as a group – we can so listen that we start to hear that group spirit greater than the sum of its parts, we can reach to heights none of us could reach on our own.

This is something about archetype supplanting ego-baggage; about prioritizing needs of place over wishes limited by personal blinkers. Something about *whole* situations, not just one-sided perceptions. It's why, in my experience, group work can produce things *more* artistic, more nourishing, beautiful, transformative, than I could ever reach by designing on my own.

Social inclusion itself has a healing role, especially for the formerly excluded. It fosters social formation for the group and inner growth for the individuals concerned. People grow visibly in the course of a one-day workshop. Their confidence, self-value, group membership and awareness all develop.

Perhaps that is why, in my desire to create places of transformative beauty – healing places – circumstance has brought me to co-design with users. Why life has led me to work with the consensus design process.

Notes

1 This is why Joseph Campbell's *The Hero with a Thousand Faces* (1968, Princeton University Press) is required reading for Disney filmmakers

2 This is the same attitude that leads to 'Abandon Earth and its problems and live in space-colonies on the Moon'.

3 Many started out well. Their residents were buoyed up by the Utopian enthusiasm. But without their design and management involvement, this couldn't be sustained.

4 Studies by John Cassel and Herb Gans in California and Boston quoted by Lindholm R. in: New design parameters for healthy places (*Places*. Vol. 2, No 4.).

PART EIGHT

Useful practicalities

CHAPTER TWENTY-FIVE

What you need

For place-study:

Clipboards and unlined paper (or note-pads), preferably stiff enough to write on without support, one per person.

Soft pencils (say 3B for ordinary paper, B for tracing or greaseproof (butcher) paper).

Erasers.

A4 (or US letter) **paper**. Useful for sketching, notes, etc. So useful, bring a whole packet.

Site plan at largest scale that will fit on table. Probably A0 size, but this depends upon building sizes and relationships. Clay modelling individual buildings any larger than A4 (12 inches) takes too long, which tends to fix site plan scale. You may need plans at several scales. Gridlines drawn at say 10-m (or 50-foot) intervals will help when you come to draw what you've modelled.

Drafting tape to fix drawings, etc.

For design stage:

Twine or string (orange or clean white – not grey, brown or green).

Pegs (bamboos are best if ground is soft enough; they are tall, cheap and, especially if cut to a 60° point, [usually] easy to stick in).

Mallet for pegs in harder ground – otherwise not needed.

Traffic cones (good markers if ground is really hard).

Greaseproof/butcher paper in large sheets (cheaper than tracing paper) for drawing plans and revised plans, with survey or previous drawing visible below. 12 sheets are probably enough. (Allow about four for each storey at each scale.) For sections, a roll of tracing or greaseproof is handy.

Clay (ordinary potter's clay is the cheapest; cellulose-fibre reinforced is the most durable). You need about one and a half times as much as the volume of the buildings at whatever scale(s) you will be modelling them at.

Glass (or acrylic[1]) to cover plan and build model on. Not essential; you can instead just trace the most up-to-date sketch plan or site plan and ruin it by putting clay on it, but the transparent cover makes life easier.

Block model If the site has a simple slope, this can just be a site plan on a sloping piece of plywood or tilted table. Neighbouring buildings can be blocks of wood or just card folded to form their roofless facades.

Scrap cardboard and kitchen scissors for balconies, overhanging roofs, neighbouring buildings, etc. Twigs, toothpicks, wooden skewers etc. are useful too.

Thin card for room-size rectangles; a different colour for each story is a luxury, but worthwhile as otherwise white room sizes keep getting lost amongst white paper.

Two tables big enough for everyone to sit around. One for clay, one for paper. You will need means (van, car roof-racks, or even wheelbarrow) for getting these, the model and everything else to and from site.

Adjustable angle lamp to simulate sunshine.

A camera to record model (I often wished I had used one to record the process – but then I was always too busy to take pictures!)

Not all these are necessary for every project. Once you've rehearsed in your mind (or, better, in discussion) what you'll be doing and the size and complexity of the site, buildable area, buildings and the people involved, what you actually will need will become clear.

Notes

1   Acrylic may be stronger and less dangerous when broken, but it's *much* more polluting in manufacture and harder to recycle.

CHAPTER TWENTY-SIX

Sample timetables

I've often had to prepare timetables for consensus design sessions. In the event, something always happens differently. Such is the life in life!

One thing, however, rarely changes: participants have limited time. Flexibility notwithstanding, this makes tight timetabling a necessity. As these sample timetables show, different scales of project, pressures on time and circumstances require different timetables.

Healing Centre

This project was for the expansion of a medical practice into multi-therapy healing centre.

DAY 1 (Evening): Aspirations, intentions, possibilities and limitations

- Introductions; individual hopes and concerns.
- Walk and silently observe, then share impressions.

DAY 2: What does the Place say? What should it say?

We will study the most significant 'journey' (probably carpark to consulting room):

- What is physically there? (Quantifiable material substance.)
- What time-related experiences, e.g. movement sequences and spatial gestures?
- What moods-of-place? What feelings do these induce?
- What does the place say it is?

We now go on to ask:

- What should the place say it is?
- What moods, therefore, would support this?
- What experience sequences and spatial gestures would reinforce these?
- What (manageably small) physical changes would effect this?

Evening: Healing environment: talk and discussion.

DAY 3: What should the project become?

We will now study the whole site in a related way:

- What is there now?
- What is the place's 'biography'? Where is this leading to?
- What are moods of its parts?
- What does it say? What enhancements and balancing does it ask for?

And then, future development:

- What should a Healing Centre say?
- What activities will it comprise, and where do these belong? (Mark out with strings and poles, then draw a loose plan.)
- What relationships, gestures and experience sequences? (Clay model.)
- What moods are appropriate?
- What physical form should this take? (Refine plan, sections, model and sketches; also check model for sun and shade at relevant times of day and year.)

Evening: How should the project grow?

- What are the present activity nodes from which new activities can grow?
- What activities are easy to start or develop? What depend upon other factors, e.g. money?

Community Centre

This project was for a village hall and outdoor facilities (sports, children's play, etc.)

Session 1	Duration – minutes
Introductions	15
Describe method, agenda	15
Identify: journey starting and end points	30
First impressions (taking roles): walk	20
Discuss	20
Physical: walk & note	30
Discuss	30
Spatial/journey sequence: walk & note	20
Discuss	20
Place biography: past	20
Future	20
Moods: walk & note	20
Discuss	20
Essence of place: discuss	20
	5 hours

Session 2	Duration – minutes
Recapitulate session 1	20
Essence of project: discuss	20
Activities generated	10
Moods to support spirit of project	10
Locate activities/moods on site	30
Plan gestures on site, string out	30
Record on paper	30
Arrange room cut-outs	60
Record rough plan	30
	4 hours

Session 3	Duration – minutes
Recapitulate sessions 1 and 2	20
Review rough plans	30
Arrange clay rectanguloids	
Clay model	60+
Revise plan	60+
Rough sections, elevations and sketches	60+
	4+ hours

Later   Enlarge scale, review plan, etc., work-up design, transition to executive architect.

CHAPTER TWENTY-SEVEN

Sample participation structure

Who should be involved in a consensus design process? Ideally everybody. But this is rarely practical. Also, like party invitations, it's easy to forget obviously important people. Rural projects affect neighbours but rarely interface with the space they use. Not so urban ones. You may not know your neighbours, but, living cheek by jowl, there is plenty of opportunity for friction. They may not be willing to take part, but if it's possible to involve neighbours, their interests and yours can be brought into coincidence.

Others also, design professionals amongst them, often can't take part in the whole process. This, refined from the ASHA involvement list (Chapter 21) is a matrix for who ought to be involved and when.

Who is involved (who)	What we do (process)	What we achieve (outputs)
	Identify players	
Neighbouring & project players	Players: fears and hopes	
Identify design group: residents/users/directors/ architect(s)/etc.		
Design-group takes part in whole process from here on (except that only the concerned/relevant members are part of housing design) Neighbours study and work on site-to-adjoining-property interface.	*Place-study*: • What is physically there? • What is its biography? • What is its future? • What moods does it have? • What does it say it is?	

	Incarnating the design: • What should the project say? • What activities are involved? • Where should these go? – so what 'places' should be where? • What moods should these have? • What flow and journey relationships between them? • What plan gestures confirm these places, moods and relationships? • What materials support these moods?	Rough plan (probably 1: 200) Clay-volume model + Area cost check
Consultants	*Functioning the design*: • Recapitulate how design has come into form • What organizing diagrams are relevant? (e.g.: social/commercial, ventilation, heating/cooling, water, goods flow including refuse and compost)	Organizing diagrams
	Reconcile clay model with organizing diagrams (if at variance, briefly repeat, including consultants in the process: • What should project say → where are activities → moods → flow relationships → plans & block-model • Superimpose organizing diagrams onto plans and sections to ensure effective function.)	Improved clay-model, rough sections, plans, flow diagrams

	Develop clay-model, sections & plans. Area cost-check	
Consultants	Enlarge scale (probably 1:100): • revise plans & sections • rough card model (block model only for housing) • check functioning with consultants • elevations, sketches, more sections • area cost-check	Card-model for volumes and structure & construction. Rough plans, sections, elevations & many sketches (of rooms & outdoor places etc.)
(If project involves several families or other diverse users) Residents	*Housing*: place-study: (but journey instead of biography)	
Each family	Incarnate design • What should it say? • What activities where? • What moods where? • What journey flow, gestures? • What plan, section implications? • Arrange paper room footprints • Plan each house • Area cost-check	Housing card-model, plans, sections, elevations and sketches
	Coordination • Incorporate detail elements (e.g. individual homes) • Check organizing diagrams • Check orientation (re: sun, view, wind, noise etc.) • Check area re cost	Total scheme rough design

CHAPTER TWENTY-EIGHT

Assessment matrix

(These matrices are relevant to many situations, not just design)

What is *physically* there?	*Biography*: past to future	*Mood*	Ideals, core *spirit*-values
What is the material situation?	How did it come to be like this? Where is this leading? OR Through what sequence of experiences do we meet this?	How do people feel about things?	How can we encapsulate the essence of the situation?
Example: evaluating a business			
Assets and accounts	Track-record Future tendencies (including competitors)	Good-will and employee-relations	Mission-statement

Decision-making matrix: turning inspiration into action

What is its *individual* spirit?	How do people *feel* about it?	*Time* continuum	What is its *physical* context?
What values, spirit, should things convey?	What qualities does this imply?	How can these grow out of the developmental currents already at work?	What material changes does this require?
Example: setting-up a sustainability course			
What is unique about this course?	What is its market acceptance?	How does it fit into the historical development of sustainability consciousness? What does this tell us about *future* needs?	Human and technical assets – how do these match what's needed?

Index